CORPORATE TRANSFORMATION AND RESTRUCTURING

CORPORATE TRANSFORMATION AND RESTRUCTURING

A Strategic Approach

Abbass F. Alkhafaji

QUORUM BOOKS
Westport, Connecticut • London

Library of Congress Cataloging-in-Publication Data

Alkhafaji, Abbass F.
  Corporate transformation and restructuring : a strategic approach / Abbass F. Alkhafaji.
      p.   cm.
  Includes bibliographical references and index.
  ISBN 1–56720–459–7 (alk. paper)
    1. Organizational change.   2. Industrial management.   3. Strategic planning.   I. Title.
  HD58.8.A6775   2001
  658.4′06—dc21   2001019188

British Library Cataloguing in Publication Data is available.

Library of Congress Catalog Card Number: 2001019188
ISBN: 1–56720–459–7

First published in 2001

Quorum Books, 88 Post Road West, Westport, CT 06881
An imprint of Greenwood Publishing Group, Inc.
www.quorumbooks.com

Printed in the United States of America

The paper used in this book complies with the
Permanent Paper Standard issued by the National
Information Standards Organization (Z39.48–1984).

10 9 8 7 6 5 4 3 2 1

To my family with love and gratitude

Contents

Preface

The rapid changes in the external environment, as well as changes in technology and increased global competition, have created evolutionary changes in management. In the increasingly competitive global economy, a business must continuously strive to become a more efficient organization. Organizations are repeatedly challenged to modify their strategies to achieve success in the global marketplace. In the past decade many companies found that the principles of operations and performance needed to be revitalized or reinvented. This revitalization can be accomplished through the process of corporate transformation. Corporate transformation refers to the fundamental changes in and altering of attitude that enable the organization to compete effectively in a global market. A successful transformation requires an organization to change its bureaucracy, policies, and existing routines. Fundamental changes must be well planned and carefully applied. Often organizations will rely on past methods that are no longer relevant. Although this reliance on past methods may fit more securely within management's comfort zone, it may not solve serious organizational problems.

Organizations must attempt to change their traditional strategies, structures, and procedures to succeed in today's global business arena.

When attempting to make this change, organizations should remain mindful of the successes and failures of their competitors. Even though every organization is unique, these organizations still can benefit from benchmarking the best practices of other competitors. Organization can improve their performance by learning from other businesses. However, merely imitating and copying the successful strategy of another organization is not necessarily enough. Successful organizational change requires appropriate conditions that limit the amount of uncertainties and that lead to better learning and successful transformation.

Today organizations recognize the need for transformational leaders who believe in change and innovation. Managers and executives of the twenty-first century have to reinvent their companies to be able to compete in a highly competitive global environment. These executives must abandon the organizational and operational principles and procedures that they have used in the past and create entirely new ones. They must create a shared vision, objectives, strategies, and a corporate culture that encourages harmony and flexibility within the new organization. They must build sustainable competitive advantages. To have a competitive advantage, management needs to invest time and resources in transforming the organization by achieving fundamental changes and development. This means that a healthy corporation needs to build long-term strengths. It is critical for companies to maintain customer satisfaction since companies would not exist if customers did not want their products or services. Quality should be built into every aspect of the tasks, processes, and systems in the organization.

Continuous improvement and innovation is no longer a privilege; it is a necessity if a business wants to survive in the future. Continuous improvement is the mindset that "We can do better," or that the current level of performance can always be improved.

To achieve successful transformation it will take a strong leader who believes in empowering the employees through effective teamwork and trust. Changes must be planned so that an organization will not be subjected to unacceptable risks.

Planning any changes will ensure that important steps are not overlooked. This will insure that the decision makers process the information more effectively. Changes that are not related to the current resources and capabilities of the firm will deter the process. Every initiative will require organizational support and the acceptance of a reasonable amount of risk. In today's business world the best leaders are those who clearly accept reasonable risk and recognize and implement continuous changes. It is up to management to motivate employees, encourage innovation, and instill the notion of continuous improvement as part of the organizational culture. Organizational resources must be allocated to upgrade employees' experiences and capabilities.

Acknowledgments

The author would like to acknowledge with appreciation the many people who made this book possible. Some of those people are as follows: Thanks go to Parameswar Krishnakumar, David Huddleson, Dineshnandini Manocha, Jerry Biberman, Len Tischler, Hooshang Beheshti, Abdalla Hayajneh, David Turnipseed, Richard Ramesey, Richard Nelson, Abbas Ali, Rogene Buchholz, Dharam Rana, Jamaluddin Husain, Roger Gledhill, David Boje, and Grace Ann for their encouragement and support. The author would also like to acknowledge with gratitude all those quoted in this book.

In addition, the author would like to acknowledge Puja Schams for his technical assistance and Emily Stolkowski, Michael Polishen, Georgette Hinkley, Kimberly Bain, Jolie Onuffer, and Megan Zurasky for their diligent work. The author would like to thank his colleagues, students, and friends at Slippery Rock University for providing a good academic environment for teaching and research.

The author would like to express his thanks to Sharon Pabst and John Beck for their efforts in editing and typesetting the entire book.

Finally, the author would like to express his love and appreciation to his family for their patience and support throughout the duration of this project. May God help us all to do the right thing right.

Part I

MANAGEMENT TRANSFORMATION

This section exhibits the need for change by presenting the challenges that management faces today. The section also presents a framework to assist management in responding to various levels of organizational performance. In addition this section will introduce the main issue of this book: corporate transformation. The meaning of transformation will be discussed thoroughly in this section. The components of corporate transformation will be displayed. A framework to help management recognize the need for such fundamental changes will be provided. This section also shows a new approach to the evolution of management thought. Total quality management, reengineering, learning organization, and benchmarking will be discussed in this section as important components of transformation management. It is the author's opinion that the implementation of each of these concepts requires fundamental changes in leadership style as well as organizational culture. Positive results can be obtained only if these concepts are applied within the framework of transformation.

Chapter 1

Why Transformation?

During the past decade, competition from abroad continued to increase. Business organizations responded swiftly to protect their market shares and regain their competitive edge. Some industries essentially disappeared. Some of the large corporations went through severe changes such as merging with one another, building strategic alliances with companies abroad, and divesting. Many companies in the 1990s eliminated a large number of management layers and employees. Small companies began reasserting their role in the economy, generating new jobs to employ some of the workers displaced by large corporations. The U.S. economy has vast natural resources, skilled labor, and capital that can be used more productively. It also has an unlimited supply of the entrepreneurial vision that allows people to utilize skills and resources to create needed goods and services as well as new jobs. The 1990s provided new challenges and opportunities for companies and their employees. Challenges such as global competition, changing technology, environmental concerns, and demographic shifts have forced businesses to move in new directions and experiment with various management approaches.

Today, competition from abroad continues to increase. The 1990s provided new challenges and opportunities for companies and their employees. In this competitive business world, organizations must continually improve the quality of their products and services. This chapter will introduce the importance of continuous change. It will present a framework to assess corporate performance and to enhance the long-term competitive advantages of the organization. It is important to mention that too much change can alter the ability of the organization to gain stability and progress. Therefore, change must be planned and have a clear purpose. A minor change that does not affect a company's strategy but improves corporate creditability does not necessary require transformation. Only the fundamental changes that affect the organization and its structure can be considered transformational. This type of change is usually risky and requires many resources.

THE GLOBAL COMPETITIVE ECONOMY

Today, globalization and integration of many cultures has become a trend in the business world. The world economy and trade between nations has been increasing rapidly. Trade by itself is not a new phenomenon, however, the continued falling of trade barriers, the opening of new markets, the goods, money, and people crossing borders as never before are new phenomena in the marketplace. Companies, whether large or small, are affected by global changes and competition. The economic integration of the world has increased as multinational corporations continue to invest overseas and expand through international alliances and joint ventures. Cultural barriers are being gradually reduced by the role of technology and information in educating societies. The explosion in information technology is both a cause and an effect of globalization. Such technology permits managers around the world to fax and e-mail information and hold videoconferences and teleconferences with one another, which has resulted in instant consultation and decision making. Globalization consists of a new form of competition characterized by networks of global linkages that bind a country's institutions and people in an interdependent global economy. A global company has to have a management structure that allows global thinking.

For the past three decades, the United States has faced strong competition from Japan, Western Europe, and the newly industrialized countries of Taiwan, Korea, Singapore, and the colony of Hong Kong. This competition will continue in the twenty-first century. At the same time, there is a move toward capitalism in many formerly communist and socialist countries, such as those of Eastern Europe and Latin America, which will provide U.S. businesses with new challenges as well as new opportunities. Many other Third World countries are fast joining the developed countries in producing quality goods and services and competing in the same global market. The developing countries will continue to supply raw materials and basic commodities. Globalization means that today's and tomorrow's managers must broaden their perspectives to go beyond their own culture, to learn to understand the way business is conducted in different cultures, and to become familiar with competitive practices around the world. All this requires new managerial skills and strategies to keep businesses healthy, competitive, and successful. Competitiveness requires businesses to continue their efforts to control costs and boost quality.

Thinking globally will provide companies the opportunity to improve quality and reduce cost in areas such as purchasing, production, and human resources. Companies go global by setting ground rules, common standards, and brand values that maintain focus and protect the company's image. The firm should then allow sufficient flexibility to satisfy local customers and market requirements as soon as the ground rules have been established. Therefore, successful globalization may be achieved by striking the proper balance between local and international needs and by creating flexibility so that local control and the customer can be satisfied.

There are a number of issues that need to be considered when entering a new market. They include

1. Choosing the area or market that needs to be explored.
2. Assessing political and economic risk.
3. Selecting entry arrangement that is appropriate for the particular market.
4. Designing a strategy that sets the ground rules and provides support and advice to the local region.
5. Providing strategic guidelines that cover the company's approach to brand image, site development, customer satisfaction, franchising, and the business process.
6. Assessing customer expectation and perceived needs, which requires the understanding of demographic and psychographic elements of the customers.
7. Developing a local management team and training them to understand corporate culture.
8. Preparing expatriates who are willing to relocate and training those expatriates on doing business in that particular market.
9. Adopting an approach which is in line with global business strategy and in tune with local market needs.
10. Keeping things simple: maintaining focus on what business you are in and what your brand stands for and replicating that positioning wherever you do business.
11. Testing the ground for moving research and development activities into that market or region.

12. Preparing to move proper control to the local area or market.
13. Considering the local culture and religion with respect and understanding.
14. Allowing flexibility and being ready to meet the needs of the local customers and adapt to the changes in these needs and expectations.

The local markets appreciate this type of arrangement. In addition this arrangement will motivate employees, satisfy customers, increase market share, and increase profitability.

THE DYNAMIC ORGANIZATION

In the coming years, the workplace will become dramatically different from what it is now, due to various changes that are taking place all around us. Factors such as technological changes (e.g., electronically linked work station, computerized coaching, and monitoring equipment), globalization, and a more diverse workforce have brought exhilarative changes to future organizations. These trends will reshape work environments over the next several years. To succeed, organizations must redefine the workplace and reinvent themselves. Today's organizations must be proactive in their measures and strategies.

Consider the following: One-third of the Fortune 500 companies in 1970 had vanished by 1983. In 1982, Petes and Waterman identified forty-three excellent companies which demonstrated superiority on six critical financial yardsticks for a period of twenty years. Five years later, only fourteen were still excellent on the basis of those measures. In ten years some had disappeared entirely, and many of the remaining were in trouble. Petes and Waterman did not anticipate the dramatic changes in information technology nor did they predict the globalization effect. We are rapidly moving toward a "spread" workforce, in which technology is used to link workers and functions at scattered work stations. This change is rapidly altering the nature of work. Today, the sales representative is in a position to give customers immediate information on new product features, pricing, and deliver times. Management is provided with reports on inventory levels, production information, sales and receivables, and lead time needed for supplying the product. The shipping employee is in a position to monitor the movement of goods to customers and invoice information.

The United States depends heavily on high technology to build its competitive advantages in a global market. Technologies of the last two decades are being used by developing countries. New fields, however, such as biotechnology, computers, robotics, lasers, fiber optics, and composite materials, will develop rapidly and will serve as the mainsprings of economic growth in the developed countries. Because of rapid development, the technology might become obsolete in a relatively short period of time. This means that the ability of U.S. firms to respond quickly and to reap a profit before competition enters the market is not as promising as it was a few years ago.

COMPETING WITH ON-LINE BUSINESSES

Information technology has been identified as a major agent for change. Today, organizations must be successful players in the on-line market. The Internet is no longer a novelty or an interesting place to pass time. The Internet business has become a very popular outlet for many companies. E-business or e-commerce, the ability to conduct business electronically with customers that you do not see, is one of the changes that has taken place recently. Today more people are leading busy lifestyles, operating businesses out of their homes, and spending more time purchasing items and services over the Internet. Traditional businesses are under pressure to conduct e-commerce to survive in the twenty-first century. This type of business will give access to people worldwide. It is also beneficial in reaching potential clients and partners. The Internet allows sellers of obscure items to reach customers and has made investing and trading in stocks, bonds, and securities of all kinds accessible to all investors. The focus is to get a higher return on investment for both the customers and the companies involved. Companies like E-Toys, E-Trade, Fidelity, and Morningstar enable people to trade thousand shares of stocks every day. These transactions can be done while at home day and night.[1]

The growth of the dynamic organization will be accelerated by the following factors:

1. The fact that the life cycle of technology is shorter than ever before; the estimated life of new technology today is only a few months or a few weeks.
2. The swift changes in the electronic technologies, which are facilitating the digital, wireless transfer of video, audio, and text information.
3. The fast spread of Internet, e-business, e-mail, and other computer networks, which helps the United States maintain a strong global advantage over all other countries.
4. The growth of telecommuting, which will enable companies to provide faster response to customers, reduce facility expenses, and help workers meet their child care and elder care responsibilities.

One implication of this trend is that individuals must redefine their role in the dynamic organization. They must distinguish themselves in what they do and be creative. Individuals need to develop better interpersonal communication and planning skills to succeed in the dynamic work environment.

DEFINITION AND MEANING

What is corporate transformation? It is the behavioral changes that occur within the organization to improve its performance. It is the reinventing and revitalization of the entire organization. The goal of all transformation is to improve performance at the individual level as well as at the organizational level. Firms have to reorganize in response to globalization and the rapid changes in technology. *Transformation* refers to redirecting organizational efforts toward the satisfaction of the major stakeholders. Businesses that like to improve their performance must revitalize and pay better attention to their major customers. It is no longer doing the assigned programs the traditional way. It is changing the foundation by building a new and more appropriate one. Transformation therefore refers to the new way of thinking about organizations and how people should relate to necessary changes. Transformation takes place when the majority of organizational members change their attitude, new initiative is utilized, and technology is modernized. It means providing an atmosphere that encourages creativity and innovation. In many cases organizations do not change unless crisis in performance has occurred. This crisis usually inspires transformations within the organization. (See Figure 1.1 for information regarding assessing crisis levels in the organization.)

Many attempts that are made to improve performance are not necessarily considered transformation. Transformation activities include innovation, reducing cycle time, building new capabilities, responding quickly to customers' demands, continuing improvements, global quality, creating a learning network, the free flow of information, thinking globally, changes in the strategies designed, cooperation with various units, and management sensitivity to customer needs. In summary, transformation involves extensive changes in how work is done.

Corporate transformation is a response to globalization and international competition. To improve the processes, organizations need fundamental changes. Creativity, innovation, total quality management, learning organization, strategy design, and reengineering are ways to improve performance and are considered the elements of corporate transformation. It is therefore a systematic and continuous process.

Buyouts, mergers, and acquisitions will effect the size of the organization or the level of debts involved, but it is not necessarily affecting the nature of management or employee work; therefore, it cannot be considered transformation as such. Portfolio restructuring deals with the significant changes of the mix of assets owned by firms or the time set in which businesses operate. It does not necessarily change people's behavior. Similarly debt for equity swaps or capital formation of the company should not be considered transformation. However, restructuring efforts, which constitute the processes involved in cost saving and creating value, such as downsizing, privatization, and strategic alliances, might be considered as transformation, especially if these efforts affect the nature of the product, process management, and employees. Similarly organizational restructuring, which includes divisional redesign and other methods to improve process, are also considered transformations.

Financial Restructuring	→ Capital reformation
	→ Buyouts
	→ Debt restructuring
	→ Debt for equity swaps
Portfolio Restructuring	→ Changes the mix of assets owned by the company, or the line of business in which it operate are not necessarily transformations

Peter Drucker said in the *Harvard Business Review*, "Every organization has to prepare for the abandonment of everything it does."[2] This means that every organization today, even the successful ones, should evaluate everything they do and be courageous enough to change, redesign, reinvent, and revitalize everything they do as they see fit to survive in this changeable environment. Management should encourage innovation and risk in their organization. Organizations need to continuously adapt to new situations if they are to survive and prosper in the new global market. The current trend is toward transforming the organization, so that all members of the organization are engaged in identifying and solving problems. This pattern of behavior will enable the organization to continuously improve and increase its capability.

Consider, for example, Jose Ignacio at General Motors who wanted to build a state-of-the-art automobile manufacturing facility that would cut the cost of production in many areas. GM shot down Jose's idea; so did Ford and Chrysler. They were unwilling to take a chance on a new technological advancement in a manufacturing facility. Jose Ignacio had to go to another company: The Big Three lost an innovative executive to Volkswagen of Germany. Volkswagen, an automobile manufacturer which has been known to take risks, hired Jose Ignacio. They considered his idea and took chances on a risky situa-

Figure 1.1
Stages of Organizational Performance Framework

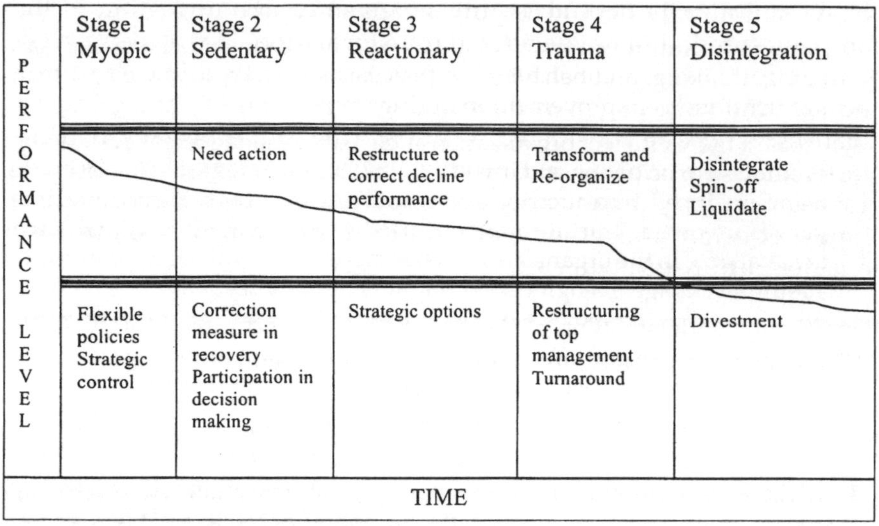

	Stage 1 Myopic	Stage 2 Sedentary	Stage 3 Reactionary	Stage 4 Trauma	Stage 5 Disintegration
P E R F O R M A N C E		Need action	Restructure to correct decline performance	Transform and Re-organize	Disintegrate Spin-off Liquidate
L E V E L	Flexible policies Strategic control	Correction measure in recovery Participation in decision making	Strategic options	Restructuring of top management Turnaround	Divestment
			TIME		

Note: Performance level can be measured by sale, return on investment, profit as percentage of sale, or simply the units produced.

tion. Volkswagen tested Jose's idea in a small pilot plant in Brazil. Jose's technological advancements in manufacturing were simple and can be summarized as follows. He believed if you located all the manufacturers of every component of an automobile under one roof, you would eliminate the need for multiple suppliers, inventory, and transportation costs; and, the union could be blocked from infiltrating the facility. GM, realizing what they gave up, conceded by saying, "You got to give him [Jose] credit; He really pushed this one through the needle."[3] Managers must not be afraid of new ideas or new technology that can transform the company. They must take advantage of the opportunity as it exists, even when a reasonable risk is involved.

ELEMENTS OF SUCCESS

The elements of success in the global market include the following:

1. Corporate transformations led by a transformational leader. A transformational leader is one who energizes the whole organization. He/she must be creative, visionary, nontraditional, open minded, curious, intellectually diverse, and have a wide array of interests. They enjoy interaction and the exchange of ideas. They are above all charismatic leaders.

2. Corporate visions that focus on how the organization can best meet the needs of its customers, and the creation of directions and goals that stretch the organization beyond its current comprehension.

3. Continuous improvement of quality and innovation and change in managing, thinking, and behaviors so that managers can advance and manage continuous improvement in their systems.

4. Create a more efficient organization and create a management system that promotes participation and involvement. This includes self-directed work teams, reduced bureaucracy, and improved communication among all parties involved. Transformation is used when capability and resources are available in the organization. When all parties involved are convinced about the change, reengineering might be used if needed.

5. A better understanding of the foreign culture and foreign market. The culture environment affects all activities international managers undertake. Therefore, study of cultural environment is important.

6. Employee empowerment and commitment through a close relationship with the leader.

7. Developing a structure in which learning, creativity, and innovation are encouraged.

8. Dedication, passion, and persuasiveness, which are critical ingredients for the future workforce.

9. Failure comes from fear, denial, avoidance, loss of control, and lack of commitment. Therefore it is the responsibility of future leaders to eliminate fear, foster trust, and facilitate the environment that creates new knowledge.

10. The commitment to unending learning will provide the tools to navigate throughout the uncertainty ahead. Thinking and behavior need to be transformed so that the employees will continuously improve and maintain an effective system.

CORPORATE TRANSFORMATION

Transformation requires a transformational leader with a new vision. This vision must touch all participants and should become the energizing force within the organization. A new corporate culture must be designed, one that permits changes, tolerates failure, reduces bureacracy, and provides flexibility to help employees adjust. Changes usually come with a cost attached to it. Employee adjustment from the traditional ways to the new ways will be difficult. We must accept some failure to occur in the beginning of this process. Employees must be informed about the need to change and also help must be provided to them to prepare for the new way of doing things through information and training. The new culture should affect our recruitment, selection, training, and performance measurment. Integrating business ethics into company practice will give a company competitive advantages in a global market. This can be considered as a part of leadership transformation. Being competitive in the global market is difficult and continuously presents ethical dilemmas for management. Ethics today is transforming itself from an academic discipline into an operating force in a socioeconomic setting. Transformational leaders must attempt to find the factual information that pertains to a particular situation and examine how it will affect their business and what are the appropriate moral standards in such a case, and then arrive at an ethical decision. This process must be institutionalized so that it becomes a day-to-day practice, and all employees should adhere to these values.

Corporate transformation is a common way of management life today. During the past decade many firms have reorganized, streamlined, and restructured their divisions in order to improve their competitiveness. While recent research on literature indicates that restructuring has had negative effects, it has been successful for the most part. The issue is not so much as to whether transformation works, but rather which restructuring works best and when should restructuring occur.

Transformational efforts must be continuous. Even when the company is doing well it should consider transformation. British Airways in 1996 was the most profitable airline in the world. Yet CEO Bob Ayling announced restructuring measures to improve the competitiveness of the organization. He predicted the severe competition ahead from European and American airlines companies. At this stage the organization can plan its transformation and prepare its employees carefully. General Electric started the efforts of transformation when its profit were rising and its market share was increasing. Jack Welch, CEO of the company, has made dramatic changes.[4] Many corporations do not consider change while they are doing well. Their argument is that "if we have been very successful, why should we change?" The board of directors evaluate management performance annually. Therefore, management's concern has been with the short-term profitability of the organization and not necessarily with its long-term viability and competitiveness. Yet other corporations or industries resist the change altogether. The result is catastrophic to the whole industry. The example of this is the auto and steel industries during the late 1960s and 1970s. The three major auto companies lost their market share to the Japanese. Chrysler Corporation was on the verge of going bankrupt in 1979. American companies stood still while they saw their sales decline way below expected levels.

In the preceding paragraphs a good case was made for the need to change. Global competition will pressure companies to change. Different companies and industries will respond differently to such pressure. In the next part of this chapter, the issue of when to change will be discussed. The message of this chapter is that continuous change of organizational culture, structure, and systems are imperative. Purely remaining in the traditional path of the organization will cause only organizational trauma. A framework is suggested to assist companies in predicting their performance and responding to the evolving globally competitive environment. The framework explicitly considers the dynamics between changing business environments and the responses to meet the challenges. It will aid in transforming the company and in designing a competitive strategy.

WHEN TO CHANGE

Businesses need to continuously reorganize themselves in view of the challenges discussed previously. Management measures corporate performance on a continuous basis. Any time the actual performance drops below expected previously set standards, a serious problem is created for the organization. Management also measures the performance of their organizations against that of their competitors. If there are any variations, management needs to take remedial action. This is sometimes called *organizational decline*. It refers to the decrease in an organization's resource base over a period of time. This should serve as a warning and then should be changed within the organizational framework.

The following framework shows how a company can diagnose their performance crisis. This framework will assist organization in their transformational efforts. It is associated with an event decline such as size reduction or restructuring. This usually follows previous success when organizations take its success for granted.

Stage 1: Myopic Stage

This stage represents the decline in the company's performance below the expected level. Sometimes it is not a big problem; therefore we should not overreact. Maybe it does not need a dramatic change. But it is important to identify the reason for such a decline. It could be the need for additional personnel or a simple delay in receiving raw materials from suppliers, or in production, delivery, or seasonability of sales.

If the issue is more serious than we first thought, and the problem might have an impact on long-term survival, then a more serious decision must be made. This decline might be the result of efficiency problems, excess personnel, rigid policies and procedures, or neglect of customer needs and expectations. To respond effectively, the company needs to develop more flexible policies and procedures to encourage employee initiatives and participation along with an appropriate strategic control system that can identify deviations from strategy design on a timely basis. A control system will provide management with the information needed to take immediate actions and correct any problems that may exist to improve efficiency and performance in a timely fashion. Management needs to focus on evaluation and control. The use of control charts and a cause-and-effect diagram is especially helpful at this stage. Employee performance is of a great concern. A biweekly evaluation system should be implemented. Employees who are not efficient, capable, and motivated should be trained or transferred. Inventory level is checked and kept at the minimum necessary for the sale of the product. New marketing campaigns may be launched to increase sales and attract new customers while retaining the current customer base.

Stage 2: Sedentary Stage

This stage represents the continuous decline of corporate performance because of efficiency problems. It is clear to the employees that something is wrong, even if management tries to deny it. Employees try to be more efficient, cutting costs where possible. They work in a team to brainstorm the causes and effects and come up with new ideas to further the growth of the company. Sometimes at this stage the problems have already been detected by the management of the business. In this case, action needs to be taken for improvement.

Careful evaluation of the information gathered can result in a proper answer for improvement. Although it is not quite necessary to panic, improvement is needed to turn things around in a positive direction. The downward trend signals a performance problem in the company. It is obvious to participants that a corrective measure is needed. However, sometimes leaders continue to deny the seriousness of the problem, hoping it will correct itself in the future. This weakens the competitive position of the company. What management really needs to do is to recognize the problem and take the necessary steps to bring the organization back to the efficiency stage. Management might encourage employees to participate in the decision-making process to reduce inefficiency and improve performance to an acceptable level instead of trying to assure concerned parties that such a problem is under control or that the problem will take care of itself if some changes are applied.

Stage 3: Reactionary Stage

At this stage, the problem is severe enough to be identified by all participants in the organization. The organization needs to correct the problem quickly before it escalates. Whether the company is following their stated objectives and strategies needs to be examined. A new strategy or a modification might be necessary. None of the participants can ignore the seriousness of such deviations. The competitive position of the company is deteriorating, and a downward trend in these stages signals a performance crisis in the company.

A strategic measure needs to be applied even if it means restructuring the organization. Management needs to develop appropriate strategic options, discuss them in detail with all participants, and explain the risks involved with these options. This measure is considered reactionary, because it is after the fact and after a long period of denial. Some of these options might not be favorable to either management or employees, especially when laying off people or a shut down of production lines is involved. Therefore some of the steps could involve reevaluating organizational strategy. The strategy selected may be not achievable or the circumstances may have changed. Management needs to identify the problems or the setbacks and identify the solution. Employees need to be motivated to do the job, and customer service needs to be improved. Employees should undergo training in each department to assure that each person is capable of doing their job. Strategy should be implemented properly with the available proper technological equipment. Employees might need a better understanding of the strategy. Businesses need to stay current with the needs and wants of their customers and insure that they are producing products that fit customer needs. Other techniques can be used, such as promotions, store location, shelf space, or display setup to see if any improvements could be made in this area. A fresh and innovative outlook of management and company environmental review and evaluation may be needed. Continuous seminars to keep management abreast of changes in the workplace may be required. It is also possible that the market is saturated, the need for the product is declining, or that there are too many companies to compete with.

Stage 4: Trauma Stage

At this stage, the company's level of performance seems to be declining rapidly. It is way below the minimum expectations. The company has ignored the problem for so long that it is less able to control the efficiency and performance decline overtime. The downward trend in this stage signals a performance crisis that might be beyond repair. Restructuring or transformations of top management and other participants is the response to this crisis stage. A change of behavior by participants is a prerequisite for any effective reorganization. Employees should take a more active role in the reorganization. A training program may be installed to help employees understand the new changes that are coming. If performance levels continue to decline, then liquidate. It is always important to find a balance between how to boost profits without destroying the quality of workers. Restructuring can be done within particular departments in the company (e.g., marketing, finance, and manufacturing) or include the entire organization. These are painful options because they could involve hiring more employees or transferring or laying off some employees if there are too many.

If the company is in the beginning part of this stage, a merger might be considered. Outsiders (independents) should be used as consultants. Sometimes management in a company can be blind to things that have been happening. A firm can fall back and regroup by getting rid of any holdings that are inefficient and that affect the company's financial well being. The company can turn around by cutting costs of distribution or employees (if really necessary), eliminating unprofitable output, and restructuring the organization. The process of changing is very important and crucial in this stage so that the company doesn't end up in liquidation.

Stage 5: Disintegration Stage

At this stage, the company has ignored the problem to the point where it continues to lose competitiveness and market shares. The problem at this stage is severe and may be uncontrollable. Management's capability to amend the product or services is limited. Management may enter into a completely new product market or line or could eliminate certain nonprofitable lines. Revenue from those lines could be reinvested in a new product or service. New market strategy may be formulated to gain public interest in the new product line. However, sometimes when the performance of a company has reached this stage, the employee's options for continued employment are limited. Divestment of unprofitable operations is another valid strategy.

The company might consider liquidation, or spinning off or spinning out of some parts or units involved in the declining efficiency and effectiveness. This means a huge loss of capital and skillful people. Sometimes the appropriate measure might include closing down the organization, which creates even higher loss than before. This shows the importance of planning strategically and developing a control system to detect any variations from the formulated plans. Executives must play an important role of leading the company in an open and participative fashion. Their responsibilities are not only to identify and acknowledge the problem in the early stages, but also to inform participants and share problem solving.

STRATEGIC IMPLEMENTATION

It is obvious that when change is introduced, some forces in the organization will support it while other forces will resist it. Change must be planned. Usually change involves strategic adjustments within the organization and the way it conducts its business. In many cases modifying the mission, goals, and objectives to achieve the desired change are considered necessary. The desired change sometimes requires a change in technology or reallocation of resources between units and groups. Technology changes are designed to make the production of a product or service more efficient. Organizations that adopt the total quality approach require changes in the product and the process. Management must make it clear to all organization members as to why there is a need for change. To start the process of implementing change, management needs to depend on those supporting the change first. They need to find a champion, either an individual or group. In many cases, management needs to change the hierarchy of authority and goals. Structural change requires altering the administrative procedures and management systems. Management should attempt to selectively remove forces that restrain changes. As restraining forces are reduced or removed, behavior will shift to incorporate the desired changes, and the driving forces will be strong enough to enable implementation.

Management must provide information about the change and communicate it well to all employees involved, especially those who may resist implementation. Building trust, education, and opportunity for training will help to soften pressure and resistance. In some cases the change must combine change in technology. Technology changes are designed to make the production of a product or service more efficient.

Training and education is especially important when the change involves new technical knowledge or when users are unfamiliar with the new way that is being pursued. Top management commitment and support is absolutely necessary for any change to succeed. Top management supports the change by being a living example that signifies to all employees that the change is important for the organization. When top managers fail to commit totally to a particular project or idea, they can inadvertently undercut it by their lack of support and undermine future new initiatives. There is no doubt that in the past the chief executive officers of any organization have borne the consequences of their strategy. Some of them were even asked to leave their company. Some of the executives who were forced to leave their job because of their level of performance and failing strategies are John Sculley of Apple, Rod Canion of Compaq, Kay Whitmore of Eastman Kodak,

Robert Stempel of General Motors, John Akers of IBM, and Ken Olsen of Digital.

Employees typically resist change when they lack information about the necessity of that change. They believe that change will take away something of value or that it will change the way they do business. Uncertainty is especially threatening for employees who have a low tolerance for change and fear the novel and unusual. A proposed change in organizational structure or the methods used may lead to a perceived loss of power, prestige, pay, and company benefits. Employees often do not understand the intended purpose of a change or they distrust the intentions behind it. If previous working relationships with management have been negative, resistance may occur. It is clear that people who are affected by the change or the innovation may assess the situation differently. Therefore, to encourage participation in the process, management needs to involve users and potential resisters in designing and implementing the proposed change. This approach is time consuming, but pays off because members understand and become committed to the implementation. Cross-functional teams help managers determine potential problems and understand the differences in perceptions of change among employees. Teams also help in finding a better way of changing.

In some cases management needs to negotiate with employees to convince them about the change, especially when sacrifice is needed. Negotiation is a more formal means of achieving cooperation among all parties involved. That is why building a trust between all units and groups will make the change much smoother. In some cases it is highly recommendable that in order to win acceptance and approval of a desired change negotiation and bargaining with employees should be utilized. In many cases bargaining is preferred over confrontation. If negotiation fails then resisters are told to accept the change or lose rewards or even their jobs. In this case managers may use formal power to force employees to change, although this should be a last resort.[5]

Management encourages creativity and innovation. Innovation requires changes in the mindset. This will lead to change in the product or the services the company provides. New product or service innovations have major implications on organizational culture. To have a successful innovation the company must succeed in preparing employees by providing appropriate reward system. Such a strategy will promote innovation and change.

Managerial Changes in a Modern Organization

1. Organizational structure change from hierarchical to more flat.
2. Managers change from supervisors to coaches, enablers, or facilitators.
3. Communication changes from vertical to horizontal.

Figure 1.2
Management Development over the Past Century

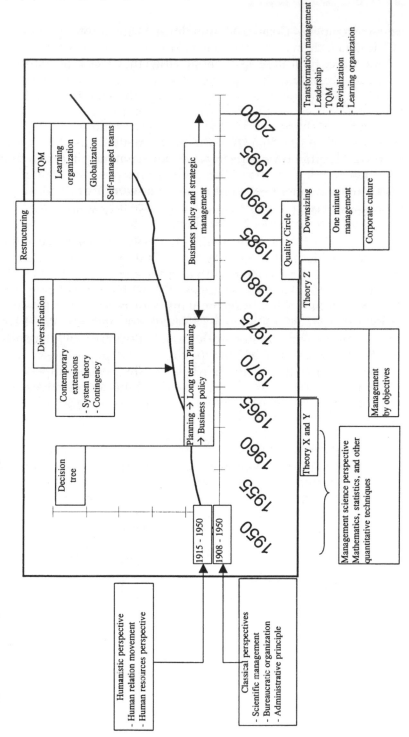

4. Workers' roles change from controlled to empowered.

5. Work unit change from functional to process unit (cross-functional).

6. Advancement criteria change from performance to ability.

7. Value change from protective to productive.

8. Job change from simple tasks to multidimensional.

9. Company strategy change from domestic focus to international focus.

10. Organizations change from public to private.

11. Focus of performance measures and compensation shift from activities to result.

12. Executives change from scorekeepers to leaders.

13. Executive decision-making changes from reactive to proactive.

Now consider some of the major changes that took place in the past century (see Figure 1.2). This figure is a summary of the changes that took place in the past one hundred years and the method or the tool mostly used to meet these changes. The focus of this book indicates the rapid evolution of management thinking over the last fifteen years. Transformation can be achieved by various methods. What worked for one company might not work for another. It usually depends on a number of factors such as the type of leadership, the size of the organization, the position in the market, the degree of competition (domestically and internationally), the availability of resources, and the level of cooperation among all employees.

NOTES

1. Nancy S. Mueller, "Missing the Competitive-Advantage Boat," *Managing Office Technology* 42 (January 1997): 33.

2. Peter Drucker, "The Society of Organization," *Harvard Business Review* 70 (September–October 1992): 95.

3. David Woodruff, "VW's Factory of the Future," *Business Week*, 7 October 1996, 52–56.

4. Alan Mitchell, "Corporate Dieting Can Make Your Company Fat," *Management Today* (May 1998): 42–48.

5. A. Khade and S. Metlen, "Gaining Competitive Advantage through Process Innovation and Experience Curve," *Business Research Yearbook, IABD* 3 (1996): 453.

Chapter 2

Transformation and Changing Attitudes

Today's firms are continually confronted with the need to develop and effectively implement strategies to achieve success in the world competitive arena. Over time organizations become more similar because they benchmark each other. Therefore, companies that change continuously have a better chance of succeeding in this global market. The objective of this chapter is to investigate the changes taking place in designing corporate strategies and innovation. Every organization's strategy is subject to change. This chapter addresses how to anticipate changes and how to align your company to succeed in this competitive environment. This chapter also discusses the current literature on strategy formulation and transformation and presents the fundamental components of transformation.

ADVANCES AND CHALLENGES

The world of business is becoming increasingly complex. Demands for acceleration in the process of providing goods and services, flexibility, quality, and innovation have increased tremendously. Today, change is occurring at a rapid geometric rate (e.g., 1, 2, 4, 8, 16, and so on). Continuous change in technology has made corporate products obsolete while customer support has drifted toward the Web. Down-loading information takes longer and longer and requires better skills. Just when you thought you were safe in your Internet usage comfort zone, the rules change. Viruses have been produced specifically to at-tack the Internet user. In recent years the growth and use of the Internet for business and personal utilization has exploded. Its infrastructure has roughly doubled each year since 1981. The size of the Internet is estimated at more than 800 million Web pages. There are more than 100 million American adults using the Internet and more than 150 mil-lion adults worldwide. As of now there are more adults in the United States using the Internet than there are U.S. adults who don't use a computer. Over 9.3 billion e-mail messages are sent each day, and 96 percent of those messages are considered Spam (e-mail sent to random people—usually used to advertise a product). With this explosion comes the inevitable confusion, frustration, and new technology, along with more advertisements than you can shake a stick at.[1]

Rigid lines of communication require organizations to change their cultural values and ways of doing business. Technology in the last twenty-five years has changed more than it has throughout the rest of human history combined. Today, consumers can watch people in their homes and order anything they need from groceries, to clothes, books, airline tickets, and much more on-line. They can listen to music, down-load music, e-mail, chat with anyone anywhere in the world, make phone calls, and receive faxes. Technology made it possible to look at the people we are chatting with, visit a library, read a book, get medi-cal advice, search for a lost friend, get a travel map, take a class, get an education, find a family tree, and send photos to the family. You can auction off your garage sale items, participate in a celebrity auction, be on a talk-show newsletter list, talk with your favorite movie star, play games, sell a house, and on and on.

The level of competition is rising rapidly. Global competition, major changes in industry structures, and an increased demand for speed, quality, and flexibility are evidence of such transformation. Partner-ships of different kinds are springing up between companies offering the same product or complementary products in the same or different geographical locations and different cultures. Because of these and other challenges, business operations, which were once relatively stable, are growing more complex. Management systems are in a state of crisis. Increasing speed and accuracy requires flatter chains of command and horizontal communication to break down the walls between franchises.

In the past, management's traditional responsibilities involved prob-lem solving. Management used to apply a problem-solving method as they saw fit. This has changed so that decisions pass downward throughout the company. Frederick Taylor's emphasis (during scientific management) was on simplifying jobs to the point where lower level employees do not have to think. Human potential was ignored, and employees were conditioned to function like simple, mindless machines that do what they are told rather than trying to contribute. Today, employees are required to think more for themselves and take corrective action. Technology has made traditional, centralized, office-based operations somewhat obsolete.

In the past, management systems were based on control. This is a reactive rather than interactive approach. We must help management to rethink its concepts of organizational attitude and organizational design and help employees to concentrate on improving their problem-solving skills. Management needs to be more flexible and willing to risk creative, new arrangements. Problem solving is the essence of any business operation. New businesses must deal with problems concerning funding, staffing, technology, competition, licenses, suppliers, record keeping, and insurance. These problems are generated by social and technical forces which grow more numerous and complex daily.

Organizations are capable of designing their own future in order to avoid problems. This defines problem solving as an integral, ongoing part of any healthy operation. There is a need for a clear understanding of the role each of the individuals within the organization must play in terms of that purpose. Learning constantly from the environment and adapting to keep its vision in tune with an increased turbulent environment makes the organization able to constantly readjust flexible structures. This chapter focuses on the variables that characterize a change in the organization, and how the company can transform its organizational structure, resources, product technologies, and its market position to develop competitive market strategies. When the company fails to respond to the changing environment, this will no doubt affect its future performance. Take for example the hesitation of the American auto industry during the 1960s and early 1970s to respond to a changing market. This delay resulted in a big market share loss to Japanese and European companies. Another good example is Xerox, the pioneer in the copying business. The company did not respond to changes in the marketplace vigorously, which caused the company to lose big during the 1970s to Japanese companies like Canon. IBM lost billions of dollars and their market share because they wanted to deal with everything related to computer business. IBM makes mainframes, work stations, midrange computers, desktops, home computers, and even software. The Japanese fell into the same trap during the 1990s where their business performance was weakened and debt accumulated. The beginning of this century will be a big test to see if the Japanese can restructure and transform their businesses and their social system to restore their prosperity.

CORPORATE TRANSFORMATION

The goal of corporate transformations is to improve performance. It is a new way of thinking about organizations and how people should relate to necessary changes. The rapid pace of the 1990s has proven to be a time of change. For many companies, the lack of quality in their operation has caused their downfall. According to Milan Moravee, "Forty-seven percent of the companies that appeared on the Fortune 500 a decade ago have disappeared from today's list."[2]

Many efforts to improve performance are not necessarily considered transformational. Transformation takes place when the majority of organizational members change their attitude, new initiative is utilized, and technology is modernized. Organizations are made up of a complex system of stakeholders such as managers, employees, major customers, and major suppliers, each having a legitimate requirement. New capabilities, continuous improvement, innovation, global quality, learning, networking, thinking globally, cooperating with other units, and showing sensitivity to customers' needs are all transformational requirements. All of this demands extensive changes in how work is performed.

Transformation improves performance and demands extensive changes in individual behavior in the workplaces to change the way people perform their jobs. A training program that emphasizes meeting the customer's requirements is a priority of most organizational agendas and is the key to a firm's survival and growth. The program should also be directed toward managing people in groups or teams and building a relationship of participation, openness, and trust among members of the organization. This will help in developing cultural change. This means creating a behavioral change. Changing only the structure of the organization is not necessarily transformation.

TRANSFORMATION IS CHANGE

It is important to distinguish between transformation and other changes such as mergers or acquisitions. Acquiring or selling in any form might change the size of the organization or the level of debts involved. However, it is not necessarily affecting the nature of management and employees' work. Creating cultural change is a long-term process that requires serious and persistent effort.

Management's immediate tasks in a merger are to change the power structure, meld work processes, and create a new source of identification. This is a difficult job, but it has to be completed. After that, management starts to build a strategy of how this new creation can compete in the marketplace and how it can enhance its position within its industry and within its macroenvironment. Competition comes after the processes of integration and operational improvement have been put in place. For example, Bell Atlantic and Nynex reached an agreement to merge for $23 billion on 22 April 1996, creating a telephone power-house. The combined entity is the nation's second largest telecommunications company, after AT&T, who has almost $27 billion in revenue, $3 billion in profits, and 134,000 employees worldwide. The Internet has made it possible for giant companies to join forces. For example, AOL has merged with Time Warner and Wal-Mart is teaming up with other companies to offer free access to the Internet, while Sears is doing the same. AT&T and Microsoft teamed up with cable companies to provide services. Almost every week in the newspaper we read about another merger or teaming of companies to plan their strategies for some type of cooperation. These companies believe that by sharing resources and acquiring synergy benefits will help them greatly in the future. There will be changes in the size, structure, and capabilities of the new established company. However, unless major behavioral changes take place, this should not be considered transformation.

TRANSFORMATIONAL LEADER ACTIVITIES

Many companies had to downsize in the not too distant past. This led to job insecurity and less loyalty to the company. Attitude is very important. A manager or employee with a poor outlook and attitude will find that outlook reflected in those that work under or with him or her. The transformed leader should resemble a coach who is willing to listen and be open to new ideas and challenges. For the company to be successful, the top management must believe in and be able to "sell" the vision of the company. This vision is not only for the present; it is for the future, too.

In dealing with the restructuring (or downsizing) that will take place in many companies, there will be chaos and some disorder. CEOs need to be able to take control of the chaos and use it to their benefit. A skillful leader can turn the chaos into an avenue for creativity and re-invention. A more open system of communication will be necessary to convey new ideas and solutions from others in the ranks. Another big requirement will be honesty about the organization's health and needs. The leaders can gain much more power and trust from their workers by being honest and open with them.

In the struggle to keep companies afloat and keep upper management positive and intact, some companies have started to send management to workshops. Allied Domecq Spirits & Wine had gone through a merger and wanted its restructuring to be successful. The executives of the company participated in a developmental workshop to reevaluate themselves and to find their strong points and abilities. They were to reassess their career goals for the future as to where they wanted to be and what they wanted to do. With this new positive outlook, the executives went back to work. The new attitude was relayed to "their people." The work atmosphere was more positive and motivating. A month after the whole process was completed, the executive held review meetings to check their progress and inquire about any new concerns or ideas. The workshop had been very successful for Allied, and they are now introducing it to a larger cross-section of their management.

The new concept of starting the change with top management is a choice companies need to make. The old hierarchy and chain of communication must be broken, and modifying a few programs or behaviors is only a temporary fix. Companies must acquire a new paradigm. A paradigm is a set of beliefs or a mindset that we use to set boundaries for ourselves and to focus problem solving.[3] This paradigm must start at the top and be relayed down through the ranks. Attitudes are contagious, and top management today must have one that is worth catching.[4]

PARTICIPATION OF TOP-LEVEL MANAGEMENT

Transformed leaders are expected to effectively lead a company along with the top managers. A transformation is necessary to ensure that the entire top management team, including the company's board of directors and operating committee, knows the direction of the company. Once the executives educate themselves about what needs to be done to transform the organization, they should prepare similar training for other members to follow. Transformed leaders must create a new vision. In 1979 and during the 1980s, Lee Iacocca of Chrysler, a visionary leader, was able to transform the company. Iacocca was able to mobilize the employees and accept the changes. He then institutionalized the changes by developing a new corporate culture. This culture allowed the creation of self-managed teams and empowered the employees. These changes have contributed to the turnaround of the company, the growth of a new stage in the life cycle, and international expansion.

The transformational process requires massive administrative changes that involve a fundamental transformation of mission, structure, and the political and cultural systems. Educating and training members of the organization on the importance of transformation can do this. Meetings can be regularly scheduled, monthly or quarterly, to ensure the methods and the concepts are successfully applied. Some of the topics that need to be covered in the initial transformation meetings are the current plans of the company and the market condition. It is important that the members of the organization are divided into various groups or teams.

Teams can be divided into two main types. The first is a team within the department, which deals with issues on a day to day basis. The second is the cross-functional team, which deals with projects or long-term issues. Some of the important issues that teams need to deal with are progress in the transformation process, strategies, financial results and projections, numbers of employees and near-term employment projections, planned major programs, and other major developments, such as updates on labor negotiations and partnership agreements.

Management teams need to address the following issues: the new product developments, other products–services in the pipelines, competitive advantages, how the company measures up in comparison to other competitors, the status and conditions of the industry itself, and what is projected for the future in the industry. The team meetings should set the company's direction and encourage opportunities for questions, answers, and discussions. In addition it is important for management to be accessible and responsive to the questions and concerns that might arise. These meetings are "ideal" opportunities to get people from various functions, business units, and locations to work together. The meeting should not be structured so that all of the communication is one way (e.g., from top executives to the audience, which is the traditional case). When the team is given a particular assignment, it is advisable to raise many questions as to why it is important. Assignments must be reviewed and acted upon. Upon completion, the teams should report back to the larger groups and discuss the information to get people to know each other. This way people are able to familiarize themselves with the other member's of the group.

Traditional Management → Transform into strategic and transformational management. Strategic management truly understands the changes in the market and is willing to modify methods and approaches to take advantage of the opportunities that exist in the marketplace.

Starting this process will require training and retraining in various issues, such as teamwork skills, management-style assessments, a planning methodology, or other topics that will enable the participants to do their team assignments. Training is a very important element of the process; it helps to ensure that every member of each team understands his or her position and role. Hospital teams include surgeons, anesthetists, and nurses. Each understand their role and position very well. The life of the patient depends on this understanding. In fact you can replace any member with a similar team member and expect the same result. Every effective team must have a clear purpose and everyone must be clear about where they are going. Sports teams and railroad teams are other good examples. Therefore training is very important. Planning exercises must be seen as making a difference, and assignments should be given with challenging deadlines.

The following list describes the new paradigm:

	Late Twentieth Century	Beginning of Twenty-First Century
Technology	Mechanical–Electronic	Electronic, electronic mail, new software, Internet service, Web pages, instant messages
Leadership	Autocratic–Participative	Mostly transformational
Power–Control	Top management	Widely dispersed
Managers	Control what people do	Managers must obtain commitment of workers
Hierarchy	Vertical	Vertical and horizontal
Workforce	Homogeneous focus only on individual work	Culturally diverse work mostly in teams
	Part of the process	People design and improve processes
Culture	Focus on stability and efficiency	Focus on change, participation, flexibility, and problem solving
Tasks	Focus on routine activities	Focus on creative activities
Process	Requires external control	Workers who run the process control it
Market	Local, domestic, national, and international	Global emphasis with use of technology
Purpose	Profit	Customers, employees, and profit
Resources	Capital and labor	Information, capital, and labor
Quality	Minimum required by the market; what's affordable; inspection-oriented	No exception; quality to meet the changing expectation of customer quality control; continuous improvement

The groups should reconvene on a continual basis in order to cover the essential issues such as updates on information given at the initial meeting, new developments, followup on action items taken at earlier meetings, planning for new actions, and further developmental activities for the group. To ensure that these meetings are valuable to all, the members must participate actively in the planning of the meeting and the meeting itself. Enabling communication among the participants between the meetings by electronic mail systems, teleconferencing facilities, computer-based bulletin boards, and conference capabilities is another vital aspect of this process. The top management group should share their newly acquired knowledge with their own employees because every employee, as well as the overall company, will benefit.

THE NEW LEADERSHIP

An individual who believes in the necessity of change must lead the transformational process. The new leader is the one who is able to predict the needs of the market and plan to succeed. In the previous example of hospital teams, the surgeon is the leader. The coaches in the sport teams are the leaders; the president of a company or university is as well. The process of change must include the following:

1. The creation of a vision can energize organizational members. Organization must break free of previous patterns and old structural processes and activities that are no longer useful. During the 1980s, GM's new strategic vision was articulated under the leadership of Roger Smith. At Chrysler, CEO Lee Iacocca during 1979 and during the 1980s established a new vision and corporate culture. Robert Eaton, the current CEO of Chrysler, fit into this category as well. He is a visionary leader and continues the process of transforming the company to meet its challenges. Managers and employees are involved in this process.

2. Above all, transformational leaders must be committed to the process. They must allocate enough time and resources to make the vision a reality. Innovation and creativity must be encouraged.

3. The process must be comprehensive and based on a total system perspective. Transformational change involves redesign and renewal of the total organization. Rethinking of previous policies, roles, processes, and values is key. A corporate culture that touches every one in the organization should be established.

4. Leaders must recruit the commitment of all participants. Participating, sharing information, and empowering the participants will enhance the transformation chances for success. At GM, Roger Smith took nine hundred top executives on a five-day retreat to discuss the vision and gain their commitment.

5. Information sharing requires adjustments on the part of managers for the inclusion of employees, major suppliers, and major customers.

6. Horizontal structure and communication replaces the familiar hierarchical pyramid, incorporating empowerment and information.

7. Operational changes improve basic work and organizational processes in different areas of the business.
8. Finally, when the majority of participants are convinced and the methods are proven successful, the changes must be institutionalized. The new practices, actions, and values must be permanently adopted. This means that major resources must be devoted to training programs to implement the new organizational style. Changes may involve the technical, financial, and marketing systems, as well as administrative structures and control systems.

Technology learning must be continuous so as to move the organization toward a new way of doing and thinking. It is important to emphasize that management must make a clear case for why such transformation is necessary and how the new efforts will lead to a competitive advantage. To encourage participation in the process, management needs to involve users and potential resisters in designing the change. This approach is time consuming, but pays off because users understand and become committed to the implementation. Participation also helps managers determine potential problems and understand the differences in the perception of change among employees. In some cases management needs to negotiate with employees to convince them about the change. Bargaining to win acceptance and approval of a desired change is preferred over confrontation. If negotiation fails, then resisters are told to accept the change or lose rewards or even their jobs. In this case, managers use formal power to force employees to change, although this should be viewed as a last resort.

THE LEARNING ORGANIZATION

Technology and globalization have forced companies to be prepared. Organizations need to continuously adapt to new technology and market changes. Learning organization refers to the degree of readiness on the part of all participants in the organization to undertake a particular project. Learning organization refers to the education and training level necessary to improve the organizational capabilities. How to construct an effective team that can engage in identifying and solving problems is a critical issue. The continuous training of employees can help a company grow and become more efficient. Employers are asking workers to work more with their heads than hands. Learning organization is an interactive system that influences all participants and units. Learning organization requires visionary leaders, empowered employees, and a new corporate culture. A proactive leader who provides vision for development of strategies can bring positive change to the organization. Management must be in a position to permit and encourage participation from all employees. They must be willing to share information with various stakeholders in the organization, employees, major suppliers, and major customers. The development of new corporate culture requires the rethinking of roles, processes, and values of all groups in the organization. The result of the learning process must be a more flexible organization where interaction and communication are encouraged. Ford Motor Company invited service managers, suppliers, and customers to a work session. By inviting such a broad range of people to the strategy table, the organization gained viewpoints that they normally do not. Learning organization therefore is an important tool for transformational change, which involves redesign and renewal of the total organization.

LEADERSHIP TRANSFORMATION: THE BOARD OF DIRECTORS

The boards of directors are the stockholders' representatives. Usually they are responsible for selection of top management and for overseeing their performance. They are expected to provide advice to top management and monitor managerial and company performance. Many studies showed that in reality the boards of directors are not effective. In order to improve this situation, many shareholder activists and institutional investors try to make an effort to be involved and hold the board members accountable. However, those stockholders and institutions rarely command enough votes to defeat management in a proxy contest. While the boards are composed of many bright and professional people, they do not play a significant role in governing the organization. The boards of directors are not necessarily the true representatives of stockholders. Many stockholders do not participate in election of the board members. Those stockholders have a small stake in the company and they believe they will not make a difference.

The expected role of the board is to oversee the strategy formulation and implementation, capital allocation, and management compensation. Efforts continue to find a better way of energizing these boards. During the last decade stockholders became more active and involved. While during the 1970s and 1980s most stockholders were thinking of themselves as investors, now they are thinking of themselves as owners.

No doubt many boards of directors are trying to conscientiously carry out their duties in the right way. In today's highly competitive environment, organizations are in need of a more involved board of directors. Those directors who recognize their responsibilities toward the stakeholders of the organization can make a difference in the governance process. The board must realize that they are held accountable for any wrongdoing in the organization. Therefore to insure the needed transformation and to better prepare the participants to do their jobs we need more involved boards of directors.

CEO TRANSFORMATIONS: RESTRUCTURING AT CHRYSLER

Chief executive officers often hold the most power and responsibility in a corporation and are in a position to implement the most dramatic turnaround when a company is failing. Never was this more evident than at Chrysler. In an article titled "Building the New Chrysler," John Bell maintains that CEO Robert Eaton succeeded in taking Chrysler from the brink of death in 1989 to record revenues in each of the last three years.[5] To accomplish this, Eaton began by changing the mission statement and taking a more simplistic approach to selling cars than had been attempted in the past. Eaton also changed the financial strategy to include selling off nonautomotive assets and restructuring the balance sheet. The company shifted to a more conservative strategy to reduce debt while instituting a new and bold development program to spur sales. In addition, a stock repurchase program was instituted to increase revenue from stockholders. Next, Eaton overhauled the entire management corporate culture. He emphasized teamwork and cited the importance of process thinking, which showed his willingness to pull apart the company and restructure. This new corporate culture focused on the people in the organization. Eaton comments that it is how well, from the top down, you train, organize, motivate, and empower those within a new culture and, in turn, lead the company in a new direction.[6] Eaton proved that widespread downsizing and excessive spending are not always needed to improve the balance sheet. Instead, he used better applications of the resources that the company already possessed. Chrysler's merger with Mercedes Benz in 1999 created a strong company that could succeed in a competitive environment.

STRATEGIC TRANSFORMATION

Strategic transformation is the process of changing strategy to regain competitive advantage. It requires redefining business objectives and creating new competencies to take advantage of opportunities in the market. If a company uses outdated strategies with little changes, this cannot be classified as transformation.

There is ample evidence that vision, mission, and goal setting and planning can positively influence organizational performance. The evidence shows that large and small businesses employing strategic planning outperform their counterparts who operate without formal planning. Today, firms are continually confronted with the need to develop and effectively implement strategies to achieve success in the world competitive arena. Business leaders can become so preoccupied with day-to-day issues that their organizations lose all sense of mission and direction. Strategic planning forces future thinking that highlights new opportunities and threats and refocuses an organization's mission.

Strategic planning is a tool for taking control of an organization. It is a way for an effective enterprise to be alert and focused. It helps organizational participants to align vision with resources and capabilities. Usually, strategic planning focuses on a business's most critical problems, choices, and opportunities. Businesses are often faced with an onslaught of problems that are difficult to address one by one. Strategic planning provides a method for resolving interrelated sets of problems in an intentional and coordinated way.

The Industrial Revolution saw the emergence of fierce competitors in a market full of new products and technologies. High rates of demand forced companies to evaluate how and where to invest. Strategic approaches that emerged in the late 1960s and 1970s provided firms with "how to" methods to evaluate the market and their resources. The 1980s and 1990s brought competition of unprecedented proportions from a multitude of sources. Faced with declining profits and loss of market shares, businesses were faced with new choices: increase revenue, cut expenses, find new markets, go into debt, change product lines, downsize, emphasize quality, reorganize the business structure, or go out of business. Strategic planning is a method for thinking through these and a myriad of other tough choices.

STRATEGY AND PERFORMANCE

The Industrial Revolution witnessed the emergence of strong competition with the development of many new products and technologies. The level of demand and competition directed companies to invest in the marketplace. Competition in the late 1960s and 1970s forced companies to develop strategic approaches that contributed to improve the position and resources of the company within the market. Many authors such as Porter, Bartlett and Ghoshal, and others describe the relationship between organizational performance and strategy development.[7] They were able to link the level of organizational performance in a changing environment to corporate strategy. They considered several environmental factors such as access to technology and natural resources, regulations and government influences, demographic and cultural differences among their customers, and the economy of local markets. Business strategy and performance are also linked to quality. Higher quality results in lower costs and improved competitiveness, which leads to increased sales and market share. Quality, like any other dimension of business, must be managed strategically. Quality ensures shortening the cycle time incurred during the production of products or services by reducing or eliminating scrap, rework, and errors or nonconformances in the production process. This increases the productive use of facilities, machinery, and personnel. This in turn reduces the total manufacturing costs and provides value-added activities.

Externally oriented strategies, focusing on competitive positioning, are interdependent with resource utilization either through internally developed technology or through strategic alliances. Technological changes must be expected and factored in when creating a strategy or plan for the future. Strategic alliances provide faster and better access to the global market. However, these types of collaborations will form new types of competitors in the marketplace. As a result, firms are looking for ways to better satisfy their major customers. The cost of keeping the customer happy is much smaller than bringing in new customers. Thus, by the late 1980s and early 1990s, theorists were redefining world market strategies.

Planning brings organizations together. It is a way for innovative leaders to share and promote their vision. Good planning requires teamwork and benchmarking. It results in improved knowledge of the organization, better communication across management and production levels, improved managerial skills, and an increased personal investment in the organization. It establishes a pattern of success and growth that businesses will want to continue into the future. It helps businesses influence and control the world, not just respond to it. While strategic thinking tells you where you want to go, planning is how you get there. In the act of transformation, organizations must be careful in collecting information and making assumptions. Incorrect information and faulty assumptions can result in the formulation of a poor or even disastrous plan that will affect all participants. Organizations need to continuously evaluate and control their strategic plans. Without evaluation, midcourse corrections fail to materialize, resulting in negative consequences.

A strategic transformation starts with a formal review of the strategic alternative, shared discussions with other levels, and takes a clear decision and commitment on major issues. Strategic transformation is also the result of changes in technology, shifts in market demand, emerging standards, and aggressive competitors. Management identifies the competencies in which to invest to obtain their goals. They must then identify strategic intent, which will provide a general direction for the whole organization. Here, we have to emphasize the role and involvement of middle level management. They are responsible for creating initiatives and experiments and developing competencies to ensure the success of the process.

Strategic management evaluates the external and the internal forces. Management should evaluate the opportunities that exist in the environment. In many cases this translates into a perceived need for change within the organization. Managers sense a need for change when there is a performance gap, or a disparity between existing and desired performance levels. The performance gap may occur because current procedures are not up to standard or because a new idea or technology could improve current performance.

Reaching clarity of the company strategy is, therefore, a gradual process that involves top and middle level managers along with other managers and employees. Strategic vision in a period of decline is important to motivate employees and encourage them to accept changes. This is especially possible when the CEO of the company has already established some degree of acceptability and credibility. If management is not committed to the strategic process, no such transformation can take place. In case of a new strategy, management roles change as company strategy shifts from one to another.

In a nutshell, the world of business and competition is in a vortex of dynamic change that will destroy all except those who carefully chart their course through the maelstrom. Companies that cannot plan strategically will have a difficult time surviving.

TECHNIQUES OF IMPROVING OPERATIONS

There are two popular techniques involved in improving operations. They are *reengineering* and *total quality management*.

Reengineering

Reengineering is a redesigning process across organizational boundaries. It is also called *Business Process Redesign* (*BPR*) or *process reengineering*. Reengineering is the fundamental rethinking and radical redesign of work processes. Its goal is to achieve substantial improvement in key performance measures such as cost, quality, service, and speed. Process improvement is premised on increasing market shares and enhancing the quality of products and service by altering system structures and redesigning processes to improve productivity and customer satisfaction. Altering systems and redesigning includes eliminating waste in terms of nonvalue as defined from the perspective of the consumer. Managers value employees and take on new roles as facilitators and coaches as opposed to the old role of supervisor. Process improvement eliminates extensive checks and controls by managers. The new approach of organizing the work is by key processes, projects, or activities. Since work activity cuts across function and stays clearly focused on customer requirement, cross-functional teams are major forces in the transformational process. Middle level management positions in many companies have been eliminated to lower cost and speed up decision making. Many large companies start thinking as small ones. They even break up the company into different units and divisions. The purpose of such changes is to be closer to the customers. Engineers, accountants, and marketing executives are closer to the shop floor. Supervision and shop operators exert a major quality influence. Many traditional sales jobs have been eliminated. Now selling and servicing products is mostly done over the Internet and by phone. New strategies and tactics to enhance the quality of goods and services are applied. The number of employees in the original companies is reduced tremendously. The managers of different units have a much greater say over their own destiny with the smaller numbers of employees.

Other companies dropped the number of purchase and personnel managers and redesigned the format of their company. They made their companies more flat with decentralization of decision making. This benefited organizational participants more quickly than if the organization had more managerial levels. Under transformation significant restructuring never stops. While all these activities improve corporate performance, we must be very careful that these changes will not carry a huge risk to the organization. We should not sacrifice people who are good at building things, such as new products and new services, and who add value to the organization.

There are different definitions to reengineering, but they have the following common elements:

1. Radical redesign
2. Rapid improvement
3. Dramatic improvement
4. Process integration
5. Information technology as a requirement
6. A change of mindset
7. The elimination of unnecessary functions
8. A continuous process of reengineering

Reengineering provides a steep change in performance in a short period of time. Employees are involved not only in designing the new process, but also in executing it on a daily basis. Proponents of reengineering encourage a continuous process improvement partnership between supplier and company. For example, Wal-Mart requested that Procter & Gamble (P&G) propose the amount of disposable diapers Wal-Mart should order. Over time, P&G skipped the purchasing recommendation and just shipped the diapers. This new relationship eliminated many cost transactions. This process refers to how one person could perform many of the transactions, which were previously performed by several individuals in various departments. In addition, no check of quantities and prices of purchased products are done at the time of receiving the products. Thus, process-improved organizations build in quality control by partnership development. In this case, process reengineering is concerned with the improvement of existing processes and short-term savings of cost and time. It is usually associated with radically improving how a company can develop, advance, and apply the commitment and talent of people.

Another example is the Alexander Doll Company, which was bought by a bank in New York City while it was in bankruptcy. Under the supervision of a TBM consulting group, "KAIZEN" (or process improvement) was conducted. The process resulted in the following:

1. The decrease in the distance each doll traveled from the beginning to the end of the manufacturing process from 630 feet to 40 feet.
2. The decrease in the time required, completing a doll from ninety days to ninety minutes.
3. The decrease in the number of unfinished doll pieces from 2,900 to 34.
4. The decrease from 2,010 to 980 in the square footage used for the line.
5. The increase in productivity from eight dolls per day to twenty-five per day. These improvements or developments will continue indefinitely.[8]

Companies that do apply reengineering spend their resources developing respect in both interorganizational and intraorganizational relationships instead of spending resources in developing and maintaining internal control. Reengineering does eliminate many costly transactions, but at the same time the elimination of these transactions causes internal control problems.

We have to keep in mind that not all reengineering is transformational because in many cases it only means downsizing or reducing management layers. In these cases, few changes to the role of employees and management are required, and therefore it is not necessarily a transformational change.

TOTAL QUALITY MANAGEMENT (TQM)

Quality can be defined as providing goods or services that meet or exceed customer expectation. Customers therefore define quality. Quality also refers to quality of work, quality of service, quality of information, quality of objectives, quality of process, quality of division, quality of people (including workers, engineers, managers, and executives), or quality of system. What is quality in one store (e.g., Kmart) is not necessarily quality in a different store (e.g., Neiman Marcus). What is considered quality today might not be considered quality tomorrow. Quality encompasses the products or services provided but also the information, planing, people, processes, and environment in which they are provided.[9] In total quality management, management learns new skills such as coaching and facilitating and utilizes less monitoring and controlling. Some people doubt that a company can adopt TQM and at the same time reduce costs. This is possible when qualities improve and demand increases. Cost reduction must be the result of less rework items, less damages, fewer products that do not meet consumer standards, and less errors and carelessness in the process. A result of a better quality is higher demand. This means buying larger quantities of raw materials at a discount prices and producing more, hence reducing overall cost (e.g., Xerox, Ford, British Airways, and many others have reduced costs through improving quality in workplaces).

TQM gives an organization a competitive advantage by increasing the productivity and quality of the product or service. This is, now more than ever, a necessity in today's competitive business environment. It requires real process improvement that involves everybody in the organization. Total quality management has been adopted for either survival or building a competitive edge. It is expected that in order for a company to transform successfully it must understand its customer's needs (both internally and externally). Many companies have come to the realization that customer loyalty is worth having. In the author's opinion, companies have done well in the past five years because they have realized the importance of customer satisfaction.

Total quality management means a total commitment to a customer-oriented and customer-satisfaction culture. Education and training are important total quality management tools for achieving total quality. But the key to quality improvement is a focus on customer needs and expectations. Before linking customer satisfaction to TQM, an organization must learn that a customer's perceived wants and needs determine satisfaction or dissatisfaction. Implementation of TQM can result in a quality perception as well as customer service leadership which ensures both customer loyalty and new customer growth. Effective TQM can change a business's culture so that there is a sense throughout the organization that the determination of customer wants is everyone's job. Marketing studies show satisfied customers tell five to seven people of their experiences. Dissatisfied customers will tell their bad experience to as many as twenty people.[10] AT&T Network Systems Transmission Systems Unit has used TQM as a way to produce state of the art equipment that has opened doors in more than fifty countries. As a result, the implementation of TQM helped AT&T to win the Baldridge National Quality Award in 1992. A team called the Wild Ones was able to reduce the number of bent pins on digital access and cross-connect panels by 81 percent. AT&T was able to reach their 1992 goal of reducing the number of circuit pack returns to thirty-four in ten thousand, which placed them among the best in class manufacturers.[11] Further, customer input in the factory to design better, more reliable products measures the equipment's performance. The factory uses this input by the customer to improve the product. Therefore, TQM is one of the transformation techniques that could be used to achieve comprehensive change. In fact, all successful implementation of TQM can be considered a transformation. Therefore, the two concepts, transformation management and successful TQM attempts, can be used interchangeably.

CHALLENGES FACING TRANSFORMATION

Transformation processes face many challenges. These include

1. Convincing management and employees that change is needed. Until management starts to question existing levels of performance, fundamental change cannot occur.
2. Giving management the tools to think strategically.
3. Implementing a new business theory, which can be difficult even when it has been defined and agreed upon.
4. The level of training, coaching, and time needed for transformation to become reality.
5. Strategic shifts, which are often more threatening to the employees than other types of changes. The following are examples of such situations: (1) experienced employees who were once greatly prized and rewarded suddenly become irrelevant to the company's success, and (2) executives who grew up with the organization, building a future with their association, suddenly become less important.

Some competencies can be developed in house with appropriate training programs. However, companies often find it necessary to hire new employees or managers with the necessary skills and competencies. Strategic transformation is more difficult, riskier, and longer than operation improvement. It is, however, necessary for companies competing in a global competitive market.

CORPORATE SELF-RENEWAL

Corporate self-renewal requires certain types of behavior such as facing reality, setting high standards of performance, and accepting responsibility for actions or results. Other behaviors include organizational change, elimination of bureaucracy, and increasing speed in the decision-making processes. The creation of a learning organization and continuous improvement programs provide the company with the capability for self-renewal. All this provides a new way of managing to help the organization stay ahead of competition.

Transformation at GE was built around one goal: to become a self-renewing organization by convincing management to be more flexible, face reality, accept criticism, engage in open communication, allow employee participation, and be more responsible for decision making. Mastering these behaviors enabled GE managers to address strategic issues effectively and launch various projects to improve productivity throughout the company. The focus was on behavior rather than on strategy, which was essential for GE's success. For other companies, where the art of management is less well developed than at GE, pushing managers to behave differently must be combined by intervention and training to address specific strategic and operation issues.

In 1993, through an analysis of our foreign operations, we found that our resources could not support 21 plants. The Board of Directors approved a management recommendation to transform the company. We decided to close 6 plants in several countries overseas and reduce our work force by 770 employees. Thus, we downsized to our present size of fifteen plants in ten countries, and eliminated excess production capacity. In the countries in which we closed plants, we left a sales staff. We tried, with success in this period, to retain and financially prop-up our other manufacturing operations. We were able to keep our company viable for our stakeholders-employees, shareholders, customers, and suppliers" (Donald F. Hastings, chairman and CEO of Lincoln Electric Company, Cleveland, Ohio, in a 1998 speech).

In summary, the transformation process requires management to understand the causes of problems before attempting to suggest any changes. In the early stages of change, management needs to play a major role in convincing all participants of why such change is needed. The attention must be given to the system as well as the people in the organization. Encouraging employees to be creative and innovative is essential to any future changes. Employees should be in a position to participate actively in decisions about change. They must understand what the company can do to improve its competitiveness. The process must be planned. Evaluation of the resources and capabilities, readiness for change to support corporate leaders, and top level management are critical factors in the process. The transformation process must start with an organization vision, the desirable future state, the future direction, and then the creation of goals and objectives that are achievable given the resources, capabilities, and the condition of the external environment. In many cases changes in organizational policies and procedures are necessary conditions for the process to succeed. Since change will involve everyone in the organization, employees must be prepared and well trained to contribute positively to the change. A transformational leader must be able to align the organization with its vision and create transformational process that can be shared by all participants. Changes are necessary to the survival of all organization. It is the fuel that keeps the organization running. Therefore, having a plan for change and using proven techniques will make this process much easier and more effective.

NOTES

1. Louis K. Falk, "The Internet: Information and Communication Overload," *Business Research Yearbook, IABD* 7 (2000): 857.

2. Milan Moravee, "Leader Must Love Change, Not Loathe It," *HR Focus* 71 (February 1994): 13–15.

3. John Refausse, "Self-Knowledge to Lift Career Spirits," *People Management* 2 (May 1996): 34–38.

4. Karen L. Newman, "Organizational Transformation during Institutional Upheaval," *Academy of Management Review* 25 (2): 602–619.

5. John Bell, "Building the New Chrysler," *Industry Week* 245 (September 1996): 10–15.

6. Ibid., 12.

7. Christopher Bartlett and Sumanatra Ghoshal, "What Is a Global Manager: Global Strategies, Insights from the World's Leading Thinkers," *Harvard Business Review* 72 (1994): 77; Michael E. Porter, *Competitive Strategy: Techniques for Analyzing Industries and Competitors* (New York: The Free Press, 1980); Michael E. Porter, *Competitive Advantage: Creating and Sustaining Superior Performance* (New York: The Free Press, 1985).

8. Philip Kotler, *Marketing Management, Analysis, Planning, Implementation, and Control* (Englewood Cliffs, N.J.: Prentice Hall, 1994).

9. Steven P. Landry and Ann Fukuhara, "Continuous Process Improvement: A Dilemma for Auditors," *The CPA Journal* 66 (August 1996): 56–61; Roberta Maynard, "A Company Is Turned Around through Japanese Principles," *Nations Business* 84 (February 1996): 9.

10. David L. Goetsch and Stanley B. Davis, *Total Quality Handbook* (Upper Saddle River, N.J.: Prentice Hall, 2001).

11. Ibid.

Chapter 3

Leadership Transformation

The rapid pace of the 1990s has proven to be a time of change. For many companies, the lack of quality of their change has caused their downfall. Today's leaders must become the leaders of change. They must leave the traditional organizational system behind and become more progressive and flexible with the changing times. This chapter will discuss the importance of leadership in today's organizations. Leadership roles, styles, and effectiveness will also be explored.

In the past, corporations wanted managers to align and change their personal goals and beliefs with those of the company. The success of a leader may depend on organizational characteristics such as size, resources, structure, and performance.

Today, organizations are changing. Companies have had to adjust their strategies to take advantage of opportunities that exist in the marketplace. When a company fails to change on time or selects a wrong direction it will end up losing market share and sacrifice profit. For example, the auto industry lost big in the 1960s. Xerox in their copying business and Sears within their financial network both lost big during the 1970s. IBM lost during the 1980s and the beginning of the 1990s. There have been radical improvements in information and communication technology and a shrinkage of the world in terms of time and distance, and most of the military and industrial blocs have broken up. This has signaled an end to the once dominant organizational hierarchy. This change will require managers to develop skills such as open mindedness and the capacity to work in teams and in a consistently high activity and changing environment.[1]

Downsizing has also led to job insecurity and less loyalty to the company. Attitude is very important to ensure loyalty. Attitudes are contagious, and top management today must have an attitude that is worth catching. A manager with a poor attitude and outlook will be reflected in those that work under that manager. For the company to be successful, the top management must believe in and be able to "sell" the vision of the company. This vision represents the present as well as the future of the company.

Many corporations will need to be able to compete on the playing field of business if they want to succeed. An energized workforce is the only way to win in business today. A leader needs to recognize that employees need to think for themselves. A leader needs to get the employees involved, get them to want to perform well, and get them to be energetic about what they do. For example, the new organization at GE depends on shared values. Their value-based organization derives its efficiency from consensus. Workers who share their employer's goals don't need much supervision.

As today's society moves toward more speed, quality, and performance, employers need employees who will act the right way with less instruction. Employees also need to be able to share some of their own ideas with their employers. That calls for emotional commitment. This is a commitment that has to be earned. It is not given freely.[2]

LEADERSHIP: DEFINITION AND MEANING

Leadership is important in every aspect of life, from government to religion to business. Leadership is a vital factor influencing the success of the work group and organization.[3] Cole defines leadership as a dynamic process in which one individual influences another to contribute to the achievement of the group task.[4] Therefore, leadership is getting things done through people.

Leadership means convincing others to accept and follow directions. It means leaving a mark. Leadership is the initiation and guidance of the future direction of the company. Through their ideas and deeds, leaders show the way and influence the behavior of others. Leadership also involves inspiring people and motivating them to perform their best and make the company's goals their own. A transformational leader is one who believes in continuous change, innovation, and creativity. Transformational leaders are those who recognize the need for change, initiate new vision that can touch all participants, and convince employees to actively pursue changes. The leader's role is to create new ideas, design strategies, build relationships, and create the infrastructure necessary to succeed. For example, Lee Iacocca was a transformation leader. When Iacocca accepted a job at Chrysler in 1979, the company was on the verge of bankruptcy. He initiated the vision of the "new Chrysler." He was able to rally all the employees behind his new vision. In a relatively short time he was able to transform Chrysler into a successful organization. Iacocca then institutionalized the changes by developing a new corporate culture, one that allowed the creation of self-managed teams and that empowered the employees. Robert Eaton succeeded in continuing the changes after Iacocca retired. Eaton overhauled the entire corporate culture and created new vision. Donald Hastings, chairman and CEO of Lincoln Electric from 1992 to 1998, was able to transform the company to be the world leader in welding and cutting products and a premier manufacturer of electric motors.

This type of leader is not limited to large organizations. Leaders of small companies can be transformational. Take for example a president of a small furniture company in New Castle, Pennsylvania who changed the way his company does business. He simply turned customer service into an excitement endeavor. He said if you want to succeed in today's environment you have to play the customer's way. His company makes the extra effort to please customers. They deliver any item any time, even if it means after work hours on nights and weekends. His employees volunteer to fix customer furniture even if they did not buy it from their store. If it costs the company, they charge the customer with that cost. Many times they offer free services. He said, "If we have the product we sell it and if we do not we promise to get it." The few employees who work in this shop work as a team and are authorized to make customers happy. "Quality and services are the key to our success."[5] They understand the value of keeping the customer happy.

Transformational leaders are the ones who promote change and innovation. They are visionaries and believe in building competencies through strategic management. Leaders who believe in change design a shared vision that touches all participants. The vision is a picture of the future and a collective product of everyone involved, even those who might disagree with their leaders. It refers to the ability of the leader to adopt and anticipate changes, and it should focus on the long term. Competitive advantage is obtained and maintained by introducing new ideas and continued innovation. A transformational leader is the one who encourages all participants in the organization to be creative, innovative, and gain new knowledge through training and development. Those leaders must accept errors and some risk from the creative members of the organization. The responsibility of positioning the company and its products and services relies heavily on the leadership capabilities.

Leaders must produce strategic vision, mission, goals, and quality values. They must provide personal commitment, and create and sustain leadership systems and environments for quality excellence. Good leaders invest in training and education of their employees and maintain a work environment conducive to the well-being and growth of employees. For leaders to be effective, they must be intelligent, able, involved, and personal. Leadership's commitment to succeed with change is the single most critical factor.

MANAGEMENT VERSUS LEADERSHIP

Organizations with good leadership share similar characteristics. These positive characteristics are common to large as well as small organizations. Some of these characteristics include

1. High productivity levels.
2. A positive attitude.
3. A commitment to the goals and the people of the organization.
4. Productive use of resources.
5. High levels of quality.
6. The promotion of creativity and innovation.
7. Teamwork.[6]

Organizations with these characteristics have a strong leadership framework. Leadership is an important and difficult job. It is the cornerstone of organizational effectiveness. However, leadership and management are not synonymous. One must acknowledge the difference between the two in order to be successful in both roles.

A manager plays many roles, and several of those roles may not be directly related to leadership. A manager plays the role of a planner, a resource allocater, a monitor, and a disseminator, as well as a leader. A manager often exhibits leadership when he or she secures the cooperation of others in accomplishing a goal.

One main difference between managers and leaders is that managers deal in efficiency and leaders deal in effectiveness. Managers are interested in how to achieve the goals and objectives of the organization on a *day-to-day* basis (or efficiency). A leader, on the other hand, is more interested in the *future* direction (or vision), goals, and objectives of the organization. Leaders are concerned with what the organization can become and how to provide passionate support to all participants.

Managers are also content when operations run smoothly, and leaders are displeased when things do not change for the better. Warren Bennis indicated several differences between leaders and managers. According to Bennis, managers are copiers while leaders are originals. Managers maintain, and leaders develop. Managers take the short view, and leaders take the long view. Managers ask how and when, and leaders ask what and why.[7]

Being a leader depends on more than acquiring technical knowledge and management concepts. Leadership is learned over time. Hence, it is evident that the term "manager" is considerably broader than the term "leader."[8] Bennis and Townsend suggested that leaders are people who do the right things and managers are people who do the things right.[9] An extremely successful manager can properly combine the worthy characteristics of both managers and leaders.

The following is a list of the differences between leadership and management:

Leadership	Management
Concern with change	Concern with consistency
Provides the vision	Carries the vision out
Concentrates more on the future	Concentrates more on the past and present
Takes initiatives	Implements initiatives
Makes the company better	Makes the company run
Makes the vision happen	Hopes the vision happens
Creates more leaders	Creates more managers

THE GOOD LEADERSHIP

Individuals who are good leaders balance their commitment to the job that needs to be done and the people who are doing the job. They also present a positive attitude and are good role models for others. This requires the leader to consistently set examples for others while on the job. A manager who is continually late will have employees who are also regularly late. To promote the quality of being on time, a good leader would be on time.

Good leaders are also individuals who possess good listening skills and communicate their ideas clearly. This is done in a nonthreatening manner to the employee. Their communication must also be persuasive. Good leaders can persuade people to follow their views and goals and to commit themselves to those views and goals.

Sometimes you wonder why companies do not establish a lunch table where employees and leaders meet regularly. How many companies leave their leaders' doors open? How many leaders start a conversation with employees about current issues? How many leaders talk to their employees about, for example, the Russian submarine crash, the wild fires in several states, or the possibility of peace in the Middle East? Effective leaders must create mechanisms that provide employees the opportunities to raise their voices and provide feedback. Such mechanisms will help management obtain needed information and ensure the effectiveness of operations. A successful leader is the one who builds trust and friendships with all participants. This will assist them in future changes as well as enforcing the values and norms of the organization. An organization must surround itself with loyal people who think that they have stake in the success of the organization.

Company leaders need to be highly charismatic individuals who create followers through personal magnetism. They are expected to inspire or motivate participants. Teams and empowerment are important tools to motivate people as well as to effectively achieve organizational goals and objectives. This motivation may involve qualities such as initiative, enthusiasm, self-confidence, commitment to the goals and the people in the organization, integrity, and trustworthiness. The leader should develop the ability to motivate individuals far beyond the scope of the present task.

The characteristics of an individual are relevant in determining leadership ability. Certain characteristics are more prevalent in leaders, such as good social skills, personal persistence, and a desire to continue learning by recognizing failures and mistakes. Similarly the capacity to challenge and motivate others is another personality characteristic. Leaders merely need to possess dedication and foresight. Effective and trusted leaders are not likely to be characterized by individual defects in personality.

LEADERSHIP STYLES

Every leader has a distinctive leadership style that indicates how they interact with other individuals. *Leadership style* is the characteristic pattern of behavior that a leader exhibits in the process of exercising authority and making decisions. The leader sets the tone for the firm's members. His or her style is a matter of considerable interest to employees at virtually all levels. It is also important in determining how committed the employees are to the firm's mission and goals and how much effort they will put into implementing the company's strategies.

There are many different types of leadership. According to Wright, Kroll, and Parnell, there are two types of leadership. The first is *trans-*

actional leadership. Transactional leadership occurs when managers use the authority of their office to exchange rewards such as pay and status for employees' work efforts. Their second type of leadership is *transformational leadership.* This occurs when managers inspire involvement in a mission, giving followers a "dream" or "vision" to follow. The transformational leader motivates followers to do more than was originally expected by stretching their employees' abilities and increasing their self-confidence. Leaders may exhibit both styles of leadership. If an organization is meeting their objectives and they do not foresee significant changes in their environment, a transactional style might be more appropriate. Because of the increasing intensity of domestic and foreign competition and dramatic environmental changes, many organizations require transformational leadership.[10]

Goetsch and Davis detail five leadership styles. They are autocratic, democratic, participative, goal-oriented, and situational leadership. *Autocratic leadership* involves the leader making decisions without first consulting with employees, and then telling those employees what to do. If the company is interested in long-term goals or if it adopts total quality management, this is not a suitable method, because total quality management involves the sharing of ideas. *Democratic leadership* involves the employees being responsible for implementing the decisions. However, the leader still makes the final decision after taking everyone's input on the subject into account. This method also has a problem, because it may lead to the enactment of the most popular method, and not the most beneficial method for the company. *Participative leadership* presents information about a problem to a team that develops strategies and solutions to correct the problem. The leader's only job is to move the team toward a consensus. This only works if all concerned have the best interests of the company in mind. *Goal-oriented leadership* also involves teams by having them only focus on the present goals. This approach may be too narrowly focused and ignores other opportunities or problems that may arise. This approach also does not take into account future goals of the company. *Situational leadership* selects the appropriate type of leadership depending on the situation the company is in at the present time. The performance of the company and employees will be dependent on the leader adopting a style of command appropriate to the situation.[11]

Factors Determining Leadership Style

The style of leadership will depend on several factors. Some of these factors are

1. The quality and strength of the leader–group relationship.

2. The degree to which the task or situation is structured or ambiguous.
3. The relative strength and credibility of the leader's position.
4. The type and the size of the organization they lead.

Corporate culture and degree of trust are two other factors that determine leadership qualities. A culture that is characterized by a preference for hierarchy and extensive application of rules, such as the United States, will be more likely to perceive leadership as important, whereas a culture that emphasizes equality and has a relaxed attitude, such as Japan, will not perceive leadership as important. The other factor, trust, dictates the type of leadership that will be applied. In a society with low amounts of trust, an authoritarian leadership style may be utilized. On the other hand, societies high in trust may utilize the facilitator leadership style.

A skillful leader can turn the chaos into an avenue for creativity and reinvention. A more open system of communication is a factor that will be necessary in order to convey new ideas and solutions from others in the ranks. Honesty about the organization's health and needs will be another significant requirement. The leaders can gain much more power and trust from their workers by being honest with them.

LEADERSHIP AS VISION

Leadership is a visionary concept. *Vision* is defined as an imagined or perceived pattern of informal possibilities to which others can be drawn, which an individual wishes to share, and which constitutes a powerful source of energy and direction within the enterprise.[12]

Leadership can be defined in terms of the capacity to create a compelling vision, to translate it into action and share it with all participants, and to sustain it. It can also be defined by the ability of a leader to organize the experience of a group or organization. By organizing the experience, the leader transforms the experience into power. The leader must have a vision that can be shared with his organization. This vision needs to be clearly defined. The role of a leader is to express a vision that touches organizational members, get buy-in, and implement it. To be a leader one needs the following visionary skills:

1. The ability to create a vision that others can believe in and adopt as their own. The vision is a picture of organizational future.
2. The ability to communicate that vision to all employees and to translate it into everyday practicalities.
3. The ability to create trust within the organization. Trust will result in less resistance.[13]
4. Since organizational resources are limited, the ability to set priorities.

5. The ability to allocate resources that insure the development of competencies and recognize the potentials for creativity and innovation.

The vision and mission of Volvo is to be "the world [*sic*] most desired and successful premium car brand." The goal is to be "number 5 in customer satisfaction (according to the J.D. Power IQS study in 1995), and number 3 in 1997 (Available at <http://www.volvo.com>, 1999).

THE ROLE OF TRANSFORMATIONAL LEADERS

The leader must be active, even when their role as president of the organization is changing. Consider the following:

1. The transformational leader has to be the person who is behind the spirit of transformation. He or she should devote most of their time on the factory floor talking to other managers, employees, and customers. A coach spends most of his or her time with their teams in the field.
2. Transformational leaders create a vision that most of the people share. This vision should indicate what kind of company we want to become in the future. Benchmarking is very important in developing future strategy.
3. The transformational leader must challenge traditional projects and programs. They must ask the question, Is this project important? Can it be done differently? What are our priorities in terms of changes? Can some of these projects be reengineered? How do other successful companies do this?
4. The transformational leader must back the effort of transformation and act as a role model so that the employees will take the change seriously.
5. Transformational leaders commit themselves to company-wide quality approaches. Accept the challenge of improvement and innovation. Establish an environment that is balanced between financial performance, customers, and employee loyalty.
6. Transformational leaders need motivation, especially when performing those tasks that often are not measured and have been viewed as irrelevant within the organization.
7. The transformational leader must also strive to save time by reducing or eliminating the less important activities in the organization.
8. The transformational leader needs to align authority, information, and skills into one harmonious concert.
9. Transformational leaders should support, coach, and facilitate employees' jobs, rather than supervise and control them. The leader's role will become one of the most essential for the success of any change needed in the organization.
10. It is important to mention that anytime the leaders are shown to not be committed to the transformation, the changes will result in failure.

The CEO does not always have to be the leader of the transformation movement, but in most cases he or she is. For any change to succeed, there must be a champion, usually the top-level management or the CEO of the organization. In some cases, the champion may come from different parts of the organization, either an individual or a team. In both cases there should be a full support of the CEO in order for the transformation to succeed.

Leadership therefore deals with creating goals and objectives, and a shared culture and values, and communicating to employees and motivating people to perform at a higher level. Successful leaders are those who produce strategic vision, mission, goals, and objectives that clearly define the organization and its future direction. They establish quality values, provide personal commitment, create and sustain a leadership system and an environment for quality excellence. Transformational leaders invest in training and education of their employees, provide them with the information needed, and maintain a work environment conducive to the well-being and growth of employees. Transformational leaders use quality teams to assist them in achieving corporate objectives. For a leader to be effective, he or she must be intelligent, able, and personal. Leadership commitment to succeed in any changes is the single most critical factor.

Lee Iacocca was able to communicate vision and energize employees into action. Another good example is Herbert Kelleher, CEO of Southwest Airlines, who has developed a shared vision and culture for employees of giving customers what they want and being happy in the work they do. Communication from the heart is the key. His philosophy is that "it is the people on the front lines, not in the front office who are the heroes"—every employee is encouraged to accept responsibility, solve their own problems, and be a leader. A package handler who does his or her job well is recognized as a leader, just as much as a manager would be.

Leadership can have a negative impact too. In contrast to Kelleher's leadership is that of Harding Lawrence of Braniff Airlines. The crew did not welcome Lawrence's appearance on the aircraft. He used to fly from Dallas to New York to visit his wife in New York City. Any time he was on the plane, arguments between him and the crew arose to the point that the crew hated to be on that flight. Fear and hatred are very much the two emotions the crew has. After the deregulation of the airline industry in 1978, a price war between the major airlines came about, and the newcomers affected the entire industry. Braniff was not able to survive the price war between 1981 and 1983. Finally the company went out of business in 1983. Most of the other airline companies lost money in this period.

LEADERSHIP AND TOTAL QUALITY

In the total quality setting, quality leadership involves taking the input from employees into consideration. This is often referred to as participative leadership, and it includes inquiring about employees' suggestions, listening to those suggestions, and acting upon the suggestions. The major difference between leadership in a total quality setting and regular leadership is that the employees are empowered by providing their suggestions.

These leaders work with their employees to improve the quality of the company by demonstrating how to improve weak proposals rather than dismissing the proposal altogether. Leaders in a quality setting also believe in rewarding their employees when improvements occur as a result of their suggestions. We can say that there is no total quality without leaderships' total commitment and support. Leaders must work to integrate quality into the process, commit resources to quality and build a partnership with suppliers, customers, and major stakeholders. Customers must define quality; therefore, ask customers what they want. I have a friend who owns a perfume shop. She told me that she tries her very best to satisfy her customers. She is willing to accept the return of the perfume bottles that do not totally satisfy her customers. One time, one of her customers asked about a type of perfume that she does not carry. She sent one of the employees to a competitor's shop to buy it for her customer. She said that she was happy to see that her customer gets what they want. She added that she personally checks with her customers to see how things are going and what she can do to serve them better. She said she uses this feedback to add new products or to drop some from her list. Simply, the customers define her business plans. She said when a problem does arise, she does not try to explain, but apologizes and offers to solve the problem according to the customer's terms. An opposite case is when the manager of a particular company refused to hear one of their customers who was complaining about their vacuum cleaner. The manager told the customer, "Good day, sir," to cut him off and hung up the telephone. It reflected negatively on the company that this manager represented and the dealer who sold this company's product.

LEADERSHIP AND CHANGE

In today's rapidly changing environment, companies have to adopt strategies for keeping pace with the change. Managers are often the ones who have to guide the company and employees through the change. For a successful transition, managers should have the willingness to change, have a high level of energy, be an effective communicator, exhibit a strong sense of responsibility, and have a clear vision and corresponding goals.[14] A manager who presents the leadership characteristics that are necessary to play a positive, facilitating role will help workers and their organization adapt to the change successfully.

A visionary company is one that is a premier institution in their industry, widely admired by their peers, and has a long track record of making a significant impact on the world around them. Some examples of visionary companies are Xerox, GE, Sony, 3M, Hewlett-Packard, Johnson & Johnson, and Boeing. Visionary companies prosper over long periods of time, through multiple product life cycles and multiple generations of active leaders.[15] A true vision is ready to break the barrier of conventional thinking and provides a powerful motivation for energizing employees. This vision must not be limited to the old ways of thinking. It should incorporate new ideas and techniques. It should allow, welcome, and encourage participation and feedback from all members.

TRUST AND THE COMPANY

A high level of trust is necessary in the workplace because of the fragility of the system. Today, employees have been trusted to deal with many problems, where and when they happen. They have also been trusted with high levels of responsibility and discretion at all points of the supply and operational process. This trust leads to a decrease in the amount of fear employees have about doing something wrong or making the wrong decision, and it demonstrates that management has faith in the ability of their employees to make the right decisions.

Trust can also increase the economic efficiency of the company by reducing transaction costs that ordinarily would be incurred. Some examples of trust are maintaining and sustaining an effective relationship architecture, holding together large-scale and impersonal organizations, dealing with interparty disputes, finding trustworthy and reliable suppliers, negotiating contractual agreements, complying with government regulations, and identifying and dealing with malpractice and fraud.

A leader can earn employees' trust through accepting responsibility for the performance of their employees. This means they share credit for successes as well as blame for failures. Another way to earn trust between leaders and employees is by maintaining consistency. Consistency tells the employees what to expect and when, which will help them to provide the expected performance on time. Also, a manager who assists employees when a deadline approaches reveals a willingness to help, which can in turn earn employee trust. When trust is built, employees will be more willing to accept new initiatives.

Trust is also important as a basis for most corporate agreements. These agreements are made easier if the relationship is based on openness and honesty. Openness and honesty decreases when the following is present:

1. The need for control mechanisms within the management process.
2. The need to specify matters contractually.
3. The need for litigation.
4. The need to hedge against unpredictable issues.[16]

Leaders should consistently demonstrate high standards for ethical behavior, because they are the role models for employees. The leader sets the ethical tone for the whole organization. The major ethical dilemma for leaders is a contradiction between what they proclaim and what actions they take. Employees notice this discrepancy very quickly, and they in turn often incorporate it into their own behavior. A code of conduct must be well written and communicated to all organization members.

The concept of starting the change with top management is what companies need to do in order to succeed in the future. The old hierarchy and chain of communication must change. By modifying a few programs or behaviors, a temporary fix will be achieved. Companies must acquire a new paradigm. A paradigm is a set of beliefs or a mindset that we use to set boundaries for ourselves and to focus on problem solving.[17] This paradigm must start at the top and be relayed down through the ranks. Every change requires its champion, either an individual or group. This role is usually performed by a manager who has a certain level of authority to utilize organizational resources and to command employees to conduct desirable changes.

Today's leaders must become the leaders of change. They must leave the traditional organizational system behind and become more progressive and flexible with the changing times. They should allow and encourage everyone in the organization to participate. This will help smooth the transition and create enthusiastic behavior toward change. Transformational leaders must encourage brainstorming, which is encouraging all participants to be creative, express their ideas freely, and think collectively. In brainstorming, the objectives of changes must be well understood and accepted by all members. All members of the teams must understand the rules of participation and each should have a chance to contribute equally. Brainstorming can be very effective if the members concentrate on the issues and not on personalities and if it is supported by management.

In summary, the successful transformational leader is someone who can deal with a complex and uncertain environment effectively. The leader must constantly monitor and assess the environment and be ready to change strategy to fit the changing environment. The transformational process must be led by a transformational leader who is creative, visionary, nontraditional, open minded, curious, and diverse, and with a wide range of interests. A transformational leader must be able to launch, sustain, and involve everyone in the organization. A visionary leader should be able to align the organization with its vision and create a transformation process that is communicated to all participants and implemented through involvement. The transformational leader must enjoy interaction with people and should be willing to exchange ideas. They should be above all charismatic leaders. The transformational leader must also have a continuous capacity to transform and a global mindset.

NOTES

1. David Weir and Clive Smallman, "Managers in the Year 2000 and after: A Strategy for Development," *Management Decision* 36 (1998): 43–51.

2. Tony Morden, "Leadership as Vision," *Management Decision* 35 (1997): 665.

3. George Manning and Kent Curtis, *Leadership: Nine Keys to Success* (Cincinnati: South-Western Publishing, 1988).

4. G. A. Cole, *Management: Theory and Practice* (London: DP Publications, 1996).

5. Sid Shenkan, owner of Haney's Furniture, in a speech at Slippery Rock University, November 2000.

6. David Goetsch and Stanley Davis, *Introduction to Total Quality Management: Quality Management for Production, Processing, and Services* (Englewood Cliffs, N.J.: Prentice Hall, 1997).

7. Warren Bennis, "Managing the Dream: Leadership in the 21st Century," *Training* 27 (May 1990): 43–44.

8. P. Wright, M. J. Kroll, and J. Parnell, *Strategic Management* (Englewood Cliffs, N.J.: Prentice Hall, 1998).

9. W. Bennis and R. Townsend, *Reinventing Leadership* (London: Piatkus, 1995).

10. Wright, Kroll, and Parnell, *Strategic Management*, 232.

11. Goetsch and Davis, *Introduction to Total Quality Management*.

12. Morden, "Leadership as Vision," 664.

13. Ibid., 672.

14. D. Shanks, "The Role of Leadership in Strategy Development," *Journal of Business Strategy* 10 (1989): 36.

15. Morden, "Leadership as Vision," 669.

16. Ibid., 670.

17. Milan Moravee, "Leader Must Love Change, Not Loathe It," *HR Focus* 71 (February 1994): 45.

Chapter 4

The Impact of TQM
on Businesses
in the Twenty-First Century

Total quality management has become one of the most talked about
subjects in the past decade. TQM is the integration of organizational
functions and processes in order to achieve continuous improvement
in the quality of goods and services. TQM means thinking about quality in terms of all functions of the enterprise. TQM strategies and methods are developed as practical, hands-on techniques for managing and
improving the company's competitive position in an increasingly competitive global environment. TQM is not a single step that occurs overnight; it is a long-term process that transforms and restructures the
entire organization to make it more competitive.

Over the past fifty years, quality management has been accumulat-
ing momentum. The concept began first in the manufacturing sector
and moved into service organizations. Many organizations have
adopted this approach recently. It seems that to survive in the global
market of the twenty-first century, quality management has become a
requirement for all organizations. You do not find anyone who argues
against the concept of quality itself. However, there is a difference between being concerned about quality and adopting the TQM concept
in an effective, coherent, and strategic way.

EVOLUTION OF THE CONCEPT

Frederick W. Taylor, the father of scientific management, revolutionized the workplace with his ideas on work organization, task decomposition, and job measurement. The publication of Taylor's book in 1911, *The Principles of Scientific Management*, marked the beginning of the discipline that grew into industrial engineering, characterized by so-called efficiency experts and time-and-motion studies. The theme of Taylor's writing is the use of the scientific method in management. Taylor developed a system that emphasized productivity at the expense of quality. This system consisted of inspection departments that checked for quality at the end of the production line. Most of these inspections were visual or involved testing the product following its manufacture. The concern for quality was limited largely to the shop floor. Methods of statistical quality control and quality assurance were added later.

Walter A. Shewhart of Bell Laboratories formulated a framework for the first application of the statistical method to the problem of quality control back in the 1920s. Shewhart wrote a note to R. L. Jones, responding to his request for some type of inspection report which might be modified from time to time, in order to provide a glance at the greatest amount of accurate information. He attached a sample chart designed to indicate whether the observed variations in the percent of defective devices of a given type are significant; that is, to indicate whether the product is satisfactory. Shewhart's example was the world's first schematic control chart. As he pursued this work, he gave birth to the modern scientific study of process control.[1] In 1931, he wrote a book titled *Economic Control of Quality of Manufactured Products*, introducing statistical quality control. Shewhart also pioneered a movement at Bell Labs in what was to be called statistical quality control (SQC). W. Edwards Deming and Joseph Juran both worked under Shewhart.

W. Edwards Deming, however, is credited with popularizing quality control in Japan in the early 1950s. After World War II, Deming attempted to involve U.S. business leaders in the application of statistical methods to control quality, but his appeal was not accepted. Then in 1950, he was invited to speak to Japanese scientists, engineers, and corporate executives on the same subject. His lecture provoked immediate interest among business people in Japan. The Deming Prize was established in appreciation of his work one year later. As a result Japan succeeded in producing economically sound products and high quality.

He believed that quality must be built into the product at all stages. While Taylor and Deming may seem to be on opposite sides, both believed that industrial progress depends upon the entire design of the organizational system, technology, and people. There are some similarities between Taylor's scientific management and Deming's TQM. Both Taylor and Deming emphasized a scientific approach to improve organizational performance. They also recognized the influence and potential for learning and knowledge in the organization. In addition, they realized the importance of training and cooperation among all the parties involved, however, they differ in the application and involvement of the employees.

The pioneers of TQM (Deming, Juran, Feigenbaum, and Crosby) believed that management and the system are the cause of poor quality. They mainly focused on techniques, processes, and systems, but not the theory behind them. There are generally two schools of thought for TQM: those who focus on technical processes and tools, and those who focus on the managerial dimensions. The TQM strategy and methods were implemented mainly to enhance and improve the firm's competitive position in an increasingly competitive and global environment. TQM techniques can be seen as a practical reaction to perceived inferiority to foreign competitors and Japanese companies in particular.[2]

After World War II, the United States emerged as a superpower, both militarily and economically. There was a huge demand for American products which enabled manufacturers to sell anything they produced. The quality of products produced in the United States declined as manufacturers tried to keep up with the demand for nonmilitary goods. American companies compromised quality for quantity. Products were made from nonstandardized materials using nonstandardized methods. The result was a product that varied in quality. The common form of quality control was inspection by the producer. Centralized inspection departments were organized to check for quality at the end of the production line.

Certain American industries that once dominated world commerce lost their market share at home and abroad. In a few industries, the American presence had all but disappeared.[3] Consumers were concerned with quality and cost of products produced in the United States. There were few suppliers from which to choose. Management's greatest concern, on the other hand, was producing quantity and not quality products. The attitude of top level management was that we know what is best for the customer, and that happens to coincide with what is best for us as a company. This shows the inward orientation and a short-term focus of some senior executives in U.S. companies. The statement made by Alfred Sloan of General Motors sums it up nicely: "What's good for General Motors is good for the country." Maybe that is why the U.S. market share of General Motors slipped from 45 percent in the early 1980s to about 31 percent at the end of the 1980s.[4] During that time Japanese companies were competing with the rest of the world. They concentrated on producing nonmilitary goods and services. The Japanese invited foreign lecturers and sent teams to study successful companies around the world. Intensive training programs were developed to educate management and employees on the new technology and how to improve quality.

The U.S. market was ready for any company to offer products that met customer needs, cost less, looked better, and lasted longer. The international competition caught American businesses by surprise. In the beginning, U.S. executives entered a deep denial phase, refusing to recognize that they were going to have to change the way business was done in order to survive. Then they realized that survival requires continuous improvement in providing goods and services.

ACCELERATING USE OF TQM

Management has come to realize that the set of principles that have shaped the structure and performance of businesses must be revitalized and reengineered. It was not until 1980, thirty years after Japan's realizations, that American industries began to incorporate quality programs into their everyday operations. In 1980 a television documentary titled *If Japan Can Why Can't We?* was aired by NBC. American companies realized that in order to succeed in global competition, they must improve quality. The strategies used in their organizations that had been in place for years were not working as expected. Therefore, there was a need for new missions, goals, objectives, strategies, and approaches. After a decade of painful downsizing and a strict focus on productivity, corporations have turned to strategic planning and total quality management. TQM can be applied to all enterprises, both manufacturing and service. TQM has been successful in Japan and comes with important lessons for American corporations. There are no easy answers to improve product or services in the domestic and international markets. The acceptance of TQM is a result of the following major trends:

1. Business responses to increased domestic and global competition, communications and resources, and the acceleration of technological change.
2. Financial problems, a large deficit, increased total debt, a decline of productivity, a lack of momentum, and weak overall job growth have contributed to the importance of finding a solution.
3. The effect of restructuring leveraged buyouts, downsizing, and takeovers on corporate growth and diversification.
4. Intensified global competition which has shown that our main weaknesses are with management techniques and workforce culture rather than technological inadequacies.

5. The European Economic Community's establishment of the International Standard of ISO 9000 as a quality measure. They demanded that all companies who deal with European concerns should have that certificate, which is issued by an outside agency. American companies had no choice but to follow the quality approach in order to continue doing business in Europe and elsewhere.

Business corporations have been quick in recent years to jump on the TQM bandwagon. TQM is a cultural transformation approach; quality and speed are complimentary rather than contradictory in nature. Companies recently surveyed consider quality criteria in compensating executives.[5] The goal is to be the world leader in business once again. Companies must provide greater attention to acquiring knowledge. Learning must be a part of any future strategy for keeping pace in the market in a rapidly changing environment. Learning through benchmarking and training is one of the most sustainable sources of competitive advantage.

VARIATIONS OF TQM

There are many variations of TQM. The four leading proponents (Deming, Crosby, Juran, and Feigenbaum) agree that management must take decisive action to ensure that quality becomes part of the company culture, rather than just waiting for it to happen.[6] The following is a list of leading proponents basic ideas:

1. Organizational vision.
2. Barrier removal.
3. Communication.
4. Continuous evaluation.
5. Continuous improvement.
6. Close customer–vendor relationships.
7. Empowering the worker.
8. Training.[7]

Underlying these eight components of TQM is the requirement that each must contain an action plan. Many books and articles have been written that explain the importance of TQM and how to implement it. Unfortunately, many are repetitious and do not add much substance.

Deming professed that most variations have a common cause, while only a few have a special cause. Deming's primary focus was to improve the system which he believed was the main cause of variations. Deming presented fourteen universal points for management to follow in order to improve quality.[8] Juran, on the other hand, focuses on top-down management and emphasizes their responsibility to achieve quality through planning, goal setting, organizing, and controlling.[9] Feigenbaum went a step further and proposed an integrated effort to develop, maintain, and improve quality through the various groups within the organization.[10] Crosby argued that poor quality in the average firm costs the firm about 20 percent of revenue, most of which could be avoided by adopting good quality practices.[11]

TQM's SUPPORTERS

Since its introduction in the United States, TQM has grown significantly. It has become a prerequisite for all firms and a strategic imperative for the twenty-first century as a result of its growing importance. Quality has now become a service issue as well as a manufacturing issue, and TQM relates to the product as well as the services that accompany the product.

The 1989 American Society for Quality Control (ASQC) survey indicated that the majority of executives rated quality of service and product as a top priority. Of those executives surveyed, 74 percent gave American-made products less than eight points on a ten-point scale for quality. Similarly, a panel of Fortune 500 executives argued that American products deserved no better than a C+.

In 1987, Public Law 100–107 created the Malcolm Baldridge Award to recognize high quality in business. A main criterion for this award is that companies utilize TQM. The award attempts to promote quality awareness, acknowledge quality achievements, and publicize successful quality strategies. There has been an enthusiastic response to the Baldridge Award. In a recent Gallup survey, 73 percent of CEOs believe that American business is committed to quality, and 84 percent of consumers agree with that.[12]

David Kearns, CEO of Xerox, organized the first quality forum. He was convinced that trade barriers do not work in the long run and believed that an understanding of total quality was one of the essential skills and insights that should be learned in order to achieve business success in today's global markets.[13]

There is more concern in the United States for product quality than for quality of services. People employed in manufacturing, however, tend to focus on production first and quality second. While many organizations may not be convinced that the quality of service they offer impacts bottom line performance, Crosby believes that it is a profit maker. For every dollar that is spent on doing something wrong over and over again, the company could earn twice as much as that on the bottom line.

Quality usually creates higher demand. This will increase market shares, according to a study by the Strategic Planning Institute of Cambridge, Massachusetts. In addition to market shares, quality will reduce the cost of rework, waste, and units that are not in conformance with acceptable standards. Reducing cost and increasing sales will increase profitability and growth, leading to improvement in both internal and external competitive positions.

CUSTOMER SATISFACTION

Customers must define quality. An organizational goal is to meet or exceed customer expectations. Studies have shown that companies rated highly by their customers in terms of service can charge close to 10 percent more than those rated poorly. This indicates the importance placed on service by customers. Customer service can thus be considered a major dimension of competitiveness. Organizations should keep asking their customers how to provide better products or services.

It is not enough to talk about customer satisfaction—one must be active in implementing processes that enhance customer satisfaction and pursue that satisfaction wholeheartedly. Some important issues of customer satisfaction are acquiring satisfied customers and knowing when you have them and keeping them. The issue should not be only how to satisfy customers but how to retain them.

The term "customer service" has become a standard part of our vocabulary. It is generally used to cover a wide range of activities, which has broadened to encompass many actions over the years. For a long time, the phrase "customer service" was used in a positive sense. It referred to service that was prompt, efficient, pleasant, and helpful. In today's economy, this term is usually modified by an adjective. There is good customer service and there is bad customer service. Thomas J. Peters and Robert H. Waterman, Jr., in their book *In Search of Excellence*, identified eight basic principles they found to be characteristic of large companies having a history of profitability and good customer service. Their research indicates that excellent companies learn from their customers. They are able to provide unparalleled quality, service, and reliability.[14]

While there is little definitive empirical data to support an absolute link between customer service and profitability, recent bestsellers provide many convincing examples. Also, Technical Assistance Research Programs (TARP) has also undertaken excellent studies and research programs in Washington, D.C. Collectively, this body of information, produced by experts, supports the theory that customer service and profitability are linked. In addition, an array of management consulting firms, such as Aim Executive, have been successful in producing customer service programs that result in higher customer satisfaction and increased revenues.

A company accepts that customers define quality:
Quality will improve. This will lead to
    improved customer satisfaction and loyalty. This will lead to
        reduced cost. This will lead to
            increased sales and profit. This will lead to
                improved productivity and increased market share.

SERVICE QUALITY VERSUS PRODUCT QUALITY

TQM has been accepted in a both manufacturing and service industries. Crosby defines quality as conformance to requirements. Juran defines quality as fitness for purpose. International Standardization Organization (ISO) 8402 explains the term quality as the "totality of features and characteristics of a product or service that bear on its ability to satisfy stated or implied needs."[15] Many writers have defined quality as simply meeting the customer's requirements. While these might explain what is meant by quality, they lack the strategic aspects of the concept. These aspects link the many variables that affect the organization internally and externally, such as management and employee involvement, control of variation, prevention of deficiency, internal customers, and the cost of nonconformance. TQM is about managing the quality of all organizational processes and systems that occur both within and external to the organization. Quality of products might be considered good if they perform accurately or conform to manufacturing specification and if they satisfy the requirement of fitness for purpose.

Deming believed that quality stems from the interaction between the product, the provision of training to the customer, and the way he or she uses the product. This illustrates the importance Deming placed on the customer. It is important for the firm to assess customers' needs today and in the future, in order to be able to satisfy customers' requirements. Dissatisfied customers are a detriment to the firm. In fact, the whole TQM process should begin and end with the customer. Customer expectations are usually included in organizational planning and development. For instance, organizational vision should be linked to customer satisfaction so that it can be measured.

TQM represents a strategic environment with seamless service, devoid of defects, errors, rework, inefficiency, and operational incompetence. TQM seeks to eradicate this in order to ensure and meet every organization's main business purpose—to totally satisfy customers–consumers. Many customers complain that organizations do not pay enough attention to their needs and expectations. They claim that they are continuously insulted, degraded, kept waiting, and treated badly by companies.

The organization must realize that what it needs to do is what the customer wants. The organization begins by asking what the customer wants. Only then can the organization plan, organize, and implement what is needed to give the customers what they require. If the customers are not totally and completely satisfied, you have not begun to achieve quality. It costs the organization much more to bring new customers in than to keep their current ones happy. This by no means suggests giving the organization away. But taking customer concern seriously is very important for any company. After assessing customer requirements, management starts the process of planning, organizing, training, and working to give the customers what they require, on time, and at a reasonable price.

PERSPECTIVES CONCERNING TQM

Global competition requires large manufacturing firms to demand quality from their suppliers who must adjust to this transformation or lose business. To obtain control over quality, manufacturing firms are minimizing the number of suppliers by selecting one principal supplier in each product area who then becomes a partner and can expect assistance and continuous evaluation from the manufacturer. Those suppliers retained should also be properly rewarded. For example, IBM has drastically reduced the number of suppliers and formed informal partnerships with those remaining.[16] The result is a product or service that meets customers needs and expectations.

In 1993, the International Quality Study (IQS) previously cited that 79 percent of manufacturers require their suppliers to be certified. This percentage has increased to about 85 percent by 1996. This certification requires very stringent quality standards.[17] TQM requires continuous evaluations of suppliers in a systematic way in order to be effective.

TQM also facilitates mechanisms of change by managers, which include training and education, communication, recognition, teamwork, and customer satisfaction programs. This is crucial to the successful implementation of a TQM program. Successful managers act as role models, encourage communication, and foster and provide a supportive environment. Management also needs to define the mission, identify the output requested by customers, and determine the activities required for fulfilling the stated objectives.[18]

TQM can be considered the umbrella that represents the body of management concepts and beliefs. Enhancing organizational performance requires the application of TQM coupled with practical tools and techniques. If it is applied successfully, it will improve quality, reduce waste and cost, and improve overall performance of the organization. For many, TQM represents a fundamental paradigm shift, a challenge to the status quo. For others, there is too much emphasis on the ethereal philosophy rather than on the key practical tools and their method of implementation. Yet others maintain that firms need to be fully aware of the organizational and managerial requirements of TQM in order to understand and appreciate the radical changes involved.

A recent study by Casimir C. Barczyk and Gideon Falk concluded that management knowledge of this concept influenced their support to the process. Senior managers of Fortune 500 firms were surveyed using a mail questionnaire. Responses came in from 173 individuals, a 35-percent response rate. It was found that knowledge of total quality management influenced the managers of major industrial firms to believe in and commit their organizations to TQM strategies and to perceive that they used a participative style of management.[19]

TQM IMPLEMENTATION

In the implementation of TQM, most organizations lack strategic vision because they drift into a program route rather than adopt a strategic approach. A program has a beginning and an end. Building quality is a continuous process. Quality management requires an innovative set of strategic and cultural interrelationships that include all parts of the organization. This set of roles begins with top management involvement and commitment, the craft of the systems and process management, investing in employees, and the cultural value and belief system. TQM also requires managerial consistency and determination of purpose. The successful application of TQM can take place effectively when organizations assess their changing environments (e.g., the strengths, weaknesses, opportunities, and threats). A basic ground for the application of TQM is the belief that it will result in the continuous improvement of organizational processes. This will be translated into higher-quality products and services. Successful implementation of this concept can be accomplished through an integrated system of training and education by using the knowledge of TQM philosophy, tools, and techniques. Implementing TQM successfully depends on several factors: a long-term perspective, customer focus, top management commitment, systems thinking, training and tools, participation, measurement and reporting systems, communications, and leadership. The effective implementation of TQM can only be achieved through a strategic management approach. This entails a radical change in the way organizations think and the restructuring of existing structures, systems, people, and processes. It recognizes that an organization cannot be truly efficient unless its people, processes, systems, and structure are effectively coordinated.

VISIONARY LEADERSHIP

In the view of many, leadership is not equal to management. By placing management over leadership, we have created one of the nation's biggest problems, and there is now a call for CEOs to be true leaders and not just managers. Creech criticized the Baldridge Award for allocating only 10 percent of total points for leadership. He believes that true leadership must permeate into every corner of the organization. TQM will not reach its fullest potential without powerful leadership that consists of a dynamic vision, motivation, and the creation of an environment where workers can achieve their best.[20]

Successful implementation of TQM requires management involvement. A strong commitment from top managers was emphasized by Deming, Juran, and others.[21] For example, Deming maintained that simply teaching people to use statistical tools aimed at achieving quality improvement is not sufficient. He thinks that only management has the power to influence changes in the organization of processes. Providing a role model and reinforcing quality values and expectations require a serious commitment and involvement. According to Naceur Jabnoun, in 2001 about 50 percent of the companies implementing TQM have failed in achieving their objectives.[22] In most of these cases, management is the cause for such failure. A reason for unsuccessful implementation of TQM may be that top managers do not understand the fundamental elements of TQM and therefore do not render their total commitment.

The principles of TQM are embodied in the strategies and leadership philosophies of nearly every major company. For example, the TQM of Procter & Gamble focuses on delivering superior customer satisfaction and can be summarized as follows:

1. Really know your customer and consumers, know those who resell our products and those who finally use them and then meet or exceed their expectations.

2. Do right things right. This requires hard data and sound statistical analysis to select the right things and to direct continued improvement in how well we do those things.

3. Concentrate on improvement. In order to achieve superior customer and consumer satisfaction along with leadership and financial goals, we must continually examine and enhance the capacity of our basic business systems and subsystems.

4. Empower people. This means removing barriers and providing a climate in which everyone in the enterprise is encouraged and trained to make his or her maximum contribution to our business objectives.

The Procter & Gamble statement of purpose captures the "what, how, and expected results" of this quality effort. They indicated that they would provide products of superior quality and value that best fill the needs of the world's consumers. They would achieve that purpose through organizations and working environments that attract the finest people and fully developing and challenging their individual talents. They are committed to provide an environment that encourages free and spirited collaborations to drive the business ahead, while maintaining the company's historic principles and integrity to do the right thing.

Chief executive officers often hold the most power and responsibility in a corporation and thus are in a position to implement the most dramatic turnaround strategy when a company is failing. A good example is the CEO of Chrysler, Robert Eaton. Eaton succeeded in taking Chrysler from the brink of disaster in 1989 to record revenues from 1993 to 1995. This was accomplished through a number of changes ranging from management style to product strategy. It began with a change in the mission statement and involved a cultural transformation. Eaton's vision for Chrysler was to be a car and truck company that designs and builds cars and trucks people want to buy, enjoy driving, and will drive again.[23]

Therefore, quality management begins at the top, with the leaders (CEOs and top management) and boards of directors. Visionary leaders are one of the most important elements of a quality management approach. The CEO of Motorola, one of the first Baldridge winners, included quality items in every board meeting. Managers need to stop blaming workers for poor quality. Many people think that the performance of American companies have been deteriorating because they lack consistent and persistent leadership.[24] Most managers apply quick fixes in response to problems as they come up and plan steps toward improving the system. Management styles and techniques directly affect worker output. Leadership vision of the future and determination will inspire everybody in the organization. Top management leads by defining, communicating, and motivating continuous improvement. Visionary leadership, therefore, is the essence of change and improvement.

THE ORGANIZATION

Another integral part of the TQM model is the organization. Organization is the structure that holds the company together and allows it to operate efficiently. Transformational leaders must assess the existence of a structure that allows the organization to reposition itself quickly with respect to the changing environment. TQM requires a flatter organization with open communication among all members involved. The reduction of the number of hierarchical levels in the organization will improve communication. Without significant changes in the organizational structure, there is a danger that the members of the company might slip right back into their old habits after a short period of time. This can be used as a measure of how successful the organization process improvement is. Continuous improvement is the aim. A tall organization with a pyramid shape and centralized structure will not insure the successful implementation of a TQM approach. Therefore, for the transformation to be successful, extensive changes in human resources management are required. New methods of communication must be developed.

To achieve implementation of TQM requires employee involvement, empowerment, self-control, autonomy, and creativity. Employee empowerment provides workers with the freedom and responsibility needed to act in the best interest of the firm and to obtain the greatest satisfaction of their customers. TQM requires that managers follow participative styles to stimulate and energize the potential of employees empowered through training and workplace involvement. The utilization of the innovative potential employees will encourage active participation. One of the major concerns for employees participating in TQM programs is the failure of senior management to become committed and actively involved in these programs.

The successful application of TQM can take place effectively when organizations assess their changing environment (i.e., the strengths, weaknesses, opportunities, and threats).

THE PROCESS

Any process is a part of an organizational system. The process refers to a number of practices that take place on a continuous basis. These practices connect operational activities and human resource management with the final product output. The result of such activities is the production of the organizational products and services. Joel Ross indicates that there are two major problems with effective process control.[25] One is the tendency to focus on volume rather than quality, and the other is not having an external performance measurement to compare to one's own process. Usually a company's financial ratios are compared to the industry in which it operates. Comparing a company's process to the industry leader or to an industry standard is a meaningful measurement. The Baldridge Award and ISO 9000 are two highly regarded standards of quality control.

The TQM concept in the service sector encompasses different factors, such as availability, convenience, usefulness, and dependability, largely because the services are provided to different people who have different and varied needs and expectations. The organization must eliminate activities that do not have value to the customer or to the process. Each service is distinct to customers. A transformative company is the one that empowers its front-line staff to respond to customer inquiries and does not put itself or its staff in a position to apologize to them for failing to meet their needs, values, and expectations. The organization needs to establish mechanisms to monitor and control receiving and to analyze customer feedback.

SUCCESSFUL IMPLEMENTATION

Many quality programs fail to deliver the expected results because of the failure to understand the importance of strategic management in applying this concept. Therefore, most companies will adopt TQM without the in-depth understanding of its underlying strategic foundation and without the evangelical involvement necessary to sustain the process. (This will be discussed further in Chapter 6.) The determination of the primary long-term goals and objectives, the shared vision, the adoption of courses of action, education, and training, and a followup by managers of all employees is the focus of TQM. A failure rate of 70 percent in the implementation of TQM is an alarming indication of the seriousness of the problem. That is why many companies are reluctant to embrace TQM. Organizations tend to give up when faced with such crisis in implementing TQM. TQM requires companies to examine and analyze the actual causes of failure and deal with them strategically.[26]

Successful quality management requires not just good policies, procedures, and documentation, but also modern technology and a good skill base. Quality management requires a new set of interrelationships that include quality communication, sustained commitment, and broad-based staff involvement. However, not many organizations implementing TQM gain the cooperation of lower level staff. Cases in TQM implementation show that management has often not secured the beliefs and commitment of those employees at the operational levels. In order for TQM to work, it is first essential to develop a strategy that emphasizes quality as an integral part of every individual and team task. It is also essential for a company to encourage the total commitment of all members of staff in order to create an organization focused on customer–consumer orientation. In addition, TQM requires the creation of a new management structure, an action plan which defines the why, how, and what of the process, and a measurement of quality to ensure that the company builds on any early returns.

In order to have a successful implementation of TQM, a major transformation must be applied. Redesigning the system, continuous training programs for management and employees, constructive and cross-functional teams, and a strategic management approach is necessary to insure the control of the *common causes* and eventually to deal successfully with the *special causes*. According to Deming, 94 percent of variations in products are a result of common causes. Common causes are sometimes called random causes and are inherited in a process over time. Somewhat predictable, they appear more frequently as random causes. They are present in any process and cannot be eliminated entirely unless a major change in the system takes place. Examples of common cause variations are the restrictions in the processes and procedures, pressure environment, poor training (if any), limits of control, or variations in materials, which all have a common cause. Special causes are variations that appear because of special circumstances. They represent about 6 percent of variations. However, they are not inherited in the process and can be dealt with and eliminated. Examples of special cause variations are incorrect or biased testing, incorrect specifications, machine breakdowns, or faulty materials. Such transformation is necessary in a global market that requires higher quality standards for survival. Adapting appropriate technology along with a horizontal and more flexible communication means should be implanted. In addition, a partnership with suppliers to insure the quality of raw materials will aid the organization in achieving one of its major goals—zero defects.

TQM SUCCESS STORIES

Frank Shrontz, a recently appointed CEO of Boeing, started the "Continuous Quality Improvement" program in 1991. This program has achieved dramatic financial results. Shrontz decided to send about one hundred of his executives to Japan to learn about their revolutionary production methods. A new team of management worked diligently with Shrontz to rewrite organizational goals and objectives. They began reevaluating the company's techniques and developed training programs for all their employees. The emphasis was more than ever on how to improve the process and promote customer focus and continuous improvement.

While these issues were not necessarily new to Boeing, it was management's commitment to change that made the difference. Management's role shifted from "fire fighting to fire prevention." The new management team was determined to improve the design and quality of the product quickly and efficiently and at a minimum cost. They have reevaluated organizational processes, from the corporate offices to the workshops of the rank and file. Customers and suppliers became heavily involved in the dynamics of the business. As a result the company was able to provide the following improvements: inventory turnover rate from 2.1 percent to 2.6 percent in 1992; the reduction of $100 million in the 1992 inventory carrying cost; and production cycle time slashed from thirty-eight to twenty-eight months. After such success with the total quality program, Boeing then requested its suppliers and subcontractors to adopt the concept.[27] The company also eliminated a number of suppliers who were less willing to implement TQM. Those few suppliers who remained were more involved in Boeing planning and commitment to quality. They have come to think of themselves as valuable members of the company's team.[28]

Another successful TQM implementation has occurred in the U.S. automotive industry, specifically, auto parts suppliers. With the arrival of the Japanese factories in the 1980s, U.S. parts suppliers were forced to face two painful facts: (1) The Japanese plants took production shares from the Big Three; and (2) Japanese car makers brought along their own suppliers to maintain quality standards because the Japanese found that U.S. suppliers had three times greater defect rates than their Japanese counterparts. The Japanese criticized U.S. suppliers as lacking coordination and having slow reaction time, poor communication, nonresponsive delivery, and uneven quality. As a result, U.S. suppliers failed to capture the Japanese business. Consumer demands and willingness to pay more for a better product have created new vehicle niches. The Japanese successfully differentiated their products to gain greater shares of these niches. The result was higher product volatility demanding the flexibility forcing them to speed up the design of a new car and production process while addressing vehicle service problem effectively.[29]

Worldwide sourcing and globalization added additional complications for suppliers. The new demand was to obtain more value added to the product and to the services provided at a lower cost. Suppliers had to quote cost-based, not market-based, prices. Auto makers expected suppliers to deliver higher value-added components around the world at a price that was competitive with local vendors.

These are some of the reasons why U.S. car companies established their own supplier quality program. General Motors, for example, produced about 68 percent of its raw materials. Chrysler developed its *Supplier Quality Assurance Manual*; Ford developed *Q-101 Quality System Standard*; and GM developed *NAO Target for Excellence*. In 1992, these programs were harmonized into the industrywide *Quality System Requirements QS-9000* to provide for continuous improvement, emphasizing defect prevention, and the reduction of variation and waste in the supply chain.

QS-9000 defines the fundamental quality system expectations of Chrysler, Ford, General Motors, and truck manufacturers for internal and external suppliers of production, service parts, and materials. These companies are committed to working with suppliers to ensure customer satisfaction beginning with conformance to quality requirements and continuing with reduction of variation and waste to benefit the final customer, the supply base, and themselves. The result was greatly improved business performance, which is the most valid outcome of successful TQM implementation.[30]

FAILURES IN TQM IMPLEMENTATION

Here are some real-world examples of failure in implementing TQM in various businesses:[31]

1. In 1984, AT&T embraced TQM, corporate groups were formed to generate training programs and manuals, and most sites developed process improvement teams applying quality to the processes. Many common themes resonated the TQM initiative: Emphasis was put on comfortable items such as the process, also team training, charter development, and correct application of the seven quality tools and the seven-step problem-solving process. The results were not encouraging and the process developed into a ritual.

2. This large utility has been both a tremendous success story and a failure. Its failure was that the TQM bureaucracy it created became so large and costly that the new president dismantled it totally. After leaving Florida Power & Light (FP&L), leading TQM practitioners formed a consulting firm to spread the FP&L brand of quality to other companies.

3. TVA adopted TQM on a grand scale. The CEO named a vice president for quality, who was given an internal consulting group consisting of industrial engineers. The newly formed quality organization began work immediately on developing a quality manual. These industrial engineers turned TQM practitioners developed the manual in isolation, instead of defining their customers' needs. The quality managers rejected the manual. The largest unit, nuclear power, then hired the former FP&L group as their quality consultants. A political fight ensued between the vice president for quality and the head of the nuclear-operating unit over who should be calling the shots. The quality vice president then ordered his group to produce TQM training programs to train all TVA employees. Both headquarters and the nuclear operating unit spent millions of dollars training employees without any demonstrable business improvements ever achieved.

4. In 1985, TQM was implemented by the IRS to develop a new computer system (called tax system modernization or TSM) due to the increased possibility of a crash in their current system. By 1995 thousands of IRS personnel had been trained in principles of TQM with heavy emphasis on statistical process control. However, the error rate at the claims processing centers remained constant, hovering between 20 and 25 percent, and approximately 100 million inquiries from taxpayers regarding mistakes,

delays, and lack of understanding were still being handled. Doing it right the first time could have prevented that workload. Regarding TQM, Congress had so little faith in the agency's ability to deliver that it pulled the plug on the funding.

WHY TQM FAILED

The focus of these businesses was more on process and activities than on achieving sustainable operating improvements and business results. These white-collar TQM initiatives tended to lack the rigor and discipline required to produce measurable outcomes. Effective TQM implementation only occurs when management pays appropriate attention to multiple areas. TQM success comes only when organizations undergo a transformation from the old way of doing business to the new. This is a massive and complex undertaking.

Many American companies are striving to implement TQM. However, many of them fail in part because their leadership lacks the knowledge to fully understand the philosophy and practice of TQM. McGrath in 1993 alleged that a major cause for the failure to successfully implement TQM in companies was the leadership in the organization. He suggested that top managers do not understand the basic elements of TQM and do not make a total commitment to it. Some companies start the quality process by delegating responsibility to a hired expert rather than training their own employees. Executives must learn how to be coaches, and employees must learn how to be effective team players.[32]

Companies need to give greater attention to acquiring knowledge. Learning must be a part of any future strategy for keeping pace in the market in a rapidly changing environment. Obtaining knowledge, learning, and training will be the most sustainable source of competitive advantage.[33]

Artzt asserts that an orientation to quality must become a national imperative. That orientation should start with knowledge. Many American companies tend to regard quality as a project with a beginning and end and not as a process. They consider it a project that is separate from day-to-day operations. This is a project people do after they have carried out their regular tasks. The Japanese, by contrast, don't talk about quality as a concept separate from their work. For the Japanese, it is simply the only way they work. American firms must embrace total quality so thoroughly and completely "that it becomes an integral part of the way we do business, educate our children, and run our government."[34] It is Artzt's contention that knowledge, belief, and commitment to total quality are fundamental prerequisites to developing a competitive advantage. Applying the knowledge of TQM to the problems that confront us is a way of making total quality a way of life.[35]

PROBLEMS WITH TQM

TQM is here to stay. It is a cultural transformation in management technique that realizes the primary need to meet customer requirements, encourage employee involvement, and embrace the ethic of continuous improvement. It promotes culture and values that emphasize work in teams and encourages initiatives, innovation, and long-term vision.

Total quality, however, is not a cure-all, and many companies have come to realize that after focusing on quality they have ended up in poorer shape financially than before. A good example of this is probably Wallace, a Houston-based pipes and valves company that dropped into major financial crisis just months after winning the Baldridge Award. One of the reasons cited for their poor financial performance was the high cost of implementing the quality processes required to win the Baldridge Award.

Both Federal Express and Xerox suffered profit slumps after winning their Baldridge Awards. In fact, Fortune reports that TQM disasters have spawned a new niche for consultants who specialize in cleaning up the mess. Two out of three firms that embrace quality fail to experience major improvement in customer satisfaction or performance enhancement. A recent study by Ernst and Young suggests that organizations have wasted millions of dollars in TQM programs while not improving quality; often, they experienced a reverse in their quality. An Arthur D. Little survey of five hundred companies found that only 36 percent of respondents felt TQM was instrumental in improving their competitiveness. Some companies adopted TQM without appropriate plans to integrate them into the elements of the organizations (e.g., operations, budgeting, marketing).[36]

There are three major problems with TQM. The first deals with the weak theoretical foundation upon which TQM is built. A house can never be stronger than its foundation. We can tailor the approach directly to specific economic, cultural, and manufacturing conditions, but we must understand this two-sided coin in order to be successful in implementing TQM. A second problem with TQM relates to finances. TQM can be very expensive to implement. Perhaps the greatest reason for TQM failures is that it has often been treated as a panacea, when in fact it cannot resolve deeply rooted problems that affect an organization's mission. TQM is an incremental process where one must build on what is already in place. If the organization has a faulty mission or the strategy does not fit reality, it matters little how much emphasis is placed on quality. You cannot transpose a defective product into an exemplary quality product.

Another problem that plagues TQM is the involvement and commitment of the workforce at all levels. TQM requires everyone's full commitment. Since quality control must be delegated to the lowest possible position, workers would be responsible for their own quality control. The employees, however, do not construct the guidelines for monitoring. Experts establish them, and the workers must comply with the requirements. Therefore, employees are not committed to guidelines, and commitment is necessary.[37]

Reports of TQM not working have tended to focus on the manner in which the TQM was implemented in the organization and/or the attitudes of top management and workers toward their TQM efforts. They can be summarized as follows:

1. Some companies follow Deming, Juran, or Crosby's approach and use only the principles prescribed in them. Quality approaches must be tailored toward the organization need.[38]

2. In many companies, preparing employees for TQM implementation means giving the employees introductory training about philosophy and attitude and not necessarily the tools they can use to do something specific and different from what they did before.[39]

3. Sometimes employees attend seminars about the importance of TQM and yet do not get involved for a number of months or even years in quality improvement initiatives. Many employees do not take the quality program seriously. They often wonder if this is just another fad or really a means of achieving a positive change that supports a continuous drive to improve performance.

4. While organizations may encourage employees' participation and involvement, however, company policy may not change to accommodate active participation, and this might create frustration and conflict.

5. In some cases the measurement techniques used are not appropriate for TQM. Managers think more in terms of getting data that will provide practice in statistical tools. The primary focus is on measuring participation in activities associated with business results.[40]

6. CEOs perceive TQM as a marketing tool that enables them to promote their company for being part of the fashionable TQM movement.[41]

7. In many cases there is an overemphasis on the format. The production division or unit is often the only focus of management.

8. After some time, the quality message is no longer new and has lost some of its excitement. The realization that those things are not going as well as expected causes disappointment, anxiety, and sometimes panic.

9. Crises in implementing TQM programs arise from two main sources: The first is change. TQM requires significant changes within an organization— changes in its methods, process, attitudes, and behaviors. It takes time for this kind of realization to sink in. Line workers receive more responsibility and authority, thereby becoming more accountable for their own work. Superiors who were experts and order givers are now forced to become facilitators and coaches. The second source is raising expectations. As

people become more knowledgeable about what a quality organization should look like, they become more sensitive to problems within the company and in their own behavior. This creates anxiety.

These results would tend to suggest that in those organizations where TQM is not successful, the fault lies not with the philosophy, approach, or tools, but in the way in which TQM is understood and implemented by top management, particularly in the United States.[42]

For TQM to be successful, the leaders must have a clear vision of destiny along with total commitment before they can embark on building a quality house. Their foundation must be solid, and their strategy should fit their environment. It is important to keep in mind that TQM is a journey, not a destination. The slogan, "If it isn't broke, don't fix it," does not relate to the TQM approach. "If it isn't broken, just make it better," should be the new practice of enlightened companies.

ISO 9000

TQM is a process of continuous improvement. The processes that produce good results are standardized and documented. If the process is changed the documentation must change as well. Standardization was given a boost when ISO 9000 became widely accepted in the late 1980s and early 1990s. ISO 9000 certification is a requirement for doing business with companies in Europe. This certification can be a positive intervention for improving organizational design and effectiveness. This requirement can be used as a means for deeper changes in management behaviors and systems.

ISO 9000 is a series of five standards developed in 1987. ISO 9000 establishes common standards for manufacturing, trade, and communication as a means of ensuring minimum levels of quality. It is also used to promote the free flow of trade between countries. The strength of ISO 9000 standards is their acceptability by nations worldwide. About 150,000 American companies are expected to seek ISO registration during this decade. Obtaining such a certificate will provide customers assurance of the minimum quality expected. It also assures that registered suppliers are using a quality system that conforms to worldwide standards. This gives organizations adopting the ISO 9000 a wider choice of suppliers worldwide.

For example, when AT&T obtained the ISO certificate, they first realized how important it was to their business in Europe. At a later date, AT&T encouraged all of its suppliers to obtain the ISO certificate. In fact, in 1995, AT&T discovered that suppliers with ISO 9000 certification had fewer defects than those without. Therefore, AT&T prefers to work with companies that are ISO 9000 certified.

Companies in the United States were not the first to take on the process of TQM. When they realized they were losing market share, they realized how important TQM is to surviving in today's global markets.

RELATED PERSPECTIVES ON TRANSFORMATION

Benchmarking

Benchmarking, reengineering, and total quality management are considered important elements of the transformation process. These elements demand ongoing improvement, customer satisfaction, and employee involvement. Benchmarking is a tool for changing the organization. It provides the means for an organization to identify those business processes that provide an advantage over their competitors in the same industry. Benchmarking can also take place between two or more companies from different industries. Benchmarking tends to help organizations find a better way of doing things, adopted after some improvement. It provides opportunities to compare processes and practices between companies in the same industry.

Deming's philosophy of quality is discussed in his famous fourteen points, which are as follows:

1. Create constancy of purpose toward the improvement of products and services in order to become competitive.
2. Adopt the new philosophy. Management must learn that it is a new economic age and face the challenge. Management must learn their responsibilities and take on leadership for change.
3. Stop depending on inspection to achieve quality. Build in quality from the start.
4. Don't buy on price tag alone.
5. Improve continuously the system of production and service to improve quality, productivity, and reduce cost.
6. Institute training on the job.
7. Institute leadership and not supervision. The purpose of leadership should be to help people and technology to work effectively together.
8. Drive out fear so that everyone contributes effectively.
9. Break down barriers between departments and encourage team working.
10. Eliminate slogans, exhortations, and targets for the workforce. They create adversarial relationships.
11. Eliminate quotas (eliminate numerical goals–quotas–standards).
12. Remove barriers that rob employees of their pride of workmanship. (Abolish merit systems that promote competition rather than cooperation.)

13. Institute a vigorous program of continuous education and self-improvement.
14. Make the transformation everyone's job.

The reason we included Deming's fourteen points here is to show that most if not all require benchmarking. Benchmarking encourages companies to learn from each other by examining a competitor's strategies and trying to adopt them after improvement. Benchmarking is developed as a part of strategic planning. Organizational competitiveness and market share are critical issues of corporate future. By benchmarking a company may examine its overall quality, costs, turnover, safety, cycle time, and productivity in comparison to other competitors.

In benchmarking the company can use the publicly available information about another successful competitor. The company can also seek the target competitor cooperation in allowing an individual or team to tour the plant and learn from their process and products. This type of benchmarking is especially helpful in redesigning a process or radically changing the system. Usually those corporations agree to provide each other with information or to exchange visits. Many strategic alliances are structured so that companies can exchange information about their markets or between members of the alliances. The warning here is to benchmark in an ethical way and not by illegal or industrial espionage. Ethics and integrity must be applied in everyday practice. Benchmarking is a cooperation between companies through some type of agreement to see how a particular product or service is structured, manufactured, and distributed. This process usually assists management to allocate resources where they are needed to lift products and services to the competitor's level.

Benchmarking: A Definition

Benchmarking can be defined as a continuous process of evaluating corporate products, practices, and services with other organizations that have the best practices in their business, whether in the same or different industry, domestically or internationally. This concept provides the organization with external measures about quality and strategies. Benchmarking is a relatively new concept, but its popularity is increasing. "In 1985, almost no benchmarking activity existed among the Fortune 500 companies. By 1990, half the Fortune 500 were using this technique."[43] Today, companies find benchmarking very helpful in designing strategy as well as in implementing TQM. The purpose of it is to produce changes and improvements in the company, whether large or small. Benchmarking is a continuous process, and it requires a long-term commitment. It is the process of assessing and comparing the internal process and operations against those in successful organizations.

Evaluation is the first purpose of benchmarking. It focuses on a business's practice–work process. Any improvement can only be accomplished by an organization making adjustments to its current processes. The objective of benchmarking is to learn not merely what is produced but also how it is produced and how it can be improved. Bayer has implemented benchmarking techniques for measuring supplier performance as well as their own to get an idea as to where the company stands in terms of quality and performance. Bayer distributes an annual "milestone" award. The award is given to the supplier(s) with the least amount of nonconformances during the year in the four areas of quality, delivery, service, and safety. The winners of the award receive continued and increased business as a result as well as recognition and prestige.

Benchmarking is also a comparison of corporate goals and strategies with competitors. It is a process for comparing the company to its competitors in the same industry and setting competitive goals and objectives that are crucial for its survival. Benchmarking is the process of finding and understanding practices that will help reach new standards of performance to upgrade the entire organization.

By showing what other companies are doing, manager and employee performance will be enhanced by discovering and adapting new methods or practices applied by others. The process involves the possibility of a significant breakthrough. It will create interactive processes with all employees. Therefore, finding the best practices through benchmarking will enhance overall performance.

Benchmarking is a long-term commitment that will help direct the entire organization to fulfill the most critical business goals and objectives. These will help the organization to meet or exceed customer expectations and requirements and insure that the best practices are incorporated into work processes in order to become more competitive. The process of benchmarking requires employees to have information technology skills, because benchmarking relies on databases to help identify which firms might be able to share information with them. These employees may also be given mass data that requires good statistical skills to interpret.[44]

There are some problems associated with benchmarking. The first is that benchmarking is a continuous process that is very costly and has an uncertain outcome. It is, therefore, not a cost-effective approach to quality control. This is especially true for companies with limited resources. Benchmarking is also only as good as the measures that are established for it. If one seeks the wrong information, the effort to get it will be of no benefit.[45] Some companies may also not be willing to share information with other companies, so benchmarking will only work if other companies are willing to help. On the other hand, benchmarking also requires that the company open its doors to other companies with no apparent direct benefit.[46]

Benchmarking supports management efforts in quality improvement. Today, customers are more sophisticated and much better informed about the quality and prices of products and services around the world. Therefore, benchmarking by learning from others is a necessity for companies to survive. It should involve management's total commitment to the process of carefully selecting the areas that need to be benchmarked and the partner that is the target of such a process. It is highly recommended that the company assign a team to select and carefully research the candidate for benchmarking.

During the early part of the 1980s, Xerox conducted benchmarking with its Japanese competitors (i.e., Canon). The company sent some of its managers to visit Canon. In 1989 Fiat Automobile benchmarked their performance against that of its competitors. The process was conducted by sending fifty of the company's managers to visit manufacturing plants worldwide. Both companies learned a great deal. Many sports teams achieve benchmarking from each other, including types of strategies, moves, and equipment.

BUSINESS REENGINEERING

Throughout history, there have been new developments as knowledge and experience have increased. The business world is not an exception. In some cases, TQM has not delivered the desired results. Organizations have poured resources into information technology, expert consultants, and process overhaul without receiving the desired outcomes. This has resulted in leaders and theorists seeking new solutions. Reengineering is one response to the dismal performance many have experienced with the implementation of TQM.

Reengineering is an outgrowth of TQM, just as TQM was an outgrowth of earlier movements. It was introduced to the world in Hammer's 1990 article entitled "Re-engineering Work: Don't Automate, Obliterate."[47] Reengineering is a strategic change for the business. It represents major organizational and cultural change. It identifies the processes that have to be redesigned, then prioritizes the key issues that need to be dealt with. The concept involves a dramatic performance improvement by radically redesigning the organization and promotes improving business performance to achieve organizational goals. It advocates the adaptation of interdependent activities within and across the entire organization.

"Radical" and "rapid" are two key words used to describe the reengineering approach. Reengineering process design seeks dramatic orders of magnitude. It can demonstrate that fast change incorporated with concrete results can be seen within a year of implementation. Reengineering also sets the stage for continuous evolution of business processes to meet rapidly evolving business needs. The concept is seen as a radical redesign because it questions the status quo and the need to change a process. It requires an innovative approach to business processes and not incremental improvements to business operations. The concept advocates major changes because simply making incremental improvements is no longer a sufficient strategy in today's dynamic environment. Through this process, the company will identify opportunities for continuous and dramatic improvements.

Reengineering has also been called *business process redesign* (BPR), because it involves a dramatic performance improvement by redesigning the processes of the organization. It also indicates that no dimension of a company's strategy, structure, processes, technology, or culture can be applied effectively in isolation. For a company to be effective, there is a need to integrate all these dimensions.

REENGINEERING–BUSINESS PROCESS REDESIGN DEFINED

Reengineering–business process redesign is still in its growth phase. Like many other new emerging theories, the concept means different things to different people. For example in 1991 Louis Fried defined the concept as a methodology for transforming the business processes of an enterprise to achieve breakthroughs in the quality, responsiveness, flexibility and cost to compete more effectively and efficiently in a chosen market. In this case the concept uses a combination of industrial engineering, operations research, management theory, quality management and systems analysis techniques and tools. Reengineering, therefore, refers to the use of information technology to radically redesign business processes to reduce cost and improve speed, service, and quality.[48]

Even though there are many different definitions of this concept, they all have common elements. These commonalties are radical redesign, dramatic improvement, and process integration. Reengineering is considered radical, because it questions whether it is necessary to perform a specific function. If that function is viewed as unnecessary, it is eliminated. The utilizing of dramatic improvements by reengineering is done so because slower, incremental improvements are not viewed as a sufficient strategy. Reengineering processes must also be integrated, because the redesign process affects all dimensions of a company.

There are a number of important fundamental principles underlying reengineering. There is some discrepancy between what various proponents claim to be the most important tenet of reengineering. One can summarize and highlight the claims by stating the following five principles: (1) Know where you are going; (2) make a major commitment of time, people, and resources; (3) identify and understand the critical elements; (4) be practical in your application and link all available resources; and (5) test your new design.

THE IMPLEMENTATION OF REENGINEERING

Before implementing reengineering, the company must understand the interaction between the organization's key objectives and core activities. This requires accurate and accessible representations of processes, events, and requirements contributing to core processes.

The company must then recognize that their information technology cannot be viewed as an optional extra, but as a necessity. According to Hammer and Champy, a company that cannot change the way it thinks about information technology cannot reengineer.[49] The organization must not only rethink its use of information technology, but its entire operational structure in order to account for the new information technology.

Companies must also learn how to consistently increase the performance of their processes while adapting to changing environments. Companies should not adopt reengineering mainly to improve the short-term performance of the stock. This might provide a greater return, but on a short-term basis only. Many companies implement reengineering so that they will not lose ground to a competitor. To be effective, reengineering must be aimed at building a competitive advantage.

The changing environment includes an increase in competition, a change in markets, and a shorter life cycle for products, business processes, and software applications. Information systems should be designed and programmed in environments that allow for flexibility so the systems may be changed as needed.

However, reengineering will not be appropriate in all environments, and not all environments will give the same desired results. Emery classified environments according to the degree of predictability, which can be assumed once one has the information of the rules and processes in context. He identified four types of environments: *placid, clustered, reactive,* and *turbulent.*[50]

In a placid environment, rules apply universally and persist over time. There is no difference between strategy and tactics. The company must adjust itself to the governing rules and procedures in order to optimize performance.

A clustered environment does not have rules and procedures that extend universally. This environment has islands or clusters that exist with different rules and norms. The clusters allow for opportunities, but may also experience threats. This environment leads to strategic thinking that would permit the organization to move toward opportunities and withdrawal from threats. Both the placid and clustered environments have a high degree of stability and predictability.

The reactive environment is very complex, because the actions and reactions of other companies must be taken into account. These companies are called oligopolies or cartels. Airlines, supermarkets, and oil companies are examples of this type of organization. The environment is theoretically predictable, but the complex interactions make the resolutions difficult.

In the turbulent environment, the rules are constantly changing in an unpredictable manner. A deregulated financial service sector or the market-driven health services are examples of companies in the turbulent environment.

Shifting from the placid to the turbulent environment elevates the level of uncertainty and risk. When risk is increased, the company may try to maintain stability, but the efforts are futile. What these companies may want to do instead is invest in flexibility. An investment in flexibility would increase the company's readiness to respond to unpredictable situations.[51]

STRENGTHS OF REENGINEERING

Reengineering offers opportunities for major improvement, as well as the potential for high cost. Hammer encourages leaders to think big and dares to offer the incentive of "cutting 75% of overhead and eliminating 80% of errors."[52] That is no small order. This is the greatest strength of reengineering, and an important one in a rapidly changing and increasingly competitive world.

Other strengths of reengineering include the demand for reassessing organizational objectives, clearly identifying and reexamining organizational processes, and clarifying the goals and objectives of the company. Insistence that the reevaluations of the processes are directed and facilitated by increasing the power and application of information technology is another strength of reengineering. By doing this, up-to-date information and technology are included and utilized in the corporation, making it more current and marketable. Many new possibilities emerge when innovative technology is incorporated. However, this does not mean that reengineering should be technically determined; but, it should be organizationally determined.[53]

PROBLEMS WITH REENGINEERING

Reengineering is a very serious and risky business that demands a high price. While rapid results are important, others emphasize that lasting change is a longer process (up to five years). Reengineering is inherently risky due to the nature of change, and it would seem reasonable to want to minimize risks by eliminating as many unknowns as possible. However, coupled with unclear objectives, reengineering becomes even more risky. It should be used when desperate measures are necessary, not as a strategy tool. It is hard for a single individual to change a bad habit. It would be harder to attempt a radical change in a complex organization.

The planning of the processes of reengineering is also an expensive and time-consuming technicality. If the reengineering processes are not followed, designing them is a waste of time and resources. Another major limitation of reengineering is the lack of research and analysis of its implementation. One reason that research in this area may be limited could be due to the short time that reengineering has been popular in the business world.

One critical problem with reengineering is the disregard for the consequences of reengineering in human and social terms. Some individuals have tried to play down the unpleasant aspects of reengineering. But, the actions of downsizing are an undesirable consideration to employees and society. Instant remedies, such as downsizing, have limited benefits. They expect lower benefits and reduced job security to increase performance, and this is foolish.[54] A company also tends not to utilize the full intelligence and flexibility of their workers if the workers must adhere to a regimented and detailed work design.

LEADERSHIP AND REENGINEERING

Leadership is very important for the success of reengineering. Executive leadership with vision is a factor that is necessary for reengineering to succeed. A true vision, ready to break the barrier of conventional thinking, will provide a powerful motivation for energizing employees. This vision must not be limited to the old ways of thinking. It should incorporate new ideas and techniques.

CEOs must also be active, even when their role as CEO of an organization is changing. The CEO has to be the person who is really behind the spirit of reengineering and who should devote most of his time on the factory floor talking to employees and customers. Top level managers must back the effort of reengineering so that people will take it seriously.

CEOs need motivation, especially when performing those tasks that often are not measured and have been viewed as irrelevant within the organization. The leader must also strive to save time by identifying less important activities and eliminating them. Finally, the CEO needs to align authority, information, and skills into one harmonious concert. This last item is even more important as decisions are moved further down the corporate ladder and diversity increases.

Indeed, the new leader should look at his role as a facilitator who aids and motivates his people to achieve their best, and not as a manager who directs the actions of his subordinates. Leaders should support, coach, and facilitate the employees, rather than supervise and control them. The leader's role will become one of the most essential for the success of reengineering. This is why most breakdowns of reengineering occur because of leadership problems.

Reengineering requires more direct participation by senior management than TQM due to the scope and magnitude of change. The success of applying this concept is largely dependent on management's support and commitment.

The CEO does not always have to be the leader of the reengineering movement. Dixon also found that in nearly every business process redesign (BPR) implementation case, there was one specific champion of reengineering. In eight cases out of twenty-three, the CEO was the leader. In the other cases, the leader came from different parts of the organization, but they always had the full support of the CEO in order for reengineering to succeed.

Dixon also found that teams were common in both the design and implementation of reengineering. These teams can vary in size and makeup, but they are always key players in reengineering. The leader (i.e., the CEO) must learn to give the teams the power and the responsibility to find their own way of reaching the desired goal.

COMPARISON OF TQM AND REENGINEERING

Similarities

For TQM and reengineering to be effective, both must have the dedication and involvement of top level management to set the proper tone for environmental change. Also, both TQM and reengineering have a starting point at process improvement, and a common preferred outcome for customer satisfaction. Both approaches attempt to improve quality and both are customer oriented.

For the implementation of TQM and reengineering to be successful, both must create an organizational culture. The implementation must be integrated at all levels of the organization in order to accomplish profound and lasting improvements. Reengineering can be applied in part or all of the process. It can be applied along with TQM. The concept may be used as a step to achieve fundamental changes in the organization. This process is taken when management and employees are convinced that the changes are unavoidable.

Differences

TQM implementation involves steady change to accomplish a competitive advantage. These advantages can be seen in small but important changes in process improvements. On the other hand, reengineering seeks radical improvements to ensure a competitive advantage.

TQM consists of a long-term commitment to quality improvement and requires having the appropriate long-term goals. Reengineering process typically involves a short duration. It is what American companies most often use to regain competitive advantage.

The implementation of TQM involves the contribution of all employees to the concepts of quality and customer service. TQM includes the participation of employees to assist in identifying problems. Reengineering usually consists of layoffs or the retraining of employees. Therefore, employee participation is minimal.

In general, most business leaders are unaware of the relationship between TQM and reengineering. A good combination of TQM and reengineering could significantly increase a sustainable competitive advantage. After reengineering is implemented, for example, the organization could provide adequate time to learn the new process and make improvements. Likewise, a more customer-oriented approach could be utilized to increase customer satisfaction.[55] It is advisable to undertake reengineering only when benchmarking is absolutely impossible.

SELECTING THE PROPER METHOD

If the company is in a highly changeable market, reengineering might be an appropriate step to be taken. If changes are gradual, then incremental steps of continuous improvement in quality may be preferred. However, sometimes a company desires changes in a particular area or section in the workplace. In this case, reengineering might be the more appropriate approach, since it does not involve comprehensive changes, for which total quality management would be more appropriate.

If you embark on the total quality management approach, suppliers and customers will be heavily involved in the change as well as those working for your organization. Part-time reengineering efforts have commonly produced limited results and will probably lead to great frustration and disappointment.

Finally, what is the level of urgency? Do you face a major crisis that you must react to swiftly and decisively to survive? In this case, reengineering would be more appropriate, because it has a shorter duration and results will be seen more quickly. Are you a new player in the quality improvement game looking for techniques to enhance the performance of your company? In this case, TQM would be a better approach.

In selecting the appropriate method, it is important to understand the company's present situation. The company should diagnose its current situation from the customer's perspective, have a clear vision of direction by prioritizing the processes and then selecting an approach, and be thoroughly familiar with the pros and cons of both involvement to gain top management commitment and full support.

CONCLUSION

Total quality management is very important in today's business environment. Over the last decade, businesses have become increasingly customer driven. Quality of product or service can make or break any company. Only those companies that are the most productive and that deliver a top quality product will survive and thrive in the world's global markets during the next decade. Most of the attention has focused on large and medium companies, which provide an opportunity for greater personal and financial wealth. These organizations have a harder time making changes because of their size and complexity. Smaller companies have a greater need, on account of their market position, to be flexible, fast-moving organization that utilizes their resources. These companies make up a substantial part of American labor and economic environment and deserve, therefore, a fair amount of attention from change agents. Those businesses that effectively apply TQM and reengineering into their culture will experience innovations in the process, product developments, and flexibility in the implementation, which is crucial for successful development.

NOTES

1. Christopher Wood, "Total Quality Management: Why It Has Not Lived Up to Expectations," *International Business Strategies*, ed. Abbass F. Alkhafaji and Zakaria El-Sadek (Apollo, Pa.: Closson Press, 1997), 17–26.

2. Joel Ross, *Total Quality Management*, 2d ed. (Delray Beach, Fla.: St. Lucie Press, 1995).

3. Abbass F. Alkhafaji, "Total Quality Management: The Role of Management Process," *International Business Strategies*, ed. Abbass F. Alkhafaji and Zakaria El-Sadek (Apollo, Pa.: Closson Press, 1997), 8–15.

4. Wood, "Total Quality Management."

5. Ernst & Young Quality Improvement Consulting Group, *Total Quality in an Executive's Guide for the 1990s* (Homewood, Ill.: Dow Jones–Irwin/APICS Series in Production Management, 1990).

6. Philip B. Crosby, *Let's Talk Quality* (New York: McGraw-Hill, 1989).

7. Bruce Brocka and M. Suzanne Brocka, *Quality Management: Implementing the Best Ideas of the Masters* (Homewood, Ill.: Irwin, 1992).

8. W. Edwards Deming, *Out of the Crisis* (Cambridge, Mass.: MIT, Center for Advanced Engineering Study, 1982), 160–174, 465.

9. J. M. Juran, *Juran on Quality by Design* (New York: The Free Press, 1992), 72–74.

10. Armand Feigenbaum, "The Future of Quality Management," *Quality Digest* 18 (May 1998): 33–38.

11. J. M. Juran, "Why Quality Initiatives Fail," *Journal of Business Strategy* 14 (July–August 1993): 35–38.

12. Ross, *Total Quality Management*.

13. James Evans and William Lindsay, *The Management and Control of Quality*, 3d ed. (Minneapolis: West Publishing, 1996).

14. Thomas J. Peters and Robert H. Waterman, Jr., *In Search of Excellence* (New York: Harper and Row, 1982).

15. Tom Taormina, *Virtual Leadership and the ISO 9000 Imperative* (Englewood Cliffs, N.J.: Prentice Hall, 1996).

16. Vincent K. Omachonu and Joel E. Ross, *Principles of Total Quality* (Delray Beach, Fla.: St Lucie Press, 1994), 293.

17. Ernst & Young, *Total Quality*, 29.

18. Procter & Gamble, "Forging Links with Higher Education," *Proceedings: The Total Quality Forum* (August 1991).

19. Casimir C. Barczyk and Gideon Falk, "Does Knowledge of TQM Influence Top Managers Beliefs, Commitment, and Management Style?" *Business Research Yearbook* 3 (1996): 463–467.

20. Joseph DePinho, *The TQM Transformation: A Model for Organizational Change* (New York: Quality Resources, 1992).

21. W. Edwards Deming, *Quality Productivity and Competitive Position* (Cambridge, Mass.: MIT, Center for Advanced Engineering Study, 1982); J. M. Juran, "The Quality Trilogy: A Universal Approach to Managing for Quality," *Quality Progress* (August 1986): 19–24.

22. Naceur Jabnoun, "Values Underlying Customer Satisfaction, Empowerment and Continuous Improvement," *Business Research Yearbook* 8 (2001): 420.

23. John Bell, "Building the New Chrysler," *Industry Week* 245 (September 1996): 10–15.

24. Ross, *Total Quality Management*.

25. Ibid., 120.

26. Wood, "Total Quality Management," 17.

27. Laura D'Andrea Tyson, "Who's Bashing Whom?: Trade Conflict in High Technology Industries," *Institute for International Economics* (November 1992).

28. James Laprecht, "Qualite a La Francaise," *Quality Progress* (June 1993): 31–35; Richard D. Spitzer, "TQM: The Only Source of Sustainable Competitive Advantage," *Quality Progress* (June 1993): 59–64; and John Templeman, "France Wants Out of Business," *Business Week*, 7 June 1993, 46–47.

29. Wood, "Total Quality Management."

30. Ibid.

31. Ibid.

32. David L. Goetsch and Stanley B. Davis, *Total Quality Handbook* (Upper Saddle River, N.J.: Prentice Hall, 2001).

33. Naceur Jabnoun, "Structure Contingency Model for TQM Completion," *Business Research Yearbook* 8 (2001).

34. Artzt, quoted in Barczyk and Falk, "Does Knowledge of TQM Influence Top Managers Beliefs?"

35. Barczyk and Falk, "Does Knowledge of TQM Influence Top Managers Beliefs?"

36. Goetsch and Davis, *Total Quality Handbook*.

37. Keith Grant, "TQM, BPR, JIT, BSCs and TLAs: Managerial Waves or Drownings?" *Management Decision* (1997): 731–738.

38. Goetsch and Davis, *Total Quality Handbook*, 211.

39. Ibid.

40. Tracy E. Benson, "TQM: A Child Takes a First Few Faltering Steps," *Industry Week*, 5 April 1993, p. 17.

41. Ibid.

42. Ibid.

43. Goetsch and Davis, *Total Quality Handbook*, 215.

44. Andrew DuBain, *Reengineering Survival Guide: Managing and Succeeding in the Changing Workplace* (Cincinnati: Thomson Executive Press, 1996).

45. Taormina, *Virtual Leadership and the ISO 9000 Imperative*, 41.

46. Ibid.

47. Michael Hammer, "Re-Engineering Work: Don't Automate, Obliterate," *Harvard Business Review* 68 (July–August 1990), 104–112.

48. Sudhir Tandon, "Re-Engineering Tradition, Traditional Product Management: Suggestions from an Empirical Study," *Business Research Yearbook* 4 (1997): 634.

49. Michael Hammer and J. Champy, *Reengineering the Corporation* (London: Nicholas Brealey, 1993).

50. F. E. Emery, *Systems Thinking* (Harmondsworth: Penguin, 1969).

51. Antony Bryant, "Beyond BPR: Confronting the Organizational Legacy," *Management Decision* 36 (1998): 25–30.

52. Hammer, "Re-engineering Work," 104–112.

53. Bryant, "Beyond BPR."

54. Ibid.

55. Sang Lee and Arben Asllani, "TQM and BPR: Symbiosis and a New Approach for Integration," *Management Decision* 35 (1997): 409–416.

Chapter 5

Total Quality Management: The Role of Management Process

Total quality management has become one of the most discussed subjects in the business circle today. TQM is a process designed to improve the quality of products and services and to meet or exceed customers' needs and expectations. The focus of TQM is continuous improvement of organizational processes that could result in higher quality products and services. The process is an integrated and interlocking sequence between customers, the organization, and the suppliers. TQM is an important element of transformation, and it is here to stay. It is a cultural transformation in management processes. *TQM refers to the systematic improvement of quality as well as to the cultural transformation in management techniques through the involvement of everyone in the organization and in all aspects of the business operations.* This requires the development of an integrated system of training to increase knowledge about the philosophy tool, the techniques of TQM, and how to implement it. This chapter will provide a more complete picture of the management functions (planning, organizing, leading, and controlling) in the implementation of TQM.

TQM strategies and methods developed as practical, hands-on techniques on how to manage and improve the firm's competitive position in an increasingly dynamic environment and complex global competition. Westinghouse Electric, Xerox, Motorola, and others have succeeded in the implementation of TQM during the late 1980s, whereas Federal Express, Marlow Industries, Cadillac Motors, and Ford succeeded in the early 1990s. Their success encouraged numerous U.S. firms to undertake integrated quality management initiatives. National and international quality awards such as the Baldrige Award and ISO 9000 series were initiated. In response to perceived inferiority to international competitors, particularly Japanese and Southeast Asian companies, the quality management initiatives were developed.

Quality improvement has become the fundamental business strategy for this century. Tom Peters mentioned in various speeches to business executives (from 1987 to 1998) that organizations should adopt TQM and fast. He said, "Get everyone involved, starting in the next 90 days, in a radical program of continuous quality improvement." Japanese companies have adopted TQM concepts and succeeded. While some of the American companies did not succeed. Tracey Benson and Richard Poe have pointed out that the Japanese, with their knowledge of Zen Buddhism, understood Deming's plan–do–check–act (PDCA) cycle as a spiritual discipline. Poe asserted that excessive reliance on logic and reason led many Westerners to misunderstand this aspect of Deming's concepts.[1]

The author strongly believes that TQM is here to stay. It is a cultural transformation in management style and techniques. The Department of Education has called for the education system to become the leader in the world. Many universities have started the process of adopting continuous quality improvements in the late 1990s. Perhaps the most attractive feature of TQM is its emphasis on improving all aspects of business in contrast to a piecemeal approach. TQM is a long-term concept, not a quick fix. Leading business people see no other way to become more competitive than to practice TQM. Evidence of the importance of TQM is the enthusiastic response to the Baldrige Award, which was inaugurated in 1988 to recognize high quality businesses.

Global competition requires the adaptation of TQM within the business community. Business has been responding slowly at first, but now it moves at a rapid pace. Japan started total quality management after World War II. The United States started in the 1980s and is still playing catch up. This chapter will introduce a strategic approach to the management processes and their role in TQM implementation.

LITERATURE REVIEW

Total quality management is a philosophy about how businesses should be run. The philosophy of TQM is filled with ideas and attitudes. The basic premise to this philosophy is the idea that the only thing certain in life is change. The bottom line of TQM is to provide greater efficiency, effectiveness, and profitability by focusing on quality and not mass production. Evans and Lindsay define TQM as the process of building quality into goods and services from the beginning and making quality everyone's concern and responsibility.[2] The characteristics of how total quality management initiatives should be implemented vary from one writer to another and from one company to another. Although TQM implementation was successful in some companies, it was not considered successful in many others. These unsuccessful attempts led to a concern that TQM was not as effective as previously believed. In 1997 Evans asked the question of why some organizations are less effective in implementing TQM than others. W. Edwards Deming stresses that top management has the overriding responsibility for quality improvement. Deming feels that if his TQM initiative is implemented, there will be a "chain reaction." The implementation of TQM will result in improvement in quality. These improvements will lead to a decrease in costs and an increase in productivity.

Writers agree that the successful implementation of TQM requires a strong commitment from and involvement of top managers.[3] For example, Refausse writes that a company's senior managers must create visible quality values and high expectations. Reinforcing these quality values and expectations requires their substantial personal commitment and involvement. Other factors cited in the literature for successful TQM implementation are the customer focus and human resource management.[4]

Without management involvement and commitment to TQM, a company can never become successful in any changes. Deming (1975) argued that simply teaching people to use statistical tools aimed at achieving quality improvement was insufficient. He stressed that only management has the power to change a firm's processes affecting the quality of its products and services. Management is also responsible for the relationships between people and their organization. Deming observed that quality control necessitates the understanding and commitment of top management.[5]

Joseph Juran was opposed to the Deming philosophy. He did not propose a major cultural change in the organization but rather sought to improve quality by working within the system. Juran focused on developing a quality cost accounting system and using Pareto analysis to focus on quality problems. His TQM program is designed to fit a company's current business and strategic plan with minimum risk.[6]

Philip Crosby places more emphasis on managerial and organizational processes for changing corporate culture. Crosby's basic elements of implementing a quality program include what he calls the four pillars.[7] These elements include

1. Management participation and attitude.

2. Professional quality management.
3. Original programs.
4. Recognition.

Bill Creech has added a new approach to implementing a TQM program. He has come up with the five elements of TQM.[8] These elements are product, process, leadership, organization, and commitment. Creech believes that there are no bad forms of TQM. Only incomplete forms of TQM produce no substantial results. He believes that for a TQM program to be successful, it must shape all parts of the management system, structure, and style. Creech's TQM approach is holistic and humanistic, which he finds to be successful in Japanese and American companies.

American companies that do business in Europe were under pressure to meet ISO 9000 requirements. ISO 9000 refers to the quality assurance standards that were established by the European Economic Community for quality certification requirements. On the other hand, many small companies are just becoming aware of the pervasiveness of TQM. The importance of this lack of awareness cannot be overemphasized.

STRATEGIC PLANNING

Management needs to include quality values and customer expectations in corporate goals and objectives. Strategic planning in TQM should not differ from strategic planning presented in management theory in terms of concern about quality, cost, and schedule. An organization can be efficient when its people, processes, systems, and structure are effectively integrated. A strategic approach to implement TQM will require the analysis of the organizational environment. To identify the internal and external environment of the firm is important in order to match internal resources and capabilities against external opportunities whilst eradicating organizational weaknesses. This will assist the organization to move away from insular thinking. Therefore, a transformational leader must develop a strategic plan and a system that is based on quality as defined by customers' and employees' involvement. Leaders who believe in continuous improvement must allocate corporate resources to improve overall quality of products and services produced efficiently and effectively. The system design must produce dimensions that are acceptable by customers, such as reliability, conformance, durability, and overall performance. When organizations do things right the first time, they save themselves the huge cost of redoing the product and do not shift their attention from other necessary development. In addition, customers will be delighted. In the next section we discuss the strategic management and quality transformation model.

FIRST: A STRATEGIC MANAGEMENT APPROACH

Stage	Analysis
Awareness stage	Initial assessment and benchmarking. Get management well acquainted with this concept.
The preparation stage (environmental analysis)	Environmental analysis: Internal (distinctive competencies) and external (within the industry and within the wider macroenvironment); the forces that shape competition.
The development stage (quality formulation)	Develop information, systems, and infrastructure necessary to start the process.
	Also specify roles, relationships, and responsibilities of steering or quality teams and the various levels of management.
	The necessary training of all involves managers and employees.
	The process requires the allocation of resources and total commitment of the CEO and management.
The strategic stage (establish organizational direction)	Adopt a coherent vision, mission, and goals; communicate functionally and horizontally; identify strategies on a time-limit basis; adopt a broad definition of quality from customer perspective.
	Systems audit: (a) identify critical business processes (those that pay bills), and (b) identify other organizational processes. • Identify customers, needs, and gaps. • Identify key issues affecting the provision of quality. • Identify measures to improve quality of employee work life. • Set new values–belief system–culture change.
The implementation stage (quality implementation)	Redesign all critical business process.
	Streamline organizational processes.
	Train and retrain employees.
	Remove quality problems when possible.
The evaluation and control stage (quality control)	Continuously measure, monitor, control changes.
	Set standards based on onjectives.
	Identify a tolerance range.
	Measure–monitor progress against standards.
	Reassess staff commitment.
	Select other improvement projects.

Total quality management is an approach that embraces a wide range of "hard" and "soft" management practices that, taken together, can transform the culture of an organization.[9]

TQM is more of a way of managing than it is a program or a set of management techniques. It focuses on customer needs and satisfaction. To have quality, cultural change is required. It focuses on the satisfaction of organizational stakeholders. The Federal Quality Institute has identified seven principles that define TQM:

1. *Demonstrating* personal leadership and support for the quality effort by leaders throughout the organization.
2. *Strategically* planning the short- and long-term directions of the organization and tying the *quality improvement effort* to the strategic plan.
3. Assuring that everyone focus on customers' needs and expectations and not their own.
4. Developing clearly defined measures for *tracking progress* and identifying improvement opportunities.
5. Providing adequate resources for training, and *recognizing worker's contributions* to quality improvement.
6. Empowering workers to *make* decisions, and fostering teamwork.
7. Developing systems to assure that quality is built in at the beginning and throughout operation.[10]

The "hard" side of TQM includes the company's strategic planning, data collection and measurement, systematic analysis, and use of statistical tools to help solve the root cause or problems. The "soft" side deals with the leadership skills, teambuilding techniques, listening, and communications skills.

TQM is hard to implement, and once it is understood, it takes years to adopt. According to Lewis, one of the greatest drawbacks of TQM is its comprehensiveness and rich underlying theory. In addition to proposing new theories about quality, managers can make certain changes if they want to improve the system, the first change being customer relationships, which consists of managers realizing their employees need quality products to receive quality work. One other factor is employee empowerment, meaning that employee input is vital to the success of the company.

Benchmarking, which Xerox popularized, is considered a fundamental guide to strategic planning. Benchmarking is the continuous process of measuring products, services, and processes against those of industry leaders.[11] Benchmarking provides standards by which the operations and improvement processes of a business are measured.

Information used for strategic planning should be collected throughout the system, with emphasis on customer needs and benchmarking.

The system consists of a cycle of demand assessments, supply of raw material from suppliers, production, fulfillment of customer demand, and feedback from the process. Planning, for any company's attempt to implement TQM, should be based on a wide range of information including its vision, mission, objectives, current and future customer needs, levels of customer satisfaction, benchmarking, government regulations, local needs, environmental issues, and an analysis of current performance. Strategy making is the process of capturing the insights of managers based on hard and soft data and synthesizing it into a vision of the direction that the business should pursue. Thus strategic quality planning is a systematic approach to setting quality goals. Planning for quality management requires an understanding of the importance of quality and the need for awareness of the total quality concept—quality of design and conformance—as well as an understanding of the planning process. Planning sets the direction and tone for future quality-related activities. Strategic quality planning should become synonymous with strategic business planning because more and more companies are finding that quality drives financial and marketing success. The planning process should reflect continuous improvement goals. Continuous improvement is considered to be the central concept of total quality management. In 1987, Motorola, after a careful environmental analysis, announced the following quality goals: ten times improvement by 1988, one-hundred times improvement by 1989, and six sigma performance by 1992 (where six sigma roughly equals 3.4 defects per million opportunities). Because of its ambitious improvement strategy, Motorola saved $3.5 billion, sales increased by 126 percent per employee and by 100 percent over the same period, and productivity increased by 12.2 percent between 1987 and 1992.

Before setting future objectives and designing strategies, organizations must analyze their environment (e.g., its strengths, weaknesses, opportunities, and threats). This analysis will help the organization to better respond to market demand and enhance its competitive position. Quality planning requires supportive policies and procedures, flexibility, and the creation of a culture that permits wider participation in the process. One important question that is usually asked in this situation is who participates in the planning process. It is generally advised that those involved in implementation participate in the planning process and that concurrent engineering be used in product development. It is also wise to include suppliers and customers in some stage of the planning process. Strategic implementation is highly emphasized in TQM because implementation is what gives a strategy its worth. Planning in TQM is considered a process that should be improved.

ORGANIZATION STRUCTURE

The organization exists within an environment. It is an entity created by law with a clearly defined purpose: to provide products and services to various customers in the context of a competitive environment. An organization is the framework that holds the firm together and allows it to operate efficiently. Designing the organization requires the firms to first be divided into various departments and then employees must be matched to the appropriate tasks required to achieve corporate objectives. Then resources should be allocated among the various activities performed by the organization based on corporate priorities. To implement TQM, continuous changes in the organizational structure are a necessity to prevent employees from reverting back to their old practices. One of the most effective ways to change behavior is to place employees into a new organizational context, which provides new roles, responsibilities, and relationships. Therefore, organizational structure should be continuously improved in order to enrich performance and to cope with changes in strategy. It is argued that TQM requires a shift from a traditional functional view of a business enterprise to one based on workflow processes. This process refers to the transformation of inputs into outputs. The inputs include materials, equipment, information, knowledge, skills, training, people, methods, and procedures, while the outputs include products, services, information, and paperwork. Hunt envisions a TQM-oriented organization to have

1. Processes rather than function as the basic fundamental unit of analysis.
2. Workers loyal to process-focused, cross-functional teams as opposed to functional departments.
3. Responsiveness to customer needs and quality rather than to department and functional rules.[12]

The TQM-oriented organization is expected to be free from bureaucratic barriers. The new structure should start with customer demand, then the request for the necessary raw material from suppliers, then production facilities, and then the fulfillment of customer needs. A company must focus on quality efforts that are relevant to customer needs, desires, and expectations. If production has no connection with customer expectations, the process is not a quality one. A company must develop appropriate methods to assess customer demand and expectations. Testing and modifying quality in the market is another way of assessing customer expectations. Then the company should plan to provide superior quality products at reasonable costs. Suppliers play a critical role in accomplishing both goals. Suppliers are considered partners in this process. The company selects suppliers based on long-term relationships. It is advisable to establish a strategic relationship with a few dependable suppliers in terms of quality of raw materials, timely delivery, and the speed of resolving disputes.

The transformation of raw materials received from suppliers into finished products that meet customer needs and expectations is the most important part of an organization's structure. Organizational structure is the method used to arrange the resources of the company (i.e., equipment, processes, and human resources) with the tasks involved. In order to effectively satisfy customer needs, the company must manufacture a quality product within a cost-effective process, using statistical process control and process-quality information management to insure the success of the process. This requires the preparation of employees for quality improvement through training, empowerment, and teamwork. TQM depends on the involvement of everyone in the organization. Training and retraining helps management to bring everyone in the organization to work together. This represents the seriousness of top management's involvement in the quality process. Cooperation of the employees and teamwork efforts are important ingredients for successful implementation of the quality system. The new structure should allow for direct communication, cooperation, and learning between various divisions in the organization. In the new organization flatter structure not only facilitates communication, but should also allow information to be exchanged freely. Technology should play a major role in paving the way for such changes to achieve effective performance.

In the 1990s many companies started restructuring and entering collaborative agreements to improve their competitiveness. They expanded their businesses abroad through strategic alliances such as joint ventures, consortia, and partnerships. During 1998, Apple continued and essentially completed its restructuring plan which commenced in 1996. This plan aimed at reducing the company's cost structure, improving its competitiveness, and restoring sustainable profitability. Apple has since created spin-outs of some of its operations. A spin-out is a separation of the strategic unit from the parent company which still maintains a long-term relationship with the parent. Many companies use aligned contractors to provide them with needed parts and raw materials. The flexibility provided by this form of structuring allows companies to provide fast turnaround for retail buyers.

These spin-outs usually result in fostering entrepreneurship and empowering management and employees. Apple benefited from this strategy by extending its scope and strength without enlarging the company. Fujisawa used this strategy of spinning-out Honda R&D as a separate, wholly-owned company with its president. Later, he spun-out Honda Engineering, responsible for all Honda's proprietary manufacturing machinery, as a second company.[13]

LEADING

Leadership refers to the process of supporting and convincing organizational members to achieve the predetermined goals and objectives of the organization. Management plays many roles, one of which is leadership. However, not all managers are leaders. The shareholders and the board of directors expect that management is responsible for the success of the organization. Because of the globalization and the changing environment, management more than ever needs the support and involvement of all employees. Leadership exists at all levels of the organization. Just like any other organizational process, leadership must be measured and improved. Under TQM, leaders are coaches and not bosses. They share responsibilities and support their employees. They assume their responsibilities as role models. Leadership at the top level (i.e., the CEOs) sets the company's visions, philosophy, and values. They create norms of behavior that will establish the corporate culture in the organization.

How to align the employees around organizational leadership is the essential issue in many organizations. To survive in a global market, many companies are struggling to implement TQM. As we mentioned in Chapter 4, about two-thirds of companies who adopted TQM have failed to succeed. Companies fail to successfully implement TQM because their top leadership lacks the commitment and knowledge to fully understand the philosophy and practice of this concept. Instead of depending on their employees, management tends to use experts from outside the organization. In many cases leaders are not ready to reform the organizational system, change traditional approaches, or form new partnerships with suppliers. Competitiveness in the global market requires the adaptation of continuous improvement, innovation, and acquiring of new technology. When managers fail to understand the importance of quality and its implication in this dynamic environment, companies suffer.

In order to build competitive advantage in this global economy, quality must be considered a priority and an integral part of the way companies do business. Management must understand that implementing the TQM approach is the only way to succeed in this century. The adaptation of TQM requires the development of participative styles of management. This will energize employees and use their unlimited potential to achieve organizational objectives. Top level management at Xerox not only acquired knowledge about TQM but also started teaching it to all employees, sending a powerful message to all employees that they are committed to the philosophy of TQM. It is crucial to build this level of commitment, because the main concern of employees involved in TQM implementation is the lack of commitment and involvement of top level management in these initiatives. A leadership evaluation and awareness process (LEAP) was established by Federal Express. Three transformational leadership behavior dimensions were identified by LEAP: charisma, individual consideration, and intellectual stimulation. It also identified six leadership qualities: courage, dependability, flexibility, integrity, judgment, and respect for others. This program resulted in lower turnover rates for management, from 10.7 percent to 1.7 percent. LEAP also solicited feedback about how subordinates viewed management's performance. This was used to improve management performance and participation at Federal Express.

CONTROLLING

Control is another management function. It is important for any company's success. Planning and controlling go hand-in-hand. The process of control consists of setting standards, inspecting the process, and taking corrective actions when needed. Companies going through the transformation process must develop control systems that facilitate the implementation process. The control system must identify the quality measures as expected by customers. The control system must allocate the necessary resources and needed authority to produce the quality required. These standards must be improved continuously. Transformation requires the establishment of a supportive corporate culture. This culture must be committed to quality, participation, and involvement. Training employee teams empowerment, quality circles, and customer surveys are important elements of the new corporate culture. In addition, innovation, research and development, and the use of outside consultants are also important to measure and improve performance.

Performance and output are periodically checked under this system. The use of statistical quality control tools such as cause and effect, the Pareto diagram, and other statistical measures will aid management and employees to identify the performance level. Anytime there is a variation within the standards, corrective measures must be taken, and they should include the performance, the organizational structure, and even the standards.

Implementing TQM invites the organization to check the possibility of improving the performance. Management has the choice to modify or reengineer the process, depending on the level of performance. These actions should take into consideration corporate objectives, resources, capabilities, structure, and future planning.

The result of such changes must be the high product quality of the end products at an economical price that satisfies customers. Today companies cannot expect to supply good products at costs higher than those of global competitors. They must therefore improve the quality of the manufacturing processes if they are to produce high-quality products at a reasonable cost and at the same time satisfy customers.

CONCLUSION

This chapter attempted to discuss the various management processes and how they could be used to support the implementation of TQM. The planning process in total quality management is the third in rank of the seven Baldrige Award criteria. Planning in TQM should consist of the components of planning found in management theory. The planning process should focus on customer satisfaction and take into account information from all over the system, including benchmarking. It also should reflect continuous improvement targets. Most importantly, the planning should focus on all the business dimensions: quality, cost, and schedule. Planning should include people from different departments and possibly suppliers and customers. Strategic implementation of TQM requires a productive cultural ground characterized by commitment, discipline, and participation.

Organizational design should be based on process; however, functional departments might be needed to provide for expertise and for economies of scale. Restructuring that promotes efficiency, entrepreneurship, spin-outs, and strategic alliances are highly recommended in a global economy. Such restructuring will provide the company with the needed synergetic network. Organizational structure should be continuously improved and changed according to the new strategies and objectives, which are in turn dependent on the customer and the environment. The organizational structure should be linear so those members of the organization can communicate horizontally and exchange information freely using the latest technology.

Total quality movement has been the first wave in building a learning organization. This requires the support and understanding of the company's leaders. Leadership in a learning organization must create a shared vision, along with accurate pictures of the current organizational position and a total commitment to the process. Leadership involvement is highly important in TQM. Leaders should play the roles of servants, supporters, and coaches rather than bosses. Leadership, like everything else, needs to be continuously measured and improved.

The control process is a dynamic one where standards can change whenever a new improvement is found. Everything in the organization can be inspected from the design stage until the end of the process. If performance does not fit standards, organizational structure or even standards might be changed. Standards will also be changed when a new improvement is possible.

NOTES

1. Tracey E. Benson, "A Business Strategy Comes of Age," *Industry Week*, 3 May 1993, 40–44; Richard Poe, "The New Discipline," *Success* 38 (August 1991): 80.

2. James Evans and William Lindsay, *The Management and Control of Quality*, 3d ed. (Minneapolis: West Publishing, 1996).

3. John Refausse, "Self-Knowledge to Lift Career Spirits," *People Management* 2 (16 May 1996): 34–38.

4. Harry Costin, *Ready in Total Quality Management* (Fort Worth, Tex.: Dryden Press, 1994).

5. W. Edwards Deming, "On Some Statistical Aids Towards Economic Production," *Interfaces* 3 (August 1975): 26.

6. Joseph M. Juran, *Juran on Leadership for Quality* (New York: The Free Press, 1989).

7. Philip B. Crosby, *Quality Is Free: The Art of Making Quality Certain* (New York: McGraw-Hill, 1979).

8. Naceur Jabnoun, "Structure Contingency Model for TQM Completion," *Business Research Yearbook* 8 (2001).

9. Lewis A. Rhodes, "On the Road to Quality," *Educational Leadership* 49 (18 March 1998): 76–80.

10. Frank L. Lewis, "Association for Psychological Type," *TQM, Leadership, and Management* 49 (6 July 1997): 31–34.

11. J. S. Oakland, *Total Quality Management: The Route to Improving Performance* (Woburn, Mass.: Butterworth Heinemann, 1993).

12. Daniel V. Hunt, *Managing for Quality: Integrating Quality and Business Process* (Homewood, Ill.: Irwin, 1993).

13. R. T. Pascale, *Managing on the Edge: How the Smarter Companies Use Conflicts to Stay Ahead.* (New York: Simon and Shuster, 1990).

Chapter 6

Strategic Planning in Academic Institutions

The changing of Category 3 of the 1992 Malcolm Baldridge Award criteria—to integrate quality planning into strategic business planning by shifting the category's focus from strategic quality plan to the strategic business plan—emphasizes the increasing realization of the interrelationship between TQM and strategic planning. This chapter illustrates how total quality management approaches, integrated with strategic planning in a variety of contexts, have and can be applied to higher education. It then describes a general framework used for total quality management and strategic planning which can be used by academic institutions.

This chapter integrates strategic management concepts as applied to the multipurpose university. Strategic planning in any academic institution depends, to a large degree, on how well educational activities are integrated into the actual institution management process. Strategic planning is the process of developing and maintaining a strategic fit between the organization and its changing environment.

The prestige and survival of any university depends on the quality of its faculty and its academic offerings. These two important factors can be assured through proper application of standards. The development of an effective administrative structure and efficiency in managing the various ingredients of it will contribute positively to the success of strategic planning. Universities face challenges by their very nature (e.g., to operate within a declining budget, to prepare students for future careers, to preserve a good academic reputation). The quality of the faculty and other academic groups are the most important elements in any university; their participation and commitment to liberal education and the quest for knowledge are of utmost importance. Their involvement in strategic decision making is critical for the entire institution and enhancement of academic reputation. Usually there is no shortage of brainpower to support strategic planning activities within an academic institution. What is missing are effective and objective tools to convince faculty and administrators to participate actively. The effectiveness of this process depends heavily on the type of leadership. It requires a visionary leader who understands the importance of institution revitalization to meet future challenges.

Managerial setting in a university is getting as complex as any organization operating in a changing environment. Such complexity is a result of the increase in multilevel relationships and increased politics in the system. This has increased the possibilities of potentially mishandling the process. The increased number and sophistication of relationships between the university and its various stakeholders and the rapid changes in technology demand that institutions continuously transform themselves into more caring organizations. Transforming the academic institutions by changing their vision and dramatically increasing the quality of their strategic planning is a requirement in this century.

IMPLEMENTING STRATEGIC PLANNING

At this stage, the use of the team management approach to strategic planning seems the most logical choice in academic institutions. Evidence suggests that companies with strategies based on TQM have obtained remarkable successes.[1] Teamwork is also one of the major components—along with a documented quality management system and statistical process control—of total quality management.[2] The need for group interaction is necessary for efficiency and satisfaction in any academic institution. Such approaches provide greater personal responsibility for all members of the top administrations.

In the past, it seemed that students were not involved in the planning process. By involving students in this process, an institution receives new ideas from those who are most affected by the implementation of different academic plans. Linda Ray Pratt asserted that university administrations want to "re-engineer," "re-trench," or "restructure" the academic part of the universities to include all areas.[3] These areas include students, faculty, staff, and administration, each having different ideas for improvement in the institution. A group comprising students, faculty, staff, and administrators is an ideal system for a university. By including the students in the decision-making process, the academic institution and the students will obtain benefits. The result is that everyone wins with this program: the school, the students, and the industry in general.

Planning and group interaction are currently being utilized in several public schools. The professors and administrators are using techniques such as benchmarking and monitoring attendance and test scores to pinpoint problems. They then use this information to brainstorm with the students to find solutions. Students are also encouraged to work in teams to identify their mistakes.

When analyzing the environment, assessment of the business community is also very important. As stated by Poorsoltan, Amin, and Tootoonchi, the academic institution must be highly involved in the businesses community's activities if it intends to increase the community's support for attainment of educational and professional objectives. Every area of this involvement should involve addressing the environment. For example, the amount and quality of services available to the community, the amount of business and economic research conducted, and how quickly the institution reacts to problems of the community, should all be thoroughly reviewed. "Higher education and business community are inseparable, and must attempt to maintain a positive relationship."[4]

The academic organization must reflect total institutional commitment towards quality in every element of its operations. The academic organization must examine the content of the current academic programs first. Then, taking the environment into consideration, the university must contemplate and facilitate the action it intends to follow. The academic establishment must demonstrate the level of commitment to implement the crafted plans and show willingness to evaluate policies and procedure as needed to insure efficiency of process. Academic institutions can benefit from TQM approaches because of their increased emphasis on quality and consumer satisfaction.

STRATEGIC PLANNING, TOTAL QUALITY MANAGEMENT, AND HIGHER EDUCATION

A number of writers demonstrate or describe a variety of relationships between strategic planning and total quality management. Chalk argues that strategic planning is essential for TQM. The TQM concept refers to the following strategic management objectives:[5]

- Continuous improvement in quality goods and services.
- Greater responsiveness to the final user.
- Greater flexibility in adjusting to customer needs.
- Cost reduction through improved quality and nonvalue-added waste elimination.

Marquardt describes how Category 3 of the 1992 Malcolm Baldridge Award criteria was changed to integrate quality planning into strategic business planning, by shifting the category's focus from strategic quality plan to the strategic business plan. He describes how the steps involved in designing and implementing a strategic plan closely parallel many of the key concepts described as being critical elements of TQM.[6] Madu and Kuei differentiate between total quality assurance, or TQM, and what they call strategic total quality management (STQM), an extension of TQM that they define as a quality management philosophy that views quality from the overall performance of the firm.[7]

Gales describes the ways in which the refining of individual schools' missions and programs, such as TQM, is being used to "reengineer" colleges.[8] Matthews says that academia and TQM meet in the four basic areas of curriculum: operations, overall direction of the institution, teaching, and research. He argues that in order to assume a real commitment to TQM, academic institutions must adopt the following seven steps:[9]

1. Identify the institution's primary stakeholders.
2. Develop a specific, competitive, quality-based mission.
3. Establish internal measures for achievement and quality in various areas.
4. Determine who has to commit to the chosen standards.
5. Establish motivation for those unwilling to commit to excellence and quality.
6. Form quality progress teams.
7. Report, recognize, and reward success.

In the beginning of 1993 the American Association for Higher Education (AAHE) has incorporated continuous improvement into its annual conference on assessment and has been an advocate of using quality and continuous improvement in all aspects of higher education.

DEVELOPMENT OF STRATEGIC PLANNING

Planning is very critical to the success of any organization. Any effort to transform the organization must be planned. Planning reduces the uncertainty by anticipating changes and developing appropriate responses. Planning helps managers avoid loss of resources, waste, delays, and sets the standards to facilitate control. Planning establishes coordinated efforts toward achieving corporate objectives. The following describes the steps for implementation of TQM in an academic setting.

A number of writers have presented steps they advocate in developing strategic planning in an organization. The following represents the distillation of steps incorporating TQM and other quality approaches into a proposed strategic planning process for institutions of higher education. Of course each institution would have to develop its own approach and the degree of people involved in the process of strategic planning. It is important to mention that the model presented in this chapter does not claim to provide a blueprint for the implementation of TQM in an academic institution. Such a model has to be tested first to prove its validity.

1. *Defining the vision* and mission of the university is an important first step in the process. The university vision is the future direction. The leadership of the institution usually initiates the vision statement. Then the members of the organization participate in shaping the shared vision through their feedback and contributions. The university mission statements form the umbrella for strategic planning in the school. "Providers of a quality education program, maintain an excellent education experience for students, and provide service for the stakeholders. Also, they maintain and develop an excellent faculty, which supports the university's ability to render an excellent education, encourage faculty to engage in meaningful research, and to provide service to its region."[10] University philosophy reflects the basic beliefs, value systems, aspirations, and philosophical priorities to which strategic decision makers are committed. Many schools establish a philosophical creed to emphasize their own distinctive outlook on services provided. This creed forms the basis for establishing the university culture.

Social responsibility of the university refers to any actions that project and improve the welfare of society along with advancing the school's own interests. The strategic decisions of any university inevitably involve social as well as economic consequences. Moreover, the social consequences of economic actions typically affect the outside claimants on the school, particularly local communities and the general public. Recognizing this, the socially responsible university builds certain social criteria or goals into its strategy formulation process. There are many good reasons why universities should be socially responsible. First, it is the noble or correct way to behave; second, it is in the self-interest of any university to behave in a socially responsible manner; and third, social responsibility is actually a sound investment strategy.

Many stakeholders such as communities, churches, cities, states, and other companies view any activity that is not socially responsible as a risky investment. Thus, if a university, like any business, wishes to maintain the support of its stakeholders, it must behave in a socially responsible manner.

2. *Develop university goals and objectives.* Students are the most important stakeholders of any school, and the university should try to satisfy their needs first. Institutional priorities must be determined after establishing goals and objectives. The university should adopt other goals to satisfy all stakeholders such as

1. Offering high-quality academic programs.
2. Ensuring an effective and efficient organizational structure.
3. Providing an environment for faculty and staff personnel that leads to positive attitudes and performance.
4. Promoting faculty research activities.
5. Ensuring that the academic programs integrate cultural diversity and global experiences.

Stakeholder participation is an important concept in today's business world. It establishes better lines of communication and encourages creativity throughout the university. It also helps faculty and administration to identify the other responsibilities of the academic institutions.

3. *Analyze the internal environment.* This involves the continuous review of academic programs and evaluating the university's strengths and weaknesses. This step also involves identifying important factors that might influence the design of the strategy, identifying constraints, the evaluation of planning policies and procedures, and identifying major trends in the internal environment such as within the board, administration, faculty, staff, business advisory council, arrangements with professional associations, or alumni.

4. *Analyze the external environment.* It is important to assess the university's position in comparison to the closest institution in the industry. This involves examining competitors and their strategies. The macroenvironment that influences the educational institution, such as the economic climate, state and federal funds and regulations, technological forces and their implications, needs to be assessed. In each of these analyses, the university assesses the market opportunity and future threats. External perceptions of the institution, nationally and internationally, should also be examined. It is important to identify major trends in the competitive environment (e.g., competing institutions and their approaches, the registrar's office, and the student recruitment office).

5. *Review available alternative strategies.* The effective process of decision making in successful academic institutions leads to the achievement of goals and objectives. This process—reflecting multilateral thinking and multilevel contributions of the whole academic community (students, faculty, and administration)—requires several implementation stages that must be integrated with other activities and with different administrative functions responsible for academic programs, student recruitment, organization, staffing, physical resources, and financing. The university, on a continuous basis, must upgrade its programs and services. In each of the previously mentioned analyses, the university evaluates the market opportunity and attempts to take advantage of it. For example, when the university is trying to upgrade its existing academic programs and performance, it must understand the following steps in the strategic planning model:

1. Identify program objectives and expected performance outcomes.
2. Identify student clientele and the social impact.
3. Initiate review of existing academic programs.
4. Assess resources allocation and develop alternatives.
5. Recommend program revisions.
6. Review program revisions with all schools involved.
7. Implement academic program revisions.

6. *Recommend the desired strategies.* After careful evaluation of the alternatives available, given the resources restriction and implementation of the recommended strategy, leaders need to approve organizational changes needed, design and recommend marketing information, planning, and control systems, and implement the strategic plan in terms of a short-term–one-year budget, medium-term tactical plans, and long-term strategic plans.

For example, almost every university has a department that provides service to students in order to help them to further their education. Such a department contributes a variety of services that range from the enrollment of students, providing housing and accommodations, and/or providing financial help, counseling, medical, and other personal services. In applying the model presented in this chapter, the department needs first to develop a commitment to quality of all services provided. Such a commitment comes after the assessment of customers needs and wants. This assessment can be collected through questionnaires or student interviews. Then a vision statement needs to be designed that represents the aspiration of all individuals involved and that meets the broader expectations of their customers. This vision is established by the leader and shared by all participants. An example of such statement may be, We strive to continuously improve the quality of all the services that we offer to all of our customers, "the students." The next step is to translate the vision statement into a series of mission statements. The mission statements should include the following:

• To assist new students' transition into higher education by enabling them to generate proper choices so that they are able to make the best use of their time while in college.

• To maintain proactive and productive bonds with academic advisors, the students' union, the health center, and other facilities.

• To maintain a high-quality counseling service to students and staff and a welfare service to students who are experiencing practical, financial, educational, or personal problems, in order to support them and enhance their educational performance.

• To provide support for tutors and their students on an individual, group, or course basis in areas related to student-support activities.

Next the department needs to address the appropriate strategies for each of the mission statements listed. The strategies are designed after careful evaluation of the institution environments. For example, the strategies of the first mission statement should include the following: proper orientation, a description of academic programs and requirements for achievements, financial advice, accommodations, career guidance, and other services. With regard to the second mission statement, the strategies should address student representation on university committees and working groups and working with the health center staff to promote close links between formal staff and student groups. The third mission statement's strategy must include counseling service, student loans, welfare service, access funds, student loans, and scholarships. The fourth statement's strategy should address consultation with course tutors, student disability procedures, equal opportunities policy, student grievance procedures, working with various organizations and groups on a regular basis and working with staff and faculty on various levels.

The next important step is for the department to identify obstacles that might lead to customer dissatisfaction. This might include prospects that can cause some delay or might add costs to the process. Adopting a system of improvement should be monitored for customer satisfactions. The number of complaints voiced by students using the various services provided by the department can measure this. It is a good practice to measure complaints from the past and compare them with the ones after the implementation of the TQM system. The people working in this department will certainly meet and continue to meet difficulties originating from the necessity to match the needs and expectations of their customers (students) with their own capacity and capability to deliver services at the level of quality demanded by those customers. These are crucial steps along the endless road to continuous quality improvement in academic institutions.

THE INTERNATIONAL CONNECTION

Just as business and academic institutions are recognizing the importance and interrelationship of TQM and strategic planning, many are also realizing the need for increased emphasis on incorporating these topics with international concerns, particularly in designing business and engineering curricula. The future of business is becoming international, and today's business students cannot afford to ignore this fact. Hoffman (1994), for example, states that international business issues were an important part of the strategic plans of the 108 U.S. CEOs he surveyed.[11] The American Assembly of Collegiate Schools of Business (AACSB) has mandated that all accredited schools should internationalize their curriculum. They also require the universities to incorporate elements of TQM and strategic planing into their curriculum.

CONCLUSION

The success of strategic planning in academic institutions depends highly on incorporating the concepts and practices of total quality management into the strategic planning process. Two such concepts are involving stakeholders and the use of teams. Team decision making involves designing the strategy process to involve people in various levels of the administration, faculty and students. In universities and colleges almost everybody is involved to a certain degree in the process of decision making. In general, those who contribute toward finding a solution are willing to try harder to make the plan a success. Here again, the TQM concept can be of great assistance to the decision-making machinery through the decentralization of authority and responsibility, the elimination of confusion in preparation of a strategic plan, and the facilitation of information flow.

The implementation of the strategy effects the future of the entire institution. Whether it is "first generation planning," or "second generation" contingency planning there are numerous situations where TQM can be used successfully. This offers a dynamic yet flexible approach that assists in analyzing activities, problems, and decisions within the institutional structure when several people are involved in either work performed or work supervised and where other people must be consulted in the process of decision making. Such situations, of course, are always encountered in strategic planning and management.

Strategic planning is the process of developing and maintaining a strategic fit between the institution and its changing environment. This process involves examining major trends in the environment; translating these trends into environmental threats and marketing opportunities; assessing the institution's resource position in terms of strengths and weaknesses—formulating objectives compatible with the major trends; developing feasible strategies for attaining the objectives; establishing the organizational structure and systems required for executing the strategies; and developing measures for evaluating performance (see Figure 6.1). The immediate challenge to administrators of academic institutions lies in dealing with accelerating change in the very complex administrative setting, with its multidirectional relationship network. They must face the inevitably increasing interdependence and learn how to deal with it successfully. With this goal in mind, the mobilizing of human potential will always be essential.

Figure 6.1
Strategic Planning within the Academic Institution

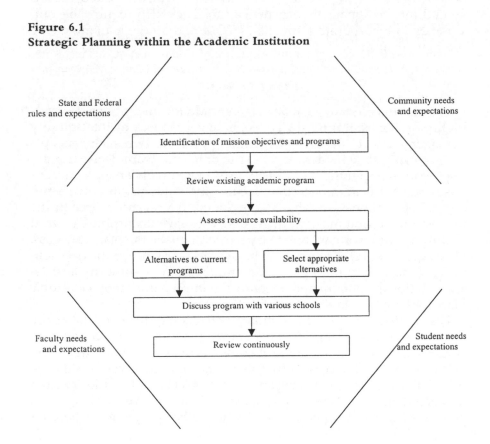

NOTES

1. J. M. Juran, "Made in USA: A Quality Resurgence," *Journal for Quality and Participation* (March 1991): 6–8.

2. David Edwards, "Total Quality Management in Higher Education," *Management Services* 35 (December 1991): 18–20.

3. Linda Ray Pratt, "A New Face for the Profession," *ACADEME* 14 (September–October 1994).

4. K. Poorsoltan, S. Amin, and A. Tootoonchi, "Business Community's Perception of Institutions of Higher Education: An Empirical Study." Presentation at the IABD conference, Washington, D.C., April 2–5, 1992.

5. Mary Beth Chalk, "Establishing a Quality Climate," *Journal of Property Management* 50 (September–October 1993): 14–16.

6. Ingeborg A. Marquardt, "Inside the Baldridge Award Guidelines—Category 3: Strategic Quality Planning," *Quality Progress* 25 (August 1992): 93–96.

7. Christian N. Madu and Chu-hua Kuei, "Introducing Strategic Quality Management," *Long Range Planning* 26 (December 1993): 121–131.

8. Ron Gales, "Can Colleges Be Reengineered?" *Across the Board* 31 (March 1994): 16–22.

9. William E. Matthews, "The Missing Element in Higher Education," *Journal for Quality and Participation* 16 (January–February 1993): 102–108.

10. Bronston T. Mayes, D. Heide, and E. Smith, "Anticipated Changes in the Business School Curriculum: A Survey of Deans in AACSB Accredited and Non-Accredited Schools," *Journal of Organizational Change Management* 6 (1993): 54–63.

11. Richard C. Hoffman and C. Gopinath, "The Importance of International Business to the Strategic Agendas of U.S. CEOs," *Journal of International Business Studies* 25, 3 (1994): 625–637.

Chapter 7

Teamwork Effectiveness

Contemporary management techniques such as transformation management, total quality management, and learning organization have put more emphasis on cooperation between management and workers to fulfill a company's objective. Dividing the workforce into teams can lead to substantial improvement in the quality and quantity of the products or services produced. Changes in consumer demand and competition have forced several companies to adopt quality leadership styles within their organizations. There are various methods to achieve employee involvement in the transformation process. This chapter will discuss productive ways to establish the self-managed or self-directed work team (SDWT).

Global competition and integration have led to increased worldwide interest in transforming the organization. Some of the important components of change are continuous improvement, empowerment, and team building and training. In the current marketplace, change is imminent. Changes in consumer demand and competition are forcing companies to transform in order to survive. Our global competitors, who are powered by a new, smarter management style, are forcing U.S. companies to restructure, reshape, and reform. Their traditional hierarchical structures, which have multiple layers of management, are dysfunctional. As a result, they are downsizing and removing excess layers in their organizations. An increased awareness has been placed on the quality of their products and/or services. As a result, quality leadership has evolved which "shifts the emphasis from profits to quality."[1] The goal is to grow healthy corporations for long-term strength, rather than short-term profits.

Quality leadership consists of three elements that depend on each other: quality, a scientific approach, and teamwork. Since quality leadership starts with the customer, a new focus on quality is utilized which requires everyone in the organization to give lasting value to the customer by meeting and exceeding their expectations. To improve products and services, a scientific approach is used. In this approach, decisions are based on data instead of guesswork by focusing on the methods of getting the work done rather than the results. Finally, to apply the scientific approach and quality elements, organizations need to capitalize on the full potential of their human resources. Major gains in quality and productivity most often result from teams, since individuals rarely have enough experience or knowledge to understand the entire process. To maximize the effectiveness of global operations, companies need to start developing multicultural teams.[2]

THE LEARNING ORGANIZATION

In the learning organization, as well as in total quality management, all employees engage in finding a problem in the workplace or identifying an issue of customer concern. After assessing how important this issue is to the customer, employees can solve the problem by providing appropriate option. This means that employees are in a position to put things together in unique ways to meet a customer's expectations. Teamwork must be accompanied with empowerment to be effective. If the team concept and spirit is not present, the remainder of the process breaks down. Therefore, special attention needs to be placed on how organizations should effectively assess, implement, and manage self-directed work teams to sustain an empowered workforce. Designing effective teams requires the careful recruitment, training, and development of the needed individuals in the organization. Those individuals will assist management in designing the work system. Quality leadership is one that involves all employees at all levels and in all functions. It also emphasizes and supports teamwork and accepts suggestions and recommendations from these teams. Quality leadership motivates the employees to perform at a high level and establishes rewards for their achievements. It is expected that quality leadership will maintain a work environment conducive to the well-being and growth of employees.

WORKER EMPOWERMENT

Organizations that have experienced success with using TQM most commonly cite worker empowerment and its consequences as a positive effect of their TQM efforts. The reported positive effects of TQM efforts can be summarized as follows:

1. For TQM to be effective, employees must be empowered. This empowerment will improve employee self-confidence and morale. This in turn results in reduced employee turnover, increased productivity, and increased profits. In addition, employees gain a personal understanding of TQM. This understanding leads to more effective employee participation.

2. Empowering employees with decision making will insure the acceptance and appropriate implementation. Employees feel more responsible and accountable for their actions.[3] Since the employees are on the front line, they know what needs improvement and are therefore in the best position to offer suggestions. In addition, potential problems get priorities. TQM provides a process that anticipates problems and provides the tools to deal with them. Such a process encourages corporate culture for continuous improvement.

3. Empowerment encourages employees to offer suggestions for improvement. This leads to increased productivity and increased consumer satisfaction.[4]

4. Management overhead is reduced because teams are self-managing and do their own hiring and firing.[5]

5. Empowered employees ensure the ongoing quality of their processes. They strive for fewer mistakes, less rework, and fewer delays, ultimately resulting in more productive use of time.[6]

The success stories reported in numerous studies tend to involve variables that in previous years have been related to employee satisfaction and intrinsic motivation.

SELF-DIRECTED WORK TEAMS

Top management empowers employees by giving them responsibility to design their job and role in the process. Self-managed teams (SMT) or self-directed work teams are good examples of employee empowerment. Usually, SMT consists of small groups of individuals who are empowered to perform certain activities based on certain procedures established with minimum management involvement. Quality circles, project quality teams, and special task teams are some examples of SMT. Management must design strategies to empower the employees and to encourage their participation. Self-managed teams are an advanced form of worker empowerment. "Empowerment is a function of four important variables: authority, resources, information, and accountability."[7] Each of the variables must be present in order for the SDWT to be successful. Empowerment is more than involvement for SDWT. It represents a high degree of involvement in which the team members are given the authority to make decisions. In order to make responsible decisions, they must possess the necessary resources and information. After the decision-making process, they need to be held accountable. For example, Robert Allen, CEO of AT&T, believed in transforming the company by allowing employees participation in all activities. His vision included turning the organization chart upside down to put the customer on top, so that people close to the customer make customer-based decisions. All the employees understood the vision and were able to carry it out without direct supervision from the top.

Employees are engaging actively in setting strategic direction. Strategy emerges from the accumulated activities of employee teams. Employees contribute to the vision and mission of the organization. An effective organization increases the size of a company's brain. This requires making specific changes in the areas of leadership, type of structure, empowerment, communications, and information sharing.

Employees in teams usually undertake a complete project or product. Chrysler decided to develop cross-functional teams. The first team was formed with eighty people to build a new car. The management located the team activities in a new research and development (R&D) center. Management provided the team with the authority and responsibility to design the car and market it. That is, the team is given a complete project of designing a new car and/or providing accounts receivable services for customers. There is usually a beginning and an end to what they create, allowing them to view their work in its entirety. It is expected that members of the team make the most of the decisions about quality issues and how their product or service is created. This may include layout of the production line in manufacturing or searching for and solving problems in both service and industrial firms. It is also expected that members establish and police work rules regarding factors such as absenteeism, tardiness, breaks, and use of the telephone. They are also in charge of establishing the criteria by which members are to be judged and evaluation forms are to be completed.

Since the team members are recognized as the experts in their jobs, they frequently play a major role in the selection of new members for their team, if needed. This can include the screening of applications, interviewing applicants, and providing recommendations to management on hiring.

When employees are involved in the creation and progress of their operations, they are more interested in their jobs. They will more likely remain involved and be committed to their work. Employee involvement through the use of SDWTs creates an environment where the employees know their mission and have a vested interest in its success. The organization needs to be proficient in selecting individuals who are capable of functioning interdependently in a complex environment. Also, as people are selected for the teams, their training needs must be assessed. Other factors, which need to be present in successful teams, are as follows:

1. Every successful team must establish its goals and objectives. Everyone must share a clear common goal and they must be able to derive some benefit from achieving the goal.
2. Team members must be prepared to have disagreements, confront conflict, and resolve issues as they arise.
3. The team must work together and gain momentum. Every member should be free to express his or her opinions.
4. The team must stay together by moving in the same direction.
5. Work is distributed among team members fairly and based on job skills.
6. To accomplish the goal, different types of skills and expertise maybe required.
7. Leadership can be changed with changing needs.
8. The tasks the team will perform must be interactive, interdependent, and multifaceted.
9. The work structure must promote interdependence and cooperation.
10. The culture of the organization must support employee involvement.
11. The managers must be willing to use the team's output.
12. Teams must assess their performance periodically and celebrate achievement of stated goals. They should be willing to move forward on other responsibilities when needed.
13. Training is essential.

Although the SDWTs are proving to be a successful management strategy for many organizations, they will not work everywhere. This concept cannot be effective when

1. Only one person is needed to do the job.
2. Decisions need to be made quickly.
3. The task requires individual accountability.
4. The task could be more efficiently performed through the current work structure.
5. The individuals do not share the same common goals.
6. Some individuals fail to complete their assignments.
7. Time is limited, and an immediate response is required.
8. The individuals do not possess the interpersonal skills required to work in teams.
9. The managers do not understand or support the team concept.

10. The culture of the organization does not support collaboration and reward the team members who share information, expertise, or success.

The implementation process begins when a company decides SDWTs
will be beneficial to their operations. It is important that the company
thoroughly plan, because during this process, assumptions and decisions will be made that will ultimately affect the success of the SDWTs.
A major change of this magnitude will require a serious commitment
from everyone involved. A clear and compelling vision, which captures the worth of the work, must be conveyed to everyone so the
individuals can clearly see how their contributions will help to accomplish an ideal. Management must ensure the strategies, structures,
and systems of the team are supportive of and become a part of the
organization's purpose and its processes. Lucas asserts that team members must share a clear sense of purpose; establish precise performance
goals; operate from a sense of interdependence; and hold one another
accountable. The organization needs to keep these thoughts in mind
when they begin to structure and build the teams. He also emphasizes
the three elements—coaching, decision making, and communicating—
as being of critical importance in team building.[8]

The first element, coaching, requires that workers be trained to manage themselves. As a result, the managers need to begin by trusting
their employees to know how to do their jobs. The managers need to
quit being bosses and start being coaches. The coach is responsible for
helping the workers do their jobs to the best of their abilities and to
help them gain a clear vision and shared sense of mission. The coach
needs to create trust and mutual respect with the team in order to
achieve winning results over long periods of time. The coach must
establish high performance standards so that everyone knows what is
expected. An open communication system needs to be created which
provides support and encouragement.

Decision making is the second necessary element required in team
building. Usually when teams are introduced, there is confusion related to who is responsible for making decisions and who has the authority. Management feels the team is responsible, and they should
begin to take charge. The teams will let the managers or coaches continue to make the decisions until they are told differently. Once the
decision making passes to the team, they are afraid they will overstep
their authority or make mistakes.

Shared decision making offers several benefits for both the individual
and the organization. The team will have a variety of ideas and perceptions that are totally different from one another. Therefore, the ideas
will result in many different alternatives for solving the problems that
can lead to better quality decisions. The team members will be challenged to think, therefore decision making will increase their learning

and personal growth. The challenge to make decisions will help to make their work become more exciting and motivating. As the employees accept responsibility for their own work, they require less management time which allows more time for managers to solve other problems and do some creative work.

Not all decisions are appropriate for teams to make, so it is important for boundaries to be set to establish what decisions can be made at what level. There will be certain instances where it is better for an individual to make the decision. When appropriate, the individual could consult the team for their input.

Communication is the third important element in team building. Communication is critical because it is the information network that is needed to connect all the players together. Teammates need to have direct communication by meeting, talking, and engaging in open give-and-take by expressing their opinions and viewing their differences. "Without this openness, the team cannot achieve understanding, hammer out the best approach, or achieve buy-in by everyone."[9]

The concept of SDWTs needs to be driven from the top down. As a result, management must be committed to the entire change process. The most frequent cause of failure is because top and middle management were not involved or because they were indifferent. As part of their commitment, management needs to provide the necessary budget and time for training to assist the team leaders and members with the necessary new skills.

Selecting the right team members is crucial. All too often, people are chosen for the wrong reasons. In selecting competent people, the decision should be based on which employees will be best equipped to achieve the team's objectives. To accomplish this, technical and personal competencies need to be considered. "Technical competencies refer to the substantive knowledge, skills, and abilities related to the team's objective. Personal competencies refer to the qualities, skills, and abilities necessary for the individual team members to identify, address, and resolve issues."[10] These skills must be balanced according to each team's objective.

The development of high performance SDWTs requires a combined effort from visionary leaders and team members who are willing and competent. To achieve high performance, the following criteria must be present in the team, and it must also be linked directly to the objectives of the company:

1. The team has a common focus, including a mission, vision, goals, action plans, and measurements of success.
2. Roles and responsibilities are clearly defined for team members.
3. Team member expectations of one another are clearly defined.
4. Resources are utilized within the team and externally.

5. Members recognize diversity and effectively deal with their differences.
6. Members are able to effectively give, receive, and solicit feedback.
7. Meetings are managed efficiently and effectively.
8. The team achieves results.

Results cannot be seen overnight. It takes several months, or even years, to develop and nurture teams to be high performers. Measuring the performance of a SDWT requires a systematic approach that takes into account the variety of work that teams perform. To be effective, the measurement system must clearly state the goals of the team, what is expected from each team member, and the priorities of the team and individual work. "Team performance standards can be developed by following several steps, these include: evaluating existing performance measures, identifying team measurement points, identifying individual achievements that support teamwork and assigning value to each accomplishment. It is also important to formulate team and individual measures and standards, and develop a system for monitoring performance."[11]

The Traditional Thinking	The Quality Thinking
Leaders design policies, procedures, and plans. Employees are expected to implement organizational strategies.	Leaders must remove restrictive policies and procedures and create supportive policies and procedures.
Jobs must be provided to qualifying individuals. Information is treated confidentially.	Education, training, and resources must be provided, information shared, and an atmosphere of trust and encouragement must be fostered.
The worker must be monitored. They are an element of organizational process that must be controlled by management.	The workers are empowered and given an opportunity to make decisions.
Management designs, improves, and controls the process.	Teams design, improve, and control the process. Management provides commitment to all teams to work with them effectively.

WHERE TQM HAS BEEN REPORTED AS NOT HAVING WORKED

Reports of TQM not working have tended to focus on the manner in which the TQM was implemented in the organization and/or the attitudes of top management and workers toward their TQM efforts. They can be summarized as follows:

1. Employees are given introductory training about philosophy and attitude and not about measurable results.

2. Management does not provide feedback after each job completed.

3. After completing their training, many participants are left in limbo for months or even years as they wait to become involved with quality improvement teams. Employees perceive the companies as using TQM as a term, and not as a real thing; when the training is over, it's time to get back to work.[12]

4. Company policy and procedures may not change to accommodate effective employee participation, creating confusion and frustration among employees.

5. The measurement techniques used are not appropriate for TQM. Managers think more in terms of getting data that will provide practice in statistical tools. The primary focus is on measuring participation in activities rather than on the impact of these activities on business results.[13]

6. Some management view TQM as a marketing tool that enables them to promote their company as being part of the fashionable TQM movement.[14]

7. Employees may wonder if management is serious about achieving a positive change that supports a continuous improvement, or if TQM is another fad that will be discontinued in the future.

8. Finally, many think that this concept is overemphasized. Management's real focus is on the production units.[15]

We must realize that TQM represents a new and different approach than the traditional way of managing. The adaptation of this approach requires changes in the traditional process and control methods. Management can only change organizational systems and culture. Both are a reflection of management thinking and values that are implanted and practiced by employees.

Leaders must encourage employees in setting goals and expectations, self-evaluation, self-problem solving, developing self-initiative and responsibility. They must provide training and encourage opportunity thinking.

HUMAN RESOURCE ISSUES

Team members and leaders alike are expected to change and take on different roles in the organization; therefore they need other kinds of formal organizational support. "Unless reinforcement systems like performance appraisals, promotions, compensation, and other rewards support the emerging role, we send a confusing message about the new expectations."[16] Human resources departments need to carefully recruit, select, train, motivate, and reward employees to ensure the success of the organization. Employees' involvement takes various forms: information sharing, dialogue, problem solving, and self-direction. Teams are constructed of a small number of people, with a common purpose and complementary skills. They usually set performance goals for which they hold themselves mutually responsible.

Typically, members of the SDWTs are trained to perform every function performed by the team. Their role description will differ from their traditional job description. The new description should focus on the shared responsibility for getting the work done for the team rather than the individual getting certain tasks done. The job descriptions will be important in selection, training, and appraisal of team members.

Appraisal of how a person functions within the team is a difficult task, since interaction with other team members might be a primary measure of individual effectiveness. An accurate appraisal of an individual's performance is needed to determine how they should be rewarded, what their developmental needs are, and what further or increased responsibilities the individual can assume in the future.

The use of a performance-based compensation structure, which is linked directly to the goals of the company through teams, may be an appropriate method of compensation. Skill-based pay can result in reduced resistance to change, encourage continuous learning and job rotation, and increase the knowledge base of cross-departmental team members. In addition, profit-sharing plans can encourage the SDWTs to find better ways to increase efficiency, effectiveness, and quality. Programs need to be developed to provide extensive training for everyone involved to teach the skills they need to operate effectively in the new structure.

WORK TEAMS IN A GLOBAL SETTING

As companies expand into global markets, they are increasingly using diverse work teams to help them with their efforts to extend their products and operations internationally. The members of these teams can come from several different countries and they can be involved in activities which can span several nations. As a result, this can present several challenges to the companies that use transnational work teams. In contrast to teams from a single culture, the employees associated with international teams will have differences in language, interpersonal styles, cultures, and group norms. Therefore, it is important for team leaders and members to be flexible and have an appreciation of these differences. The teams should be encouraged to capitalize on the differences, rather than suppress or ignore them. Otherwise, barriers will be created that will interfere with the team's work.[17]

The communication of the team will be difficult since the members will be geographically dispersed. The geographic distance will make it difficult for the members to meet face to face to share information and make group decisions. Therefore, a good communication system needs to be established so that team members can communicate with other team members, others in the organization, and outsiders. The international teams will rely heavily on telephones and voice mail, computers and e-mail, and fax machines. In addition, when available, teleconferencing and videoconferencing should be utilized.

CONCLUSION

Through quality leadership, using self-managed work teams effectively will help the organization meet the demands of its customers. The best approach to teamwork requires commitment and shared responsibility from top management down, and there must be a shared vision by everyone involved. It will take time to implement a change of this magnitude. Communication and training is needed up front. Technical and personal competencies need to be identified before team members can be selected. The team must be empowered to plan, improve, and control work processes. The team can discipline or replace any member of the team if they think it is necessary. These teams set goals and inspect their own work, schedule and review performance, and hold themselves accountable. Transforming supervisors into team leaders is essential. Identifying and developing training programs, pay structures, and performance measurements is critical. To ensure the ongoing success of the teams, evaluation and taking corrective action to strengthen performance is needed. International or transnational work teams will be established when companies expand into the global markets. Therefore, consideration is needed to avoid problems that could arise because of cultural differences among the team members. Through careful planning, self-directed work teams will increase productivity, efficiency, and effectiveness, which will lead to customer and employee satisfaction. Recognition and rewards to team members whether monetary or nonmonetary are essential. The rewards must be tied to the quality of the teams. Peers and customers should be encouraged to nominate and recognize superior performance.

NOTES

1. Peter R. Scholtes, *The Team Handbook: How to Use Teams to Improve Quality* (Madison, Wisc.: Joiner Associates, 1988), 1.

2. Dean Elmuti, "Self-Managed Work Teams Approach: Creative Management Tool or Fad?" *Management Decisions* 35 (March–April 1997): 233.

3. Richard Hamlin, "A Practical Guide to Empowering Your Employees," *Supervisory Management* (April 1991): 8.

4. David Niven, "When Times Get Tough What Happens to TQM?" *Harvard Business Review* 71 (May–June 1993): 20–24.

5. Elizabeth Erlich, "The Quality Management Checkpoint," *International Business* (May 1993): 56–62.

6. Ibid.

7. Kimball Fisher, *Leading Self-Directed Work Teams* (New York: McGraw-Hill, 1993), 13.

8. Richard J. Lucas, "New Twists on Teams," *Internal Auditor* (April 1996): 30.

9. Ibid., 33.

10. Carl E. Larson and Frank M. LaFasto, *TeamWork* (Newbury Park, Calif.: Sage Publications, 1989), 62–63.

11. Jack Zigon, "Team Performance Measurement: A Process for Creating Team Performance Standards," *Compensation and Benefits Review* 32 (January–February 1997): 38.

12. J. W. Dean, Jr. and J. R. Evans, *Total Quality Management, Organization and Strategy* (Minneapolis, Minn.: West Publishing, 1994), 18.

13. Tracey E. Benson, "A Business Strategy Comes of Age," *Industry Week*, 3 May 1993, 40–44.

14. Terry Walker, "Creating Total Quality Improvement That Lasts," *National Productivity Review* 2 (Autumn 1992): 473–478.

15. Fisher, *Leading Self-Directed Work Teams*, 7.

16. Charles C. Manz and Henry P. Sims, Jr., *Business without Bosses* (New York: John Wiley & Sons, 1993), 210.

17. John Kotter, *Leading Change* (Boston: Harvard Business School Press, 1996), 3–7.

PART II

RESTRUCTURING

The process of restructuring usually starts when one company initiates an attempt to buy another. The buyout process can be conducted in any of several different ways. One company may announce their intention of buying another company (the target) for a specified price. After careful evaluation by the board of directors (BOD), the proposal is either approved or disapproved. When the owner or the BOD approves the sale, it means that the target has been taken over by the buyer. This type of buyout is categorized as a friendly takeover. It can be done through leverage buyout, management buyout, or mergers, and/or acquisitions. In some cases the target company resists the buyout because the company wants to stay independent or they expect a higher price. At the same time the buyer remains firm to take the company over. This attempt is categorized as a hostile takeover. This type of buyout was popular during the 1980s and early 1990s. While the amount of successful hostile takeovers is declining, the fear of such bids continues. The legal measures taken by many states during the 1990s have been much more protarget. These measures made the companies and their board of directors a little bit safer than they were during the 1980s.

Chapter 8

Restructuring:
The Takeover Game

Today, American companies are paying more attention to creating value for their stockholders and customers. That is why the stock market in the United States has been booming during the last three to four years. In the past two decades however, Wall Street has been infiltrated with many greedy minds concentrating on making quick money. This process outburst has caused a rise in the restructuring of American companies. This restructuring has resulted in changes in corporate strategies and has affected negatively its competitive situation. This takeover craze has also left many unanswered questions about the ethics and morals of trends and where they lead. This increase in the restructuring of corporate America has also led to some shakeups inside the companies. This chapter will discuss the importance of restructuring and its implications on corporate performance.

When a company, a group of people, or an individual acquires another company whose management is opposed to the arrangement, this action is known as a hostile takeover. Those who make a practice of instigating these unwanted takeovers are known as corporate raiders. During the 1980s and the beginning of the 1990s, financial analysts and smart corporate executives had begun to identify companies in which the stock prices underestimate the true value of the company's assets. Making names for individuals such as T. Boone Pickens, Carl

Icahn, and Sir Martin, companies quickly realized that it was cheaper to buy than to build new plants. Once a company had been successfully taken over, it was much more profitable to sell the company's assets as opposed to selling the company as a whole. There were few hostile takeovers before 1980. However, the intensity of competition and the advent of creative financing of the 1980s multiplied the frequency and complicated the process. In making a bid for a company, a raider will usually tender an offer to current stockholders, offering to buy their stock for an amount well above current market price. In this manner, the raider acquires enough stock to gain control of the company. In the past few years, hostile takeovers in Europe have increased tremendously. For example, since the beginning of 1999, Europe has seen more than $400 billion worth of hostile deals, which is over four times the combined total from 1990 to 1998. In 1999, over half the bids launched produced favorable results.[1]

Corporate hostile takeovers, and the fear of a takeover, have been a fact of a fast-paced business world. All managers fear that they must make short-term profits to ensure their jobs. They are afraid of the takeover-minded investment bankers, who have been running rampant on the stocks of Wall Street. J. Michael Shepherd, a San Francisco banking lawyer, was quoted as saying, "Though hostile takeover efforts will never be numerous because of the difficulty and expense, they will always be with us."[2]

The manager of the twenty-first century can never be completely sure whether their company might be the focus of a hostile takeover. The number of hostile takeovers is likely to take off, especially in the banking industry. Investors want a good return, and when bank stocks and performance levels continue to perform poorly, shareholder patience may diminish.[3] Some investment bankers have mentioned Regions Financial and Summit Bancorp as possible future takeover targets. Both banks suffer from low performance and low price–earnings ratios. On the other hand, banks with high performance and high price–earnings ratios, such as Fifth Third Bancorp of Cincinnati and Firstar of Milwaukee, can be expected to get aggressive. Other corporations, such as Catellus Development, with a depressed stock price, have adapted a "poison pill" plan to fend off hostile takeover bids.[4]

This chapter will explore the reasons for increasing popularity of buyouts and takeovers and its implications. This chapter will also examine the takeover phenomenon in Japan and Europe.

THE RESTRUCTURING PROCESS

Companies continue to explore restructuring for the acquisition that will increase sales and stock prices. The United States is paying a tremendous price for the restructuring game which takes place in the form of buyouts and hostile takeovers. Few benefits stem from such activities. Raiders walk away with millions of dollars in profits. Also, companies divest themselves of unprofitable divisions to prevent hostile takeovers. Financial manipulators, speculators, lawyers, and investment bankers are big winners. Investment bankers provide the corporate raiders with financial assistance. Although they don't initiate the takeover process, they are considered the main ingredient in this process. Without the investment bankers' funds, this process would come to a screeching halt. Stakeholders—workers, consumers, and the local community—lose. The economy suffers. While American managers focus on the possibilities of takeovers, the ability to compete is lost to foreign competitors who are concentrating on product technology. The loss of jobs, ranging from top level executives to blue collar employees, as well as the decline of research and development, are the direct result of hostile takeovers.[5]

Eastman Kodak bought Sterling Drug in 1988 then sold it in 1994. Matsushita bought MCA and sold it in 1995. Sir Martin of WPP Group bought Y&R Advertising for $4.2 billion in 2000.

Another major effect of hostile takeovers is the loss of employment at every level of the affected company. According to Lane Kirkland, president of the AFL–CIO, about 90,000 union members have lost jobs due to restructuring activities in the last ten years.[6] In addition, many thousands more have been forced to take wage and benefit reductions. Blue-collar workers are not the only ones affected—low, middle, and top level managers' jobs are also frequently on the line as a result of corporate restructuring. A survey conducted by the author in 1988 shows that most of the companies who moved from public to private have lost employees and managers. The survey shows that 54 percent of the companies who responded laid off some of their employees and about 30 percent laid off some of their managers. Those who stayed on the job often distrusted the acquiring company. Employees put their energy into defending their interests and protecting their turf, resulting in decreased productivity.

Another problem created by the takeover atmosphere is that top level management has to spend time and money devising takeover prevention strategies. This detracts from the effort put into basic considerations such as growth, return on investment, product quality, sales, and distribution. When a hostile takeover occurs, the company is saddled with a large debt. The company will trim the budget up to 15 percent by firing employees. Employees are now protecting themselves by constructing golden and tin parachutes. Usually, the targeted companies are encouraging employee stock ownership programs (ESOPs), which allow the employees to control the interest of the company. Also, hostile takeovers saddle the company with a large debt, which can be used as a tax shelter.

Another effect of hostile takeovers or buyouts is cutting back on R&D. Studies show that R&D is the first department where spending is cut as a direct result of a buyout. Sixteen companies that underwent mergers showed a 4.7 percent drop in R&D spending. Even more drastic, in fending off a takeover attempt, Owens Corning was forced to take on a $2.6-billion debt. The net result was that R&D was slashed by 50 percent. Other companies such as Allied Stores and SCI Television both incurred a total of about $1 billion in debt in their buyouts transactions. When the R&D budget is cut by 10 to 20 percent, it deters the company from increasing its market share. The acquired company in a takeover or a buyout transaction usually pays huge debts and interest. In return this will decrease its capital expenditures, the consequence being a significant reduction in R&D activity. Increased company debts plus a significant reduction in R&D might threaten the company's survival or affect negatively its competitive station.[7]

Raiders claim that they help America succeed; however, their main objective is to satisfy their own greed. After a company is taken over, it can either go bankrupt or restructure. Restructuring has a great impact on the company itself as well as society. In this process the company must redefine its mission and direction. A change in the business vision, mission, and objectives will most likely result in a change in the company's strategies. If corporate strategy revised its polices and procedures, restructuring will become essential. Companies often slash jobs and reduce overhead. The real issue here is that the buyout and hostile takeover game is no more than changing ownership or transferring resources from one group to another. This definitely threatens the long-term stability of the American economy. The importance of restructuring continues to grow daily. Companies with strong cash flow and a long list of assets will become more of a takeover target than a lower income company that is not performing as well. This fact underscores how damaging the hostile takeovers game is to our long-term competitive advantage as a country.

Since few people benefit from buyouts and takeovers, one can assume that something should be done. There are always some people who look for quick money and do not consider the effect of their action on others. In order for today's businesses to prevent themselves from being a target, they must structure themselves as strong firms with long-term strategies. Top level management must prepare for long-term results instead of just the next quarter's profits. Corporations must give leeway within one quarter in order to advance in the long run.

The corporate restructuring not only takes place when there is a threat for a buyout, but also when a corporation feels a change is necessary in the organization. If, for instance, debts exceed profits, a change would be necessary, and certain steps should be taken to increase the corporation's profits. In the past four years, the stock markets have increased tremendously. The stock markets become more influential than ever before, demanding much higher returns. When companies cannot produce the expected returns through normal operation and growth, they tend to restructure by adopting one or more of the restructuring methods. These strategies are expected to reduce cost and improve profitability. If a corporation wants to exist as a vital entity capable of competing in the long run, then it should continuously scrutinize its environment to determine its strength and weaknesses along with its competitive advantage in order to redefine its future direction. These analyses help the organization to better understand its products, services, and resources. It will give a better indication as to where the company must allocate its resources. Restructuring has become very important in today's businesses, and if a company is incapable of doing it, most likely its business will deteriorate.

Usually takeover increases the wealth of the stockholders significantly, but other stakeholders suffer. The consequences are plant closings, employee layoffs, productivity loss, and restructuring. For these reasons, many states passed antitakeover laws that allow boards of directors to consider the impact of such bids on stakeholders.

The following terms are essential to the understanding of this chapter.

Golden parachute This agreement indicates that senior management will receive hefty compensation if they leave the firm as a result of a merger or takeover.

Greenmail The target's repurchase of its own shares from a hostile acquirer. The raider, often obtaining a high premium, is referred to as a greenmailer.

Junk bonds Unsecured bonds, whose payment of interest and repayment of principal are potentially in doubt. As a result, interest rates and the risk are typically higher than those of high-grade bonds.

Proxy battle A battle between a company and the unhappy shareholders. The battle is precipitated by the solicitation of proxies by dissident shareholders in order to obtain approval of a shareholder resolution.

White knight A corporation that comes to the aid of the target in a takeover battle.

RESTRUCTURING IN EUROPE AND JAPAN

Japanese companies are different from American companies in that they did not go through hostile takeovers in the past. Mergers and acquisitions were common in both markets. The slowdown in Japanese economy has resulted in the urgent need for restructuring. Banking collapses have affected many Japanese companies because of its *Keiretsu*. *Keiretsu* is a loose grouping of a number of formally independent companies, usually centered on a bank or large trading company, and linked by cross-shareholders (i.e., the reciprocal holding of shares).[8] Japan's first-ever hostile takeover was in June 1999. Cable & Wireless plc, a British company, outbid Japan's Nippon Telegraph and Telecommunications (NTT) for control of International Digital Communication (IDC). This takeover was seen as a blow to Japanese corporate tradition and a victory for market forces.[9]

Similarly, European companies did not use hostile takeovers to the same extent as the American companies did. In fact Veba, a German company, was advised to take over Mannesmann during a transformation period from engineering to telecomms. But Veba rejected this advice, finding this sort of idea to be unacceptable.[10] However, after the unification of Europe and the birth of the euro, the hostile takeover became very popular. In 1999 takeover deals in Europe were valued at about $1.5 trillion, a record for European companies.[11]

THE CORPORATE RAIDERS' GAME

Throughout the years, corporate raiders have hunted vigorously through the business world for possible buyouts. They have financed these buyouts by borrowing billions of dollars. Today, analysts as well as businessmen feel that the era of hostile takeovers is coming to an end. Forces behind mergers and acquisitions have stammered. The number of potential companies for takeover due to undervalued stock prices has declined, and management has slowed down the process of growth and profits for the satisfaction of the shareholders.

Corporate raiders buy up stock and threaten to try to take control of a corporation. To ward off this threat, sometimes the company buys the raider's stock at a much higher price than the raider had bought it. These higher costs are transferred to the consumer in the form of higher prices and to the bondholders in terms of higher risks. In addition, employees suffer lower wages. This will place the company in a less competitive position.

Two methods of corporate takeovers are typically available. First, the raider may attempt to buy the necessary shares on the open market. This open-market method has its disadvantages. If the market is not perfect and the operations are not kept secret, the price of the stock is indubitably going to rise as purchases rise. The second method is known as the takeover bid. A bid takes place when the raider publicly announces that he will buy all the existing stock at a stated price, provided the raider has sufficient acceptances so that he or she may receive the desired degree of control. This method has a disadvantage because the public announcement would increase the price of stock higher than the market value. This type of takeover often invites other bidders into the field. Often the initial bidder is bought out and makes enormous profit on his attempt. In practice, the most efficient is usually a combination of the two, where a raider can acquire all the stock he needs without affecting the price at all. Management does not discover the takeover attempt until it is too late for them to defend themselves.

To resist the threat of corporate raiders, management is told it must work to keep the price of the company stock high and give shareholders a good return for their investment. But this frequently means mortgaging the future of the company for current stock price gains.

CAUSES FOR TAKEOVERS

The globalization of the marketplace and the reevaluation in technology has encouraged the free movement of capital. The globalization resulted in the breakdown of traditional borders, which led to many local firms giving way to institutions with global presence and expertise across a wide range of industry sectors. The forces at work today were emerging by the mid-1980s and have continued to impact how business conducts itself in this global market. "In the 1980s, we felt we were adding value by defending against selfish corporate raiders. In the 1990s, we created value by helping inefficient and fragmented industries to consolidate. In the 2000s, I expect to see the creation of global champions that will move the global economy into the future."[12]

Over the years there have been a number of different theories assigned to the causes of corporate takeovers. Recently it has been argued that in a modern corporation characterized by a separation of ownership from control, the salaried managers will be less interested in maximizing the profits or stock market value of the firm than they will be in maximizing its rate of growth. Managers shoot for what is related to the size of the firm as opposed to its profitability.

Other writers have argued that, as far as the modern corporation is concerned, it is no longer possible to talk about any single fixed goal of the firm, but rather its profit maximization or growth maximization. The present-day corporation is viewed as a bureaucratic organization whose goals are neither predetermined nor given and whose decisions are not automatically translated into practice. It possesses a diversified group of people from top level managers to factory workers whose interests differ and may not include profit maximization or the size of the firm. There are several reasons for the causes of corporate takeovers. Among these reasons are desires to achieve an economy of scale in production, distribution, and advertising, and to extend control of patents, as well as tax advantages and the ability to limit competition.

With regard to the community, corporate raiders are merely involved in the "hostile takeover game" to reap personal benefits. It matters little to the average raider whether a community is completely broken up because of job loss through the restructuring of the company. In many cases, older employees who have devoted their lives to the company lose their entire pension plan, and these employees often have little hope of finding new jobs. Those who initiate hostile takeovers are merely financiers and speculators who are not serious about the operations of the companies and are solely in it for quick profits.

One may argue those hostile takeover threats force managers to focus on short-term goals in order to keep their stock prices high. This keeps the attention away from longer-term investment and growth. Raiders' defense can keep management from running the day-to-day operations of the company. Alfred D. Chandler, a distinguished business historian at Harvard Business School, notes the rising trend of unfriendly takeovers. He argues that takeovers provide no productivity, services, or functions. He adds that "while our managers are fighting takeovers, the Japanese are finding it easier to take over their markets."[13]

There is little doubt that corporate raiders represent a threat to All-American businesses. Companies should implement the necessary defense strategies that will discourage raiders from causing chaos in the economy. If this is accomplished, then strong corporations can continue to survive, and the raiders will be the losers.

Government and society are not completely aware of how much damage these hostile takeover tactics cause to the economy. Lately, certain state governments have addressed the issue of corporate raiders by supporting an antiraider, antitakeover law such as the one introduced in the state of Pennsylvania. The law requires management to weigh the interests of specific stakeholders, such as employees, customers, and the community, when considering a takeover.

If insider trading is illegal, then why shouldn't corporate raiding be illegal? This is due to the fact that insider trading means finding out information that is not made public, and hence are not fair to the public, for normally this forces companies to cut jobs in the long run. Business ethics is beginning to play a major role in society, and corporate raiders are very unethical in their money-making tactics.

TAX ADVANTAGES OF A TAKEOVER

Certain transactions will create tax advantages while others will have disadvantages. Kaplan found that tax benefits are an important source of wealth gains in a buyout. There is a very large gray area, which is pointed out by Kaplan. He states that anyone embarking on a program in this field should be aware that each case is unique and has its own trade-off; therefore, professional counsel and an accountant may be necessary. There are three tax advantages reported by Kaplan. The first potential advantage is a tax loss situation, which needs to have special conditions met; otherwise, it could turn into a disadvantage. Second, the purchase may have hidden assets or hidden net worth and is shown as real property and assets with a depreciation factor, which would be a loss. The tax savings in the use of this method could equal or surpass the total purchase price. Third, the method of payment must be considered. Equity capital could avoid interest payments. To determine if there is an advantage the accountant should add up the comparative advantage of dilution of equity, cost of interest on borrowed money, and the tax savings afforded on this interest. Raiders who can substitute debt for equity may be giving money to the shareholders at the expense of the country's tax revenues.[14]

TAX DISADVANTAGES

Any liquid asset that can be converted to cash might seem very desirable. However, the cash could be fully taxable. Another aspect is the internal situation of the undistributed dividends, which have a tax liability. Finally, this purchase could bump you into a higher tax bracket, which could do away with any other advantages.

RESISTING TAKEOVER STRATEGIES

Hostile takeovers can pose a major threat to any company, but many defense strategies are available to prevent them. Resistance strategies are techniques that corporations use to avoid violent or hostile takeovers. Several such strategies are as follows:

1. *Corporate Restructuring.* This has become a byword for the complex, intertwined process of maximizing current shareholder value by increasing debt while preserving a company's independence. By repurchasing stock, a company will increase its debt to equity ratio, making it more difficult for corporate raiders to purchase.
2. *A Poison Pill Strategy.* The poison pill is a legal device that makes a company unaffordable without permission from the board of directors and

requires the raider to launch a proxy contest to oust the board. Thus, companies that attempt the takeover must deal with existing management and offer a high price for the shares to convince the other shareholders to remove the board. Examples of corporations that have used this technique include Merrill Lynch and Bristol-Myers.

3. *The Pac-Man Defense.* This is rarely used in practice. This is when the company being acquired attempts to acquire the company that is trying to acquire them. The technique provides security for the present employees of the company.

4. *The Lockup Defense.* This strategy is not used to prevent a takeover; rather, it is used by the target to influence its choice of acquirer. The principle of the lockup strategy is mainly to block a raider from gaining sufficient shareholder control to consummate a takeover attempt. It can be designed to deprive a hostile bidder of the primary reason for its offer by promising the target's prized asset to a white knight. It can also be designed to make it much more expensive for the hostile bidder to acquire control. Use of the lockup is often thought by the target to deter competing bidders and as a result increase the white knight's assurance of success.

5. *The Leveraged Buyout Defense (LBO).* LBOs usually consist of a group of investors, including existing management, who are attempting to buy the company out. When a LBO is used as a defense strategy, the target is typically a public company or a subsidiary of a public company that is made private with a significant portion of the cash purchase being financed by debt. This debt is secured not by the credit status of the purchaser, but by the assets of the target firm. Golden parachutes protect management by providing a handsome compensation for management in the event of a takeover.

6. *The Self-Tender Defense.* Some companies protect themselves through the issuance of new stock, while other firms protect themselves by attempting to buy back voting stocks to increase their control. A self-tender defense occurs when a firm undertakes a tender offer for its own shares as a method of defending against a hostile aggressor. After the purchase, the shares are taken off the market and commonly referred to as treasury stock. This type of strategy is often employed to defend against a two-tier hostile takeover. Also, some companies' charters contain provisions that require very high levels of stockholder approval of takeovers.

7. *Caring for the Stockholders and the Employees.* The company should pay attention to what the shareholders and the employees have to say. It can use a "fair price" provision, which requires all stockholders to receive the same price for their stock in a takeover bid. The company can also install an unusually high stockholder approval clause (often higher than 80%) in its charter for takeover approval. Recently companies facing unwanted tender offers or stock accumulation programs have resorted to using employee benefit plans as part of their defense strategy. Because of the percentage of stock held by employee plans, companies have endeavored to use their plan as a defense against takeovers. Four methods of this defense are utilized. The first method involves the company using the em-

ployee plan to accomplish a leverage buyout. A second method calls for the employee benefit plan to refuse to tender its shares. In a third approach the plan purchases the target company's stock, and the final method entails using the plan's surplus assets.

8. *Proxy Defense.* This could be used in a takeover game. There are three variations of an aggressor's proxy strategy. The first is a formal solicitation of proxies, usually mailed separately from the firm's proxy materials. This is the most common form of a proxy contest. The second type is a shareholder resolution that is mailed with the firm's proxy material. The third variation, a proxy contest, may take the solicitation of shareholder's consents. While proxies must be submitted at a shareholder's meeting, consents can be solicited without having to wait for a meeting. The use of shareholder consents is less frequent.

9. *The Antitrust Defense.* This is used for two primary reasons: first, as a signal to the aggressor that pursuit of the target will be opposed vigorously and will result in a potentially long and costly courtship for the aggressor; and second, as a long-shot business decision with a potentially high return. In this case the odds of success in the courts may be small, but if the target should win, the target is able to maintain its independence, at least until the next aggressor makes his appearance.

Although there seems to be a large variety of defense strategies that management is able to choose from when their company is in danger of a merger or takeover, sometimes they accept defeat as being unavoidable. Companies often consider restructuring to resist hostile takeovers. One of the most used forms is a stock buyback. The extreme version of this is through a leveraged buyout. That means taking a public company private.

10. *The Establishment of State Laws.* Laws such as the Pennsylvania antihostile takeover law in 1990 has severely curtailed the incidence of takeover. Other states have established similar laws to deter hostile takeovers. The author gave testimony to defend Senate bill 1310 in the state of Pennsylvania and this is attached as an appendix to this chapter.

In 1999, the General Assembly passed the most significant Maryland corporate takeover legislation since the enactment of the Control Share Acquisition Stature in 1989. This bill is intended to discourage hostile takeovers of Maryland corporations and real estate investment trusts. Part of this bill permits the target company's board to consider the effect the action would have on the corporation's stakeholders, such as employees, suppliers, customers, creditors, and the community, as well as the effect on stockholders.[15] We can say that the antihostile takeover legislation in the United States has made it difficult to mount hostile takeovers. The incentives of such a strategy have been reduced significantly.

Takeovers have harmful effects on stakeholders other than just the target company and its employees. Major suppliers are adversely affected by the loss of business. And the tax advantages for the acquiring company are passed on in the form of increased taxes for individuals. Another negative effect is that restructuring gives foreign companies the opportunity to gobble up large chunks of American industry. This threat in turn leads to calls for protectionism, to the detriment of our economy.

THE STAKEHOLDER SOLUTION

A more revolutionary, and in the long run more effective, approach would be a basic change in our country's corporate governance. Stakeholders mentioned earlier are defined as those groups who have a direct interest in the survival of the corporation, and without whose support the corporation could not exist. Instead of viewing the corporation as concerned exclusively with maximizing returns to stockholders, the stakeholder approach preaches that there are other constituencies in the corporation whose claim and interest should be protected. This issue needs to be considered seriously in order to find a solution that satisfies the demands of stakeholders.

In the stakeholder model of corporate governance, the firm's objectives would be reached by balancing the conflicting claims of stakeholder groups. Social, political, and economic interests would all be represented on a "stakeholder board." This board, which would have representatives on the traditional board, would focus not just on short-term economic considerations, but on the corporation's long-term well-being and the effect on society as a whole. As a result, the corporation would become much more socially responsible. Long-term effects of takeover actions on all stakeholders would be weighed and balanced before reaching a decision. Therefore, it is logical that the stakeholder approach would inherently deter hostile takeovers. A board comprising responsible stakeholders would ensure that only takeovers and mergers that would benefit the company, and all its constituencies in the long run, would take place. And all of this would rely on internal controls, without the need for government intervention or other outside measures. What is the long-term solution to acquisition fever? The answer is simple: the stakeholder approach to corporate governance.

CONCLUSION

A hostile takeover can be targeted at almost any corporation. The takeover occurs when one purchases enough stock to gain control over a company. A hostile takeover is a dramatic experience for the target company. This causes concern and worry, affecting the company's morale, stability, and most important, its future. Unfriendly takeovers provide no productivity.

Corporate raiders are merely involved in the "takeover game" to harvest their own personal benefits. It matters little to the average raider whether a community is completely broken up because he or she comes in and slashes jobs through restructuring of the company. In many cases, older employees who have devoted their whole life to the company lose their entire pension plan. These older employees often have little hope of finding new jobs. According to investor Warren Buffet, "American industry should not be restructured by the people who can sell the most junk-bonds."[16] Those who initiate hostile takeovers are merely financiers and speculators who are not serious about the operations of the companies and are solely in it for quick profits.

Hostile takeovers and raider activities are forcing management to adopt a short-term perspective because there would be no long-term planning necessary if a hostile takeover takes place. Another concern after a takeover is that the corporation would spend much less time, knowledge, and money toward research and development of new technology.

The solution may be in the restructuring of the internal control system. Directors could take into account the impact of takeovers on employees, suppliers, consumers, and the communities in which the company operates. By considering their interests (and those of the shareholders as well), values will be maximized. In addition, in discharging their fiduciary duties, directors should consider the long-term as well as short-term interests of the corporation and all its stakeholders. In addition, the company should continuously examine its environments to determine its strength and weaknesses along with its competitive advantage in order to redefine its future direction. These analyses help the organization to better understand its products, distinctive abilities, skills, and resources. This will help the organization to redirect its resources along with its markets.

APPENDIX

Testimony Supporting Senate Bill 1310 to Preserve Pennsylvania's Economy and Keep It Competitive Given by Abbass F. Alkhafaji

To make Pennsylvania competitive again we have to stop the ruthless practice of takeovers. This changing of ownership leads to the wasting of our resources in a non-productive and non-economical way. Our country is paying a tremendous price for the restructuring games that take place during buyouts and takeovers. It is true that there are a few who benefit from a takeover. Raiders walk away with millions in profits. Financial manipulators, speculators, lawyers, and investment bankers are also big winners. But the stakeholders—workers, management, consumers, and the local community—lose, and the economy suffers as a result.

Without restrictive legislation, hostile takeovers at present are relatively easy. This is because when the rumor mill gets wind of a takeover, the word spreads and the price of stock soars. By this time, a substantial portion of that stock is already in the hands of arbitrageurs. These are not stockholders in the classical sense, but merely speculators. They have no interest in the corporation as an institution, feel neither affection nor loyalty to the institution, and are active only in the hope of a quick profit.

Opponents of this bill would have us believe that takeovers are good because they will eliminate inefficiency and incompetence, and will benefit shareholders and the economy. While in some cases this may be true, all too often takeovers are just pointless exercises in rearranging the economic landscape.

No wealth is created—rather it is merely transferred, resulting in no economic benefit. An ever-growing body of evidence is proof of this. Takeover attempts are not made on poorly managed companies, rather they are made on ones that are well run because a strong company can support the high debt level involved in buyouts, has assets to sell, and has good cash flow. Good examples of this are American Airlines, Dayton-Hudson, and UAL, all recent takeover targets. In addition, the restructuring that takes place after a takeover or takeover attempt forces management to take a short-term view. Long-term investments and research and development efforts suffer as a result. Debt levels increase, workers are laid off, employee morale and loyalty suffer, and community tax bases are reduced as a result of layoffs and plant closings. And even though the raiders realize large profits, the average shareholder's wealth does not increase. Even if short-term financial gains are realized, there are offsetting losses from other sources such as reduction of investments due to debt, the selling of assets to finance debt and transaction costs in the form of lawyers' and investment bankers' fees. In fact, the RJR Nabisco deal cost almost $1 billion in fees. The implications of takeovers for the economy and society are disturbing indeed.

The most immediate problem stemming from takeovers and takeover attempts is their staggering cost. Many unethical raiders have no intention of actually taking over a company—they are interested only in temporarily inflating stock prices. They buy low and sell high making millions in profits for themselves, while leaving their target financially crippled from its battle to prevent the takeover. Lee Iacocca, chairman of Chrysler Corporation says of this practice that "greenmail is nothing but blackmail in a pin stripe suit."[17] T. Boone Pickens, well known in the past ten years for short-term stock manipulation, has yet to actually take over a company. He even boasts in one of his books that the prospect of acquiring Gulf was "unthinkable."[18] Carl Icahn is in the same league as Pickens. An interview with Newsweek in 1986 quotes Icahn as saying, "I do it for the money. . . . I do it with a profit motive. That's how you score in this game and those are the points."[19]

We are not opposed to profits—everyone wants financial security—what we are opposed to is the misuse and abuse of our system for personal gain, while workers lose their jobs, communities suffer, and competitiveness is weakened. Raiders suggest that they are out to help America succeed, but the truth is that they are out to satisfy their own greed. The need to quickly pay down debt, the loss of jobs, the disruption of the economy, and the sacrifice of commitment for R&D are all costs resulting directly from takeovers.

Takeovers are very profitable to the acquiring companies because the stock prices of many companies don't reflect the value of their assets. An investor group decides to buy the company from shareholders. To fund the deal, the investors borrow up to 90 percent of the money needed, pledging the company's assets as collateral. Ideally, the debt is paid back within a number of years, but in reality, the debt is so staggering that the acquiring company often is forced to sell off subsidiaries and close down branches. In extreme cases, bankruptcy results.

Even if a company does not go bankrupt, there can be a great impact on jobs. To pay down debt, investors sell off subsidiaries and streamline what's left, slashing jobs and reducing overhead. According to Lane Kirkland, president of AFL–CIO, about 90,000 union members have lost jobs due to restructuring activities in the last ten years.[20] In addition, many thousands more have been forced to take wage and benefit reductions. Not only should American blue collar workers be fearful for their jobs, but also lower, middle, and top level managers' jobs are frequently on the line as a result of corporate restructuring.

Restructuring also creates distrust and pressure on those who stay in the job. It seems like one group's gain is another one's loss. Without trust people won't dedicate themselves to common goals. They put all their energy into defending their own interests, which means declining productivity.

These realities imply that managers of today and tomorrow should be concerned about the implications of the many buyouts that have taken place, are currently taking place, and will continue to take place unless something is done to curb them. Top level management now spends more time and money on devising strategies to prevent their companies from being taken over than they spend worrying about the quality of their product and how it can be distributed more efficiently. If nothing is done managers will have to work harder to monitor the external dynamic environment in order to watch for hostile outsiders.

Buyouts also impact our economy adversely. Because they lead to reduction of top management, our economy is more vulnerable to bad decisions; mistakes made by large companies affect the economy more than those made by small firms.

Takeovers lead to the pursuit of short-term goals at the expense of long-term competitiveness. In an effort to save money and their jobs, management may skimp on R&D; competitors may surpass them, as in the case of the American steel industry.[21] Studies by the National Science Foundation show that R&D is the first department where spending is cut during a buyout. Sixteen companies that had undergone mergers showed a 4.7 percent drop in R&D spending.[22]

Restructuring gives a foreign company buying into American industry the opportunity to snap up a larger chunk at one time. Such threats encourage protectionism, to the detriment of the economy. We will not be able to compete with the foreign countries when it comes to research and development of new products.

The tax advantages for the acquiring company is passed on to individual taxpayers. This creates more problems for society as a whole.

From a social point of view, a corporation is a sociological institution as well as a collection of financial assets. Employees understand that corporate change is synonymous with corporate survival. However, they will not accept abrupt, radical change imposed from outside that has nothing to do with current business conditions. Takeovers involving dismemberment create real suffering for individuals whose jobs are eliminated or whose lifelong careers are ruined. Entire communities that experience abrupt economic dislocation are harmed in the aftermath of takeovers.[23]

PUBLIC OPINION

Polls have consistently shown that the majority of Americans disapprove of takeovers. A 1989 Louis Harris & Associates poll showed that, by a margin of 6 to 1, the general public believed that takeovers do more harms than good to the economy. Two-thirds of those polled favored legislative response to limit hostile takeovers. Seventy-seven percent requested information about the impact of the takeover on the employees, stockholders, and communities where the companies were located.[24] Another survey conducted by the author showed that 72 percent of the companies that went through restructuring laid off employees, and 35 percent of them laid off some management. In 1988, 73 percent of those polled by the National Association of Manufacturers (NAM) agreed that hostile takeovers have hurt the industrial base of their states. Forty-one percent of the respondents believe R&D is no longer a priority when there is a hostile takeover.[25]

Since public opinion is so strong, politicians are unlikely to accept the current takeover craze. Already, antitakeover laws are being passed at the state level, and it is only a matter of time before Congress intervenes. The Supreme Court handed down an important securities law decision in March 1988 designed to protect investors against stock manipulation. It prohibits a public company from making untrue, misleading, or incomplete statements about facts that are "material" to its fortunes. Companies must now disclose merger talks right away rather than wait until talks reach fruition. A wrong move can invite challenges from the SEC and from stockholders who say they were misled. Because shareholder lawsuits are often brought as class actions, the potential damages could amount to millions of dollars.[26]

Unfortunately, legislation that has been passed to restrict takeovers to date has been relatively ineffective. Those who favor takeovers argue that such laws favor existing management no matter how inefficient or self-serving. The board of directors can hardly be expected to rectify this situation; the board was chosen by management, and will challenge or dismiss management only in the most extreme situation. Stockholders need protection from this type of management; workers, executives, and communities need protection from corporate dismemberment.

So the real issue is that the takeover game is no more than changing ownership or a transfer of resources from one group to another. This definitely threatens the long-term stability of our economy. In fact, since corporations are financially weakened, they are less effective in competing internationally. They also cost the government money because interest on debt is tax deductible. There is also a great opportunity cost, because minds that could be applied to improve products and services are diverted to the lure of quick profits to be made in the takeover game.

By supporting Senate bill (S.B.) 1310, we can restrict the hostile takeover attempts that result in layoff and large debt for Pennsylvania companies and create an atmosphere where job loyalty suffers. This bill attempts to restrict making huge profits through the use of greenmail, junk bonds, and golden parachutes. It also makes clear that the board of directors is not only accountable to stockholders for short-term profits—rather its responsibility lies in the long-term health and growth of the corporation, its employees, the community in which it functions, its major creditors, and its major suppliers. In short, S.B. 1310 embraces the stakeholder approach. Only by passing this bill can we prevent what Kirkland so eloquently describes in his testimony: "Whether or not we crash and burn is not the question, only when and how many casualties there will be." Give your support for S.B. 1310, and lessen those casualties.

NOTES

1. "Marriage a la Mode," *The Economist* 355 (29 April 2000).

2. Gordon Mathews, "Hostile Takeovers Won't Fade, Some Say, Despite Easy Market," *American Banker* 162 (29 September 1997): 33.

3. Richard Epstein, "Where Have All the Hostile Takeovers Gone?" *Management* 47 (March 2000): 58.

4. Abbass Alkhafaji, *Restructuring American Corporations* (New York: Quorum Books, 1990).

5. Epstein, "Where Have All the Hostile Takeovers Gone?"

6. Lane Kirkland, "Testimony before the House Ways and Means Committee on Leveraged Buyouts," 1 February 1989, 1.

7. Douglas Robson, "Catellus Adopts Poison Pill Plan to Ward off Hostile Takeovers," *Business Journal Serving San Jose & Silicon Valley* 17 (7 January 2000): 14.

8. Peter C. Kostant, "Exit, Voice and Loyalty in the Course of Corporate Governance," *Journal of Socio-Economics* 28 (1999): 203.

9. "Too Friendly," *The Economist* 353 (13 November 1999): 66.

10. Michael Edelstein, "Lloyd's Helps Fend Off Unwanted Bids," *Mergers & Acquisitions* 13 (19 June 2000): 6.

11. Steve "Mac" Heller, "Adding Value from Hostile to Global Times," *Investment Dealers' Digest* 66 (22 May 2000): 43.

12. "Lloyd's Market to Offer Protection for Shareholders Against Hostile Takeovers," *PR Newswire*, 2 May 2000.

13. Alkhafaji, *Restructuring American Corporations*.

14. S. Kaplan, "Management Buyouts: Evidence on Taxes as a Source of Value," *The Journal of Finance* 44 (1998): 611–632.

15. Eric G. Orlinsky and C. James Harris, "Corporate Takeover Bill Protects Stockholders," *Baltimore Business Journal* 16 (16 April 1999): 20.

16. Quoted in Kirkland, "Testimony," 1.

17. Lee Iacocca, "A Plague of Corporate Raiders," *Japan Economic Journal* (24 January 1987): 8.

18. T. Boone Pickens, Jr., "Boone Speaks," *Fortune* 115 (16 February 1987): 42–56.

19. Carl Icahn, "Confessions of a Raider," *Newsweek*, 20 October 1986, 51.

20. Kirkland, "Testimony," 1.

21. Douglas K. Sease, "An Appraisal: Analysts Wonder if Takeover Pace Will Continue," *The Wall Street Journal*, 25 April 1988.

22. Anthony Ramirez, "What LBOs Really Do to R&D Spending," *Fortune* 119 (13 March 1989): 98.

23. Henry F. Myers, "Will Mergers Help or Hurt in the Long Run?" *The Wall Street Journal*, Eastern ed., 2 May 1988, 1.

24. Louis Harris and Associates, "Public Opinion," on-line 26 March 1989, Roper Center, University of Connecticut.

25. Ramirez, "What LBOs Really Do."

26. Wayne E. Green, "Confusion over Merger-Disclosure Law," *The Wall Street Journal*, Eastern ed., 24 June 1988, 1.

Chapter 9

Restructuring:
The Downsizing Game

Organizational restructuring sometimes requires extreme and painful measures. In this case organizational restructuring refers to the reduction or elimination of organizational employees. It is a fundamental change that effects the entire organization. This usually takes place either at the corporate level or radically reconfiguring activities and relationships at the business unit level. It involves rebuilding the strength of an organization to ensure that the structure and allocation of assets properly matches the size and makeup of various units and human resources. There is one form of restructuring, downsizing, which has increasingly been used in the near past and more than likely will continue to gain a lot of attention in the future. This is the focus of this chapter.

In the past decade competition increased tremendously. Most firms' strategies at that time were to outperform their domestic competitors. Information technology and better transportation techniques enabled many companies to expand operations into the global marketplace. Businesses therefore changed rapidly in this global environment. Firms have grown in size and scope of operations. In many cases, those firms have become too large with many organizational layers. Large organizations brought excessive cost and severe bureaucratic complications. The huge personnel costs added to inefficiency and less competitiveness in the marketplace. This has contributed negatively to their capability of meeting the needs and expectations of customers. Strategic decisions could not be implemented quickly through the bureaucratic complexity of organizational structure. It was often difficult for these companies to bring together managers to discuss important issues on short notice. In these cases, change becomes necessary. Management needs to reconstruct the company to meet these challenges. Companies need to continuously renew themselves if they want to survive.

When management is forced to restructure to combat the inefficiency or to change corporate strategy, they are faced with many challenging questions. Some of these questions include the following:

1. Is the restructuring limited to a particular area?
2. Which hierarchical layer should be eliminated?
3. Can the employees in these layers be redistributed to other areas in the organization?
4. Will this satisfy stakeholders' interests?
5. What type of communication needs to be installed?
6. How do we improve overall performance?

These are just a few of the issues that managers must consider with restructuring. This chapter will discuss downsizing strategy as a form of restructuring.

DEFINITIONS

Downsizing strategy refers to the reduction or elimination of one or more hierarchical levels from the organization and then transforming the decision-making process into a more decentralized form. It is becoming a very popular strategy in both the public and private sectors. This strategy was widely used over the years. In the United States, employees can be fired immediately and without substantial reason given. Organizations usually downsize to reduce costs and to enable them to compete in their respective industries, both domestically and internationally.

Downsizing is essential for many organizations to survive or to remain competitive in a particular industry. When the turnaround strategy works, the company can save many people their jobs. But when this strategy fails, it will cost everybody their jobs. By reducing or eliminating one or more hierarchical levels from the organization, personnel costs are reduced, as well as the time in which critical decisions are authorized. This contributes to efficiency and competitiveness.

Customer satisfaction will also become enhanced in that the consumer can better communicate with key organization employees. Downsizing usually involves reducing costs by eliminating middle managers and those who work under them.

The argument for downsizing is that in order to prosper, a company has to learn how to be efficient. Efficiency is defined as the ability to do more with less. For example, a company is efficient if it can produce more products with less labor input. This newfound efficiency leads to better profits, which is often a corporation's primary goal. This is where downsizing comes into play. A company may downsize by eliminating or changing jobs or products. The company can move its operations to a more cost-efficient location, which is often overseas in countries with less strict labor laws and where laborers are willing to work for less money in poor conditions.

However, employees, customers, and the public at large see downsizing as negative. This is mostly because many people lose their jobs, and this affects the whole society. Today, almost everyone knows someone who has been affected by downsizing. It should be noted, however, that people outside of the public sector are also affected by downsizing. In fact, the U.S. government has recently undergone its own form of downsizing. The Officer Corps of the U.S. Army suffered cutbacks of about 30 percent between 1990 and 1995.[1]

A study in 1994 showed that hospitals that downsized had a 200 to 400 percent higher mortality and morbidity rate than other hospitals. The 311 companies that downsized employees by more than 3 percent have failed to improve their financial or stock performance. Reasons are poor planning, poor leadership, and poor communication. A study conducted by Ronald Burke showed that two-thirds of firms that downsize end up doing the same thing a year later. One of the main failures of corporate downsizing is credible leadership. The senior presidents usually have little communication with the employee, which does not help to build their morale or a future for the institution.[2]

FORD MOTOR COMPANY

In the early 1980s, Ford Motor Company decided to adopt total quality management. At that time the company was stressed with high overhead and administrative costs. In their efforts to improve quality and efficiency, they focused on their accounts payable department, which consisted of over five hundred employees. At that time they were involved with Mazda. They decided to benchmark with Mazda. Mazda and Ford had formed a strategic alliance a few years back. Mazda handled their accounts payable duties with only five employees. Ford introduced a new accounts payable process shortly after the visit.

After restructuring, Ford's new design was completely different from its original structure. The employees in the accounts payable department were reduced from 500 to 125, a 75-percent decrease in the total number of personnel. When a buyer in the purchasing department makes an order, the order is automatically put into the accounts payable database. When the products arrive, a check is sent immediately. Before, clerks on the receiving docks handled the process of clearing and sending checks, which accounted for considerable late fees and other significant problems.

The implementation of such a downsizing strategy created a few difficulties for Ford Motor Company. First of all, the process took nearly five years from design to complete implementation. Ford spent considerable time trying to insert former accounts payable workers into other areas of the organization, if at all possible. Another problem was that suppliers seem to have benefited the least from the new design process. These suppliers found that they received payment, in most cases, more slowly than when the original system was still in use. This could be a potentially dangerous situation for Ford because these suppliers may cut off the shipments and refuse to do business altogether.

AT&T

AT&T eliminated about 128,000 jobs between 1992 and 1996. Executives claim that global competition, advancing technology, and market forces were behind this radical change in the organization's workforce. CEO Robert Allen was quoted as saying, "I truly wish we did not have to do this downsizing. I understand how wrenching it will be to remain competitive."[3]

This quote triggered a jump in AT&T's stock price of over two points; however, employees and their families lost in a big way. There was a push by customers and former employees to boycott AT&T in an attempt to protest these layoffs. This is another difficulty and consequence associated with downsizing.

STAGES OF DOWNSIZING

When the organization discovers that an area or a department has created cost inefficiencies, the organization must restructure. Costs can be associated with excess personnel, too much red tape, and overall inefficiency. The process starts with assessing the nature of reduction. For example, should the employees be temporarily or permanently laid off? Vice presidents, middle managers, and project heads are those who are most frequently affected at this stage of downsizing, not to mention the lower level employees who work under these middle and upper level managers. Next, when one or more of the hierarchical levels in the organization are eliminated, there are fewer levels for decisions to pass through the chain of command. The number of employees which upper level management must now control becomes significantly larger after a couple of layers have been terminated. If every decision were to be approved by these upper level managers, an overload would occur and the organization may become inefficient once again. In order to combat this situation, decision making is pushed downward into the organization after the first part of the downsizing is completed.

As mentioned earlier, the elimination of one or more hierarchical levels and the push of decision making downward in the organization are the two main changes involved in downsizing an organization. The main goal of organizational restructuring is to achieve customer satisfaction by making the company more efficient. Reduced costs, better communication throughout the company, and decentralized decision making are all factors in the equation to achieve better overall efficiency in the organization. All this will improve corporate performance.

COSTS OF DOWNSIZING

Downsizing is often very costly to a corporation. More than 50 percent of companies that downsize fail to reach their financial objectives. More than one million people are permanently laid off each year. For example Boeing eliminated 60,000 jobs between 1989 and 1997. The company's orders for jets increased from two hundred to nine hundred within two years. The company has had a difficult time hiring qualified people. This caused the company to stop producing 747s.[4]

Downsizing was very costly to AT&T, who spent over $23 billion restructuring itself. Beyond the financial concerns, companies who choose to downsize also have to worry about employee morale, as well as public perception of the company. Downsizing reduces employee morale and the customers and the public in general develop a negative image of the company. In addition, those who survive the cut will be left in an environment where they are expected to do more with less.[5]

Al Dunlap, who was hired in July 1996 as the new CEO of Sunbeam, has been given the nickname "Chainsaw." "Chainsaw Al" cut 34 percent of 33,000 jobs at Scott Paper, and announced that he is eliminating 50 percent of jobs at Sunbeam and closing eighteen of its twenty-six factories.[6]

Between 1980 and 1990, Fortune 500 companies cut 3.4 million jobs. Since 1991, twenty-five of the Fortune 500 companies announced an additional 624,000 cutbacks in employees. The list included IBM, AT&T,

General Motors, Sears, Boeing, GTE, Eastman Kodak, Xerox, and some other well-known organizations. Between 1985 and 1995, AT&T cut 114,000 employees, and an additional 40,000 in 1996. Downsizing has become a growing trend since the early 1970s, and it is not going away anytime soon.[7] By the mid-1990s, downsizing reached its highest level. It is estimated that about 3,100 employees lose their jobs every day.

In summary, some of the reasons why companies downsize are the following:

1. To be able to survive in a competitive market.
2. To gain competitive advantage by producing the same quality product or services with fewer or more efficient employees and better technology than competitors.
3. To improve efficiency and productivity. Downsizing usually involves those workers with higher salaries.
4. To boost share prices. When the company announces downsizing, it is usually accompanied by an increase in the price of its stock.

NEGATIVE EFFECTS ON THE ORGANIZATION

There are some negative effects to be felt by the company when downsizing is chosen. The firm must be prepared to deal with decreased productivity of the remaining employees, by as much as three to four hours a day.[8] Downsizing leaves more work for fewer employees, and it is not done as well. They must also find a way to deal with the bad feelings of the surviving employees, brought about by watching their friends and coworkers lose their jobs. The company will need to retrain, reskill, and adapt the working culture of the remaining employees, which could be costly.

THE EMPLOYEES

There are two types of employees in the downsizing environment: those who are leaving and those who are staying. Those who are leaving can be categorized by several criteria. Usually, the two groups that go first are the youngest and the oldest: the youngest because they lack experience and the talent to do certain jobs and the oldest because they are the highest paid. Employees may also find themselves targeted if they are not up to date on the latest technology, are at the bottom of the power chain, or earn more money than others who do the same work as they do. Those targeted to leave feel hurt, foolish, betrayed, and scared. They may be unable to find another job for the same reasons they were given for losing their previous job. They may be told they are too young and lack experience or that they are overqualified, which is the legal way of saying too old. The employees who retain their jobs experience feelings of loss of control, fear, uncertainty, and mistrust. A survey of thirty-one Fortune 500 firms found four major factors that cause employee morale loss during restructuring of the company. These are the flow of inaccurate gossip, lack of leadership, concern for coworkers losing their jobs, and inconsistent information.[9]

The loss of coworkers through downsizing has the same effect on employees as would other types of losses. Therefore, the remaining employees must go through a process of recovery in order to regain morale. According to Chip Bell, manager of Performance Research Associates, a Minneapolis-based consulting firm, the most important thing for management is to admit that a loss has occurred. "To assume there is no grief is always inaccurate, incomplete, and insensitive."[10] It is also important to recognize that people are under social pressure to act "normal," when in reality they feel hurt, angry, and guilty. They feel guilty because their coworkers had to leave; hurt because they were left behind; and angry because (most likely) their workload has increased.

Most people have difficulty dealing with feelings of anger, frustration, and confusion alone. Without the help from others, employees may react in ways that are inappropriate or misdirected. For the company, this may mean assuming blame for homicide, suicide, or being the target of sabotage.

Amabile and Conti, quoted in Tootoonchi, indicated that layoff decisions were politically based, rather than being rationally founded in assessment of the company's needs. They also reported that "our results suggest that, not surprisingly, downsizing has a negative impact on the work environment for creativity and innovation, on actual creative and innovative behaviors, and on employees [sic] feelings about their work and their organization."[11]

DOWNSIZING STRATEGIES

The first downsizing strategy that can be used by an organization is horizontal restructuring. This involves downsizing the organization by eliminating one or more layers of management in order to create a more flat, decentralized structure. Xerox used this technique to reduce administrative costs and improve customer satisfaction. The executives felt by eliminating hierarchical levels in the company, the decision-making process would be speeded up. The main objective of this strategy is limiting the chain of command in which a decision must pass in order to be approved. This results in customers receiving notice on key organizational decisions in a very short period of time.

Also, many administrative costs will be eliminated due to the reduction of the number of offices, secretaries, and personnel after the downsizing strategy is implemented.

Another strategy of downsizing that can be implemented by an organization is an evaluation approach. Every year, employees at all levels of the organization are evaluated based on their annual performance. Managers are asked to rank their respective employees and to pick out those who they feel are in the bottom 5 percent in performance. These employees are then targeted for coaching by their superiors. Along with encouragement and skill training, these lower performance employees are given operational goals, which are to be achieved within the next two years. If the employee fails to improve on his or her performance in that amount of time, the company will be forced to terminate them. This strategy allows employees a fair chance at keeping their jobs.

An organization does not have to resort to massive downsizing in order to effect austerity measures. There are a variety of alternative actions available that cause less upset and chaos among the workforce survivors. Suggested by Rosen in "The Healthy Company: Eight Strategies to Develop People, Productivity, and Profits" are the following strategies: temporary salary cuts, layoff rotations, shortened work weeks, flexible employment, early retirement, delay of projects, tin parachutes for hourly workers, and rehiring employees.[12]

Many companies have used these strategies with great success. For example, Intel reduced employee salaries proportionate to their pay level. Nucor employed a shortened workweek for everyone, the CEO included, by initiating a bonus system. Employees were encouraged to maintain the production schedule to avoid the loss of jobs. They received smaller bonuses and worked fewer hours during sluggish periods. An innovative idea utilized at Anheuser Busch was successful in avoiding layoffs. The completion of a project was deferred for two years because of impending retirements. The cost savings realized by postponing the project were offset by employee wages. Downsizing occurred naturally, through attrition, without the upheaval in the ranks that accompanies major layoffs.

THE DANGERS OF COST CUTTING

Downsizing occurs because of changes in the industry and environment and poor management practices. Unfortunately, many executives are reactive, rather than proactive; if costs are managed as part of strategic planning (proactive), less cutting would be needed (reactive). It has been noted that executives who have undertaken cost containment measures (restructuring, downsizing, or cost reduction) often repeat the process in the near future. Cost cutting, when unsuccessful, leads to further efforts of reduction and is generally frustrated by five factors. They are

1. Cost reduction is often not relevant to the strategy of the company. When organizations cut into the segment of their business that they are known for, it weakens their foundation (e.g., loss of skilled employees, low morale leading to a decrease in productivity, reduced R&D capabilities, or deficiencies in quality).

2. Cost cutting is destined to be ineffective, since many managers do not have a clear understanding of true operating costs. Cost information is often presented in a complex fashion that is not easily understood by lower level managers. In order to control costs companywide, employees must understand their part in the process. Harley Davidson, for example, has undertaken a long-term project to revise their cost procedures in order to account for the "true costs" of production. Their goal is to simplify the system so that all employees gain an understanding of their part in managing costs.

3. Organizations put too much emphasis on technology at the expense of their human resources. While it is necessary to introduce the use of innovative technology, cost savings will not materialize without upgrading the skills and knowledge of the labor pool. Education is an ongoing process. People are naturally reluctant to change; they often sabotage the efforts of the firm to move forward because they do not understand how it will affect them.

4. Cost cutting is often prompted by a crisis. If costs were managed effectively all the time, there would be fewer occurrences of massive downsizing. Efficient cost-containment policies result in higher levels of quality and service to the organization because they avoid the disruptions that accompanies large-scale job terminations.[13]

Downsizing must be done gradually and must be a rational process. This is driven by clear objectives that are clearly communicated. The process must be well planned by providing direction and strategic context, committing to common values, developing a social contract, designing the right performance environment, creating a learning environment, and building infrastructure.[14]

CONCLUSION

The main goal of downsizing is to help financially troubled companies reduce or eliminate unnecessary costs and improve performance. Companies are choosing to cut personnel, which is a quick fix to an unprofitable situation. However, only less than 50 percent of those companies met cost reduction targets, and less than one-third raised their profits. Take, for example, Eastman Kodak, who has restructured five times since 1985. It has cost the company $2.1 billion and it cost 12,000 employees their jobs. As of 1992, their profits are half what they were in 1985, stock prices are less than desirable, and the bottom line is not much better than a decade ago.

The devastating effects of downsizing on survivors, the victims, and the society at large are undeniable. However, in some cases downsizing is unavoidable due to the changing environment (e.g., technological changes and global or domestic competition). Downsizing has changed the old rule of codependency between employers and employees. As a result employees today are more willing to develop their knowledge, improve their skills, accept more risks, and take more challenging work. The message of this chapter is that downsizing should be avoided when possible. Future jobs expect employees to be technologically literate.

NOTES

1. American Management Association, *Survey of Downsizing and Assistance to Displaced Workers* (New York: AMA Report, 1995).

2. Richard Doust, "Downsizing: Making It Work," *CA Magazine* 131 (December 1998): 20–26.

3. Matt Murray, "Amid Record Profits, Companies to Layoff Workers," *The Wall Street Journal*, 4 May 1995, A1.

4. Doust, "Downsizing: Making It Work."

5. Art Bonros, "The New Capitalism and Organizational Rationality: The Adoption of Downsizing Programs, 1979–1994," *Social Forces* (September 1997): 229–250.

6. Ahmed Tootoonchi, "Downsizing: Is There a Bright Side to It?" *Business Research Yearbook, IABD* 4 (1998): 338.

7. Robert H. Rosen, "The Healthy Company: Eight Strategies to Develop People, Productivity, and Profits," *Canadian Banker* 100 (March–April 1993): 59.

8. Robert M. Tomasko, "Downsizing: Reshaping the Corporation for the Future," *The Management Magazine*, 18 September 1995, 19.

9. Tootoonchi, "Downsizing: Is There a Bright Side to It?" 338.

10. Ibid., 339.

11. Ibid.

12. Rosen, "The Healthy Company," 119–121.

13. T. Quinn Spitzer and Peter M. Tobia, "Has Cost Cutting Gone Too Far?" *Across the Board* 31 (April 1994): 54–55.

14. Doust, "Downsizing: Making It Work."

Chapter 10

Mergers and Acquisitions

Surviving in the beginning of this century requires building sustainable competitive advantages through the formation of various strategies. The fast changes in technology, the intensity of competition, the slow growth or the recession of some economies, and the globalization of the market have pressured companies to seek cooperative relationships with other firms. The new collaborations and mergers of yesterday's competitors have become the dominant trend in corporate America and corporations worldwide. Corporate leaders are changing their attitude from a paranoid worldview, centered on images and fears of being dominated, to one of allying with other firms.

Companies pursuing vertical integration or diversification approaches employ the strategies of merger and acquisition. The number of companies that have used merger and acquisition strategies to become vertically integrated or diversified over the last five years is staggering. For the past five years, more than 20,000 mergers or acquisitions took place. In fact in 1994, there were more than 5,800 mergers or acquisitions with economic value of more than $344 billion. *Economists* stated that the volume of transactions in 1996 worldwide totaled $1 trillion. In the United States, 10,000 transactions worth more than

$650 billion were completed.[1] While mergers from the 1960s to the 1980s were effective in expansion and/or diversification, in the 1990s merging changed dramatically. This chapter will focus on the merger and acquisition strategies in the end of the 1990s. It will evaluate the effectiveness of these strategies and expectations in the coming years.

DEFINITION

Many organizations prefer to buy an existing firm than to create one from scratch during an expansion. In 1995 Wheelen and Hunger defined a merger as a friendly arrangement involving two or more similar-sized corporations in which stock is exchanged and one corporation survives with a name that is a combination of the original companies. The Federal Trade Commission (FTC) has been given the responsibility of evaluating the competitive implications of proposed mergers or acquisitions. The FTC disallows any acquisition within the United States that has the potential for generating monopoly (or oligopoly) profits in an industry. The FTC has defined five types of mergers.

The first is a vertical merger, which is the vertical integration forward or backward of a firm through its acquisition efforts. The second is a horizontal merger, which involves acquiring a former competitor. For example, when Coca-Cola tried to acquire Dr. Pepper, the FTC concluded that such a merger could have led to an oligopoly power for Coca-Cola. The third is a product extension merger, which is how a company acquires complementary products through their merger and acquisition activities. The fourth is a market extension merger. This is how a firm gains access to new geographic markets. The fifth is a conglomerate merger. This is in evidence when firms have no vertical, horizontal, product extension, or market extension links between them.[2]

THE HISTORY OF MERGERS AND TAKEOVERS

It is important to mention that mergers and takeovers have been taking place for hundreds, perhaps thousands, of years. However, these two terms have come into focus during the past one hundred years. John Pound states that the term "company raiding" has its roots in the late 1800s, when the market had very few controls and raiders were known as "barons."[3] These conditions continued with little change (the Great Depression notwithstanding) until the 1950s, when a new conservatism emerged. By this point, the public was wary of the "faceless" management that takeover artists claimed they would overcome if their bid was successful. Proxy fights are as familiar to this decade as LBOs were to the 1980s.

The precursor to the debt-financed purchases of the 1980s occurred during the 1960s, when high-priced shares and convertible securities (at the time a departure from the norm) were utilized instead of cash to secure large industrial conglomerates. Randall Smith states that this *conglomerate theory* holds that companies operating in many different businesses would be less vulnerable to downturns in individual sectors and could benefit from centralized management. When the market fell during the 1970s, these industrials lay vulnerable with many parts to them. The time was ripe for picking.[4]

Many organizations became victims of the raider's axe during the 1980s. This decade has had the largest measurable number of mergers and hostile takeovers. The overwhelming thesis of these transactions seemed to focus on sacrificing long-term management objectives in exchange for short-term profits ("churn and burn"), since the breakup value of a company was always higher than its consolidated value. Drastic cost-cutting measures were destroying jobs and lives, and these effects crossed all social barriers.

The most powerful takeover force during this period was Kohlberg Kravis Roberts (KKR), a firm well-known for leveraged buyouts. KKR was responsible for the $25 billion buyout of RJR Nabisco in 1988. When a leveraged buyout occurs, the target firm is saddled with a huge debt due to the high cost of financing the buyout and the high rate of interest that must be paid on junk bonds.[5] Yet, even with the amount of capital invested in such deals, KKR and firms like it held onto their acquisitions for only three to seven years on average, at which time they "cashed out." This practice slowly started to change, however. Raiders and LBO firms alike stood up and took notice of the strategic gains to be made in business holdings, as this country's economy became increasingly global.

The 1990s witnessed a change in attitude toward mergers and acquisitions. They still occur with regularity; however, the focus now rests on strategic positioning of the company. This is a marked departure from the "get rich quick" schemes so prevalent in previous years. In his essay "The 'Barbarians' in the Boardroom," George Anders states that many corporate raiders who own large stakes in major industrial companies simply move into the boardroom. Further, these former buyout specialists are defying expectations and implementing model management practices.[6]

The new political approach to governance thus draws its strength from both the collapse of takeovers and the rise of informed institutional investors.[7] Takeovers founded on faulty visions and mismanagement exacted a toll on the American economy at the end of the 1980s. By 1992, the lesson was clear: Focus on long-term, stakeholder interests (to regain the trust of investors), and provide a forum whereby the legitimate interests of all may be addressed.

The assumption of mergers is that shareholders will be enriched by the synergies that are created. As indicated in the previous chapter, that downsizing announcements often result in increasing stock prices, similarly, merger announcements usually result in improving the stock price of the companies involved as well.

In fact, some Wall Street analysts believed that the proposed merger between Citicorp and the Travelers Group was strong enough to send the Dow through the 9000 figures. Mergers usually result in layoffs. In general, about 11 to 15 percent of the workers may lose their jobs when mergers take place. For example, 12,000 employees lost their jobs during the merger between Chase Manhattan and Chemical Bank. At the same time stock prices rose about 12 percent.[8]

THE VALUE OF A TARGET FIRM

Management needs first to understand not only the value of a target firm when combined with their own company, but also the value of a target firm when combined with other potential bidders. It is the difference between the value of a particular bidding firm's relationship with a target and the value of other bidding firms' relationships with that target that defines the size of the potential economic profits from an acquisition.

Next is the ability to keep information away from other potential bidders. One of the keys to earning superior performance in an acquisition strategy is to avoid multiple bidders for a single target. If only one bidding firm knows the information, and if this bidding firm can close the deal before the full value of the target is known, then this bidding firm may earn above-normal profits. To keep the possibility of profits alive, bidding firms must not fully reveal the value of their synergies with a target firm.

The third thing to remember is that to "win" a bidding war, a bidding firm will often have to pay a price at least equal to the full value of the target. Many times the winning bid may actually be larger than the true value of the target. This decreases the above-normal profits. Only when the market for corporate control is imperfectly competitive might it be possible for bidding firms to earn above-normal profits from implementing a merger or acquisition strategy.

Fourth is the concept of time and information. It takes time for other bidders to become aware of the economic value associated with acquiring a target; it takes time for the target to recruit other bidders; information leakage becomes more of a problem over time; and so forth. A bidding firm that begins and ends the bidding process quickly may forestall some of these processes and thereby retain some superior performance for itself from an acquisition.

RULES FOR TARGET FIRM MANAGERS

One way in which a bidder can attempt to obtain superior performance from implementing an acquisition strategy is by keeping private the information about the source and value of the strategic relatedness that exists between the bidder and target. By inviting other firms into the bidding process, the target firm increases the competitiveness of the market for corporate control, thereby increasing the probability that the value created by an acquisition will be fully captured by the target firm.

Target firm managers can engage in a wide variety of activities to delay the completions of an acquisition. Some of these actions have the effect of reducing the wealth of target firm shareholders, some have no impact on the wealth of target firm shareholders, and some increase the wealth of target firm shareholders.

Strategies that reduce the target company's value

1. Greenmail: A maneuver in which a target firm's management purchases any of the target firm's stock owned by a bidder, and does so for a price that is greater than the current market value of that stock.

2. Stand-still agreements: A contract between a target and a bidding firm wherein the bidding firm agrees not to attempt to take over the target for some period of time. It prevents the current acquisition effort from being completed, and it reduces the number of potential bidders.

3. Poison pills: Creative devices that target firms can use to prevent an acquisition. In one common poison pill maneuver, a target firm issues rights to its current stockholders, indicating that if the firm is acquired in an unfriendly takeover, it will distribute a special cash dividend to stockholders.

Strategies that do not reduce the target company's value

1. Pac-Man defense: Targets using this tactic fend off an acquisition by taking over the firm or firms bidding for them.

2. Crown jewel sale: A few of the businesses currently being operated by the target firm that a bidding firm is interested are the target firm's "crown jewels." The target firm can sell off these crown jewels, either directly to the bidding firm or by setting up a separate company to own and operate these businesses.

3. Shark repellents: A variety of relatively minor corporate governance changes that, in principle, are supposed to make it somewhat more difficult to acquire a target firm (e.g., super majority voting rules).

An imperfectly competitive market for corporate control can exist when a target is worth more to one bidder than it is to any other bidders and when no other firms are aware of this additional value. In this setting, the price of a target will rise to reflect public expectations about the value of the target. Once the target is acquired, however, the performance of the special bidder that acquires the target will be greater than expected, and this level of performance will generate above-normal profits for the shareholders of the bidding firm.

Strategies that increase the wealth of a target firm include the following:

1. White knight: Another bidding firm that agrees to acquire a particular target in the place of the original bidding firm. The entrance of a white knight into a competitive bidding contest for a target firm increases the wealth of the target firm shareholders.

2. Creation of bidding auctions: RJR Nabisco accomplished this in 1988 when it orchestrated a series of competitive bids from several potential bidders. In the end, the competition came down to a group led by the firm's top management team and the leveraged buyout firm Kohlberg Kravis Roberts. At one point in this auction, KKR increased its bid by $12 per share to a final offer of about $25 billion.[9]

3. Golden parachutes: A compensation arrangement between a firm and its senior management team that promises these individuals a substantial cash payment if their firm is acquired and they lose their jobs in the process.

BENEFITS FROM A MERGER

Usually, both companies benefit from a merger. The merged firm's profits are greater than the sum of each of the original firms. Boeing and McDonnel Douglas were considered competitors in the domestic market. Today, they are collaborators in the international commercial aircraft industry. The threat of outside competition, overall decrease in defense spending, and the effects of the worldwide recession have brought Boeing and McDonnel Douglas to work together. Boeing's market share is about 55 percent of the global market for large commercial transports. Though there has always been substantial competition in this industry, Boeing has been able to maintain its leadership primarily due to its new technologies, new markets, economies of scale, complementary skills, and its continued focus on quality and service.

An apparent increase in shareholders wealth helps the shareholders to vote favorably on the proposed merger. For example, when Pepsi and Lipton Tea established a partnership in 1991, their sales increased by about 500 percent in 1996 (from 9.5 million cases sold in 1991 to 56.2 million cases sold in 1996). They became a very successful company. Each company brought their strength into this partnership. For example, Pepsi brought a strong distribution system, a dynamic marketing strategy, and knowledge about the competitive market. Lipton brought in 108 years of tea technology, experiences, and the best-known trademark in tea. A key to successful mergers is knowledge. Past experience is good, but knowing a current market's trends will surely help any manager with deciding about a merger's future potential. Consider the previous example. The two companies designed some goals to their partnership:

1. Pepsi wanted to become the first total beverage company and Lipton represented the all-important first step.
2. This partnership was run as a joint venture.
3. The new company was managed and controlled by a board of directors to guide and continue innovating. Technical development, service, marketing, and research were all shared in thinking, innovating, and executing.[10]

Another example is the friendly merger between Proffitt's and Saks in 1998. The two companies combined by exchanging their stock. The shareholders of both companies approved the merger on 17 September 1998. A new name will emerge from this merger. This agreement will enhance the value of the shareholders and it will give the new company a better future. Proffitt's is one of the fastest growing specialty retailers in the United States. The company has been involved in many mergers and acquisitions since becoming a public company in 1987. Saks is the most recent merger. Saks operates more than fifty full-time Saks Fifth Avenue stores in areas such as Beverly Hills and Palm Beach. Once the merger is completed, Saks Fifth Avenue will become a subsidiary of Proffitt's. Proffitt's has annual sales exceeding $3.5 billion, and Saks has annual sales exceeding $2.1 billion. By combining these two companies, revenue will be in excess of $6 billion. The two companies expected to realize cost and growth exchanges of about $10 to $12 million in 1998 and $25 to $85 million by the year 2000.[11]

The two companies expect to benefit more from each other. Proffitt's will provide Saks the support and funding to successfully profit on its growth opportunities. Proffitt's expects to expand Saks on a global basis with its primary business and new retail business. They are able to share technology and system by combining the two companies. Mergers take place usually when both parties benefit from each other.

Another merger example is Berkshire Hathaway, a diversified investment company that took over the insurance company General Re Corporation. The deal was first announced on 19 June 1998. The cost of their takeover was $22 billion. The shareholders of General revoted to approve this acquisition by a 90-percent margin. Hathaway is labeled by their consistent investing in "blue chips," which is defined as a company that will provide a large rate of return on their investment.[12]

From the previous examples we can say that there are important issues that need to be considered during any merger. These include

1. The importance of knowing the new markets of both companies.
2. The implications of cultural differences between both companies.
3. Adequate resources available to complete the merger process.
4. How this merger strengthens the globalization efforts of the companies.
5. The various management skills needed for each stage of the merger.
6. The level of communications that exist between the two companies and how it can be improved.
7. Accounting and reporting systems.
8. Domestic, national, and/or international laws governing the separate companies.

We can also conclude that there are at least four main objectives of this strategy. They are as follows:

1. The strategy is designed to stay competitive in an ever-changing environment. A good example of such activity is the merger involving Alltel and 360 Communication Company. This merger will create the third largest wireless communications carrier. Alltel bought 360 Communication Company for $4.1 billion in stock enabling Alltel to become one of the biggest communication companies. Before the merger, Alltel had about 3 million customers in fourteen states. The merger with 360 Communication Company will give Alltel a 5.6-million customer base in twenty-two states. Alltel annual revenue will also increase to about $4.5 billion and its assets will increase to $8.6 billion.[13]

2. It is necessary to sustain or enhance profits by reducing cost and eliminating redundancies. The same merger listed previously could also enable Alltel to challenge one of its chief rivals, Bell South, in providing local, long distance, wireless, and Internet service. The merger was also expected to save both companies more than $110 million a year by the year 2000. Together the two companies became more powerful competitors in a broad marketplace. The two companies before the merger dealt in mid-sized and smaller communities. Now they can expand their service to larger geographical areas.

The merger is the best scenario for both companies to stay competitive in an ever-changing environment by trying to enhance profit by reducing cost. It will save both companies enormous amounts of money. It will enable them to cover a larger area and to gain more customers to maybe become the top communications carrier.

3. Another goal is to become more competitive in the global marketplace. A good example of such merger is the one between Daimler and Chrysler. The merger expects to promote better competitive power for both companies. Stockholders from both companies approved this merger in September 1998. Chrysler is the third-largest auto maker in the United States and Daimler is the largest industrial company in Germany. The two companies share reputations that are among the strongest in the world. This merger will create the world's fifth largest auto manufacturer. The deal is valued a $40 billion and is expected to generate more than $130 million in sales. This merger is also expected to save over $100 million. This would come as a result of the economies of scales from joint purchases of raw materials and savings on research and development costs. Both companies will share much information about technology. Chrysler Chairman Robert Eaton told shareholders this merger is different because it is not a desperate attempt by two weak companies to survive by leaning on each other. He continued that "this is not a merger to rationalize costs. . . . It's a merger to produce growth." He added that "we aren't destroying redundancies, we are creating opportunities." The new company will be called Daimler Chrysler AC. Because of the cultural differences of the two companies, they decided to complete the merger in a three-year period. The size and complexity of this merger offers advantages and disadvantages to this marriage. Among the advantages is the increased market share for both companies. For example, Mercedes, a subsidiary of Daimler, now has access to the minivan market, which it so badly desired and Chrysler could provide. Meanwhile, Daimler's large cash flow may allow Chrysler to enter the high-priced luxury car market. Other similar mergers include German VW merging with British Rolls-Royce, Ford's equity interest in KIA, Jaguar, and Mazda, and finally GM's ownership of Germany's Adam Opel AG.

There is a fear that Chrysler may lose some Jewish customers from Daimler's Nazi involvement in World War II. Another fear involves listing the new company on Standard and Poor's 500 stock interest. Chrysler stockholders could lose value in their stock. The two companies expect to save $1.4 billion without laying workers off or closing plants.

4. Finally, companies want to increase market share. For example, IBM spent $3.5 billion trying to vertically integrate into the personal computer software by acquiring Lotus Development Corporation. Seagram's $5.7 billion acquisition of 85 percent of Matsushita Electric Industrial's share in media giant MCA can be seen as a diversification move by Seagram. And Disney's almost $20 billion acquisition of Capital Cities/ABC can be viewed as a vertical integration move into the entertainment industry. The incidence of mergers is on the increase; it is a global phenomenon and shows little signs of abating.

ACQUISITION

An acquisition, as defined by Wheelen and Hunger, is the purchase of a corporation that is completely absorbed as an operating subsidiary or division of the acquiring corporation.[14] This volatile–nonvolatile acquisition can be between corporations of different sizes. A nonvolatile acquisition is similar to a merger in that the different corporations discuss desires for the outcome of the one company.

A hostile acquisition or takeover is where the acquiring firm ignores the other firm's pleas (demands) and begins buying stock until a controlling interest is held. This was very popular during the 1980s. The takeover target tries to block this from happening in one of three ways:

1. Starts buying its own stock to keep it from going to the takeover firm.
2. Calls in the Justice Department to initiate an antitrust suit.
3. Tries to find a merger partner to block the takeover firm.

Technological advances have created increasing pressures on smaller, single market companies to point where significant shakeout in the hub market is predicted. This is a viable reason for an acquisition. NetCo drew ComNet's attention because of the complementary technology and advancements in per port network-bridge switching technology.

COLLABORATIVE AGREEMENTS

The major advantages of mergers and acquisition are

1. Achieving the economy of scale, innovation, and speed in producing and marketing a new product or service.
2. Joint product and project research and development activities.
3. Gaining avenues to new markets and technologies.
4. Sharing the risk of such activities.
5. Taking advantage of the know-how located outside the boundaries of the companies involved.
6. Combining the strengths and weaknesses of companies involved.
7. Avoiding political risks in host countries.
8. Strengthening positions in a global market.

Contractor and Lorange in 1988 believed that many companies are motivated to pursue collaborative agreements when the synergies outweigh the problems, such as technology dissemination and reputation erosion.[15] Neighboring countries are forming regional trading blocks and a more encouraging cooperation in this competitive market. The new technologies have connected the world through advanced telephone systems, fast transportation, fax machines, and advances in computer technology and telecommunications. Technology has made the world smaller and well connected.

WHY PURSUE MERGER AND ACQUISITION?

Mergers and acquisitions have been an integral element of corporate strategy. Such collaborative arrangements have been practiced domestically and internationally. It may be necessary for interested companies to engage in merger and acquisition activity to ensure their survival. If all of a bidding firm's competitors have been able to improve through a particular type of acquisition, then failing to make such an acquisition may put a firm at a competitive disadvantage. The purpose of this merger or acquisition is not to gain competitive advantages and above-normal economic profits but rather to gain competitive parity and normal economic profits.

Free cash flow is simply the amount of cash a firm has to invest after all positive net-present-value investments in a firm's ongoing businesses have been funded. Free cash flow is created when a firm's ongoing business operations are very profitable but offer few opportunities for additional investment.

Merger and acquisition strategies can benefit managers in at least two ways. First, managers can use mergers and acquisitions to help diversify their human capital investments in their firm. Second, managers can use mergers and acquisitions to quickly increase firm size. If management compensation is closely linked to firm size, managers who increase firm size are able to increase their compensation.

Another reason why managers might continue to pursue merger and acquisition strategies is the potential that these strategies offer for generating above-normal profits for at least some bidding firms. A reason for this is the ability to cut double upper management. Since upper management receives higher wages, then the cutting of two highly paid managers leaves money open for other projects.

PROBLEMS IN THE MERGER

Despite these advantages many problems keep mergers and acquisitions from being completed and even started. Employees encounter many problems that arise from uncertainty regarding the organizational and personnel changes that usually follow mergers and acquisitions. Such stress cannot be easily avoided since many of the changes associated with mergers and acquisitions are evolutionary, and final outcomes are often not known during negotiations. Auster stated in

1987 that the number of national and international business agreements is increasing dramatically. Also in 1987 Morris and Hebert were convinced that national and international business agreements were well known for being unstable, subject to failure, and at best, difficult to govern. To combat these problems, some general considerations need to be made. These include an analysis of the target company, a reexamination of the reasons for making the acquisition, and the buyer's previous experience in acquisitions.[16]

A study by *Business Week* reported that only 17 percent of transactions from 1990 to 1995 met buyer's objectives. Fifty percent of the transactions actually eroded corporate value. A similar study by Mckinsey showed that 40 percent of all cross-border deals failed to meet expectations. It has also been found that 33 to 60 percent of all mergers ultimately destroy the value of the target company.[17]

Some of the failures resulted from

1. Incomplete data collection during the due diligence process (activities that are intended to provide information concerning the risks and opportunities associated with potential investment opportunities).
2. Poor understanding of the implications of the data in another cultural context. Marks and Mirvis in 1992 noticed that most companies believed that they had a relatively thorough understanding of key areas, such as market growth and technology, but were less comfortable with the implications of foreign laws, business practices, and cultural traditions.
3. Not using appropriate resources during and after the integration process. The acquiring company tries to use too many markets or too many products with too few resources.
4. Lack of communication. Companies may downplay issues or show indecisiveness when naming new leaders or managers in the new organization, contributing to employee distrust or unease.

Instead of concentrating only on top level strategic issues, the acquiring company needs to examine strengths, weaknesses, and unique characteristics in the individual companies. In order for the newly acquired company to grow and gain loyalty to its new structure, an integration management team should create small teams to conduct analyses and make recommendations. These teams should consist of members of both companies. They can identify present structures and practices, get rid of redundancies, and develop strategies for communication and training.

The target company's employees are invaluable to the integration process. They know their markets, customers, government rules and regulations, and their culture. Both companies must work together in order to make the merger or acquisition succeed.

CULTURAL BARRIERS

In different countries a person can find different cultures. When a company is trying to make a deal with another company in a foreign country, then each of the companies should have a language that is of equal fluency between them. An interpreter may be helpful, but unfortunately some vocabulary between countries can be mistaken. For instance, in the Japanese language there is no word for the word "no." When a Japanese person wishes to express "no," then the phrases that are used are, "It's very difficult," and "We will think about it." In America these phrases mean that the person still has hope and therefore goes on and tries to convince the other company. Also, in the Japanese language the English term decision making has no direct translation. Also consider the Daimler and Chrysler merger. It could be difficult to blend the two separate cultures the two companies have. The laws in Germany differ slightly from those in the United States. One example of a difficult issue is how to deal with codetermination or worker participation at the board level in Germany.

Forms of intercompany culture should be looked at. In the United States many managers have an open door policy and prefer oral communication to written. In France, however, corporate culture is very formal. Written communication is always given and a closed door policy is administered.

In Latin American countries, how much information is shared depends on how well the other individual is known. This is accomplished at the beginning of the negotiations. Many business people from this country will not even begin negotiations or talk about the company until certain pleasantries are over with. This is how an atmosphere of mutual trust and respect is established. In Asian countries no personal questions are asked, even if the negotiators have known each other for a long time.

LEGAL BARRIERS

Host country definitions of what a national, resident, and nonresident are may cause some problems if the host country has certain restrictions on staffing, ownership, and building restrictions. Mexico, for instance, required all foreign company partners to only hold minority ownership until recently. In 1994, Egypt informed Owens Corning that if they were planning on building a factory, they could not own the land that the factory would be built on. Saudi nationals must fill technical positions in Saudi Arabia. Expatriates cannot staff foreign-owned companies in Nigeria.

Some localities require that any products sold in the area must contain a certain percentage of the area parts or resources contained within. In Kenya, for example, Unilever had to alter its detergent formulas to use the local soda ash and indigenous oils.

POLITICAL RISK

Government's instability has become the greatest threat to countries that would like foreign investment. When a company checks into the country's background, a company must look at the stability of the current government (e.g., how long it has been in power, what are its political motivations, how much public support does it have). A government attitude about foreign investment (past and current) should also be looked at. If the government has a habit of changing its mind about foreign country investment, then a company should consider its possible position for future investment within that country.

CASE STUDY: THE BELL ATLANTIC–TCI MERGER

Consider the merger between Bell Atlantic, the most aggressive of the Baby Bells, and TCI, a cable company that serves 10 million cable subscribers. The cost of this merger was estimated to be $22 billion. The key players in the deal were Ray Smith and John Malone. Ray Smith assumed the position of chairman at Bell Atlantic six years after the breakup of AT&T. John Malone serves as chief executive at TCI, a large and very successful cable company. During May 1993, Smith approached Malone with the idea to merge their two companies (Bell Atlantic and TCI, along with its sister company, Liberty Media). Having come to a general agreement on the terms of the plan in August, Smith and Malone announced the deal on a New York hotel stage on 13 October 1998. This was an all-stock deal. For Bell Atlantic, the price of the merger started at $11.8 billion in its own stock (220 million shares at a set price of $54) for the majority of TCI's assets.[18]

The aspects of this mega merger had drawn its share of praise and criticism. A proponent of the Bell Atlantic–TCI mix was Representative Ron Wyden, a Democrat from Oregon. Representative Wyden saw a "boon for consumers" based on the argument of procompetitiveness. He viewed the merger as the opportunity "to create more choices, to promote technological development, and to keep the bedrock of telecommunications, which is universal service."[19] Malone and Smith argued also that their deal is procompetitive. They stated that their merger will accelerate development of the industry and give consumers new choices.[20]

Senator Howard Metzenbaum (D-Ohio), chairman of the Senate antitrust subcommittee, among others, had objected to such a merger by calling it a "double whammy for consumers." Senator Metzenbaum asserted that if this merger took place, overcharges for cable and telephone service should be expected.

Bell Atlantic and TCI agreed to join forces and reap the benefits of synergy. There was a price, however. With increased technology comes an increased cost, especially when one considers Bell Atlantic's prodigious use of fiber optics.

EVALUATION OF THE LITERATURE

We are currently in the midst of a merger boom that rivals that of the 1980s. The price for such deals is high, as are the risks. Edward Kerschner, chief investment strategist at PaineWebber, acknowledges this. Yet he and others considered the 1991 crop of deals to be generally sound (despite their high prices) because companies are pursuing logical business strategies within closely related fields.[21]

The literature indicates that past leadership styles used before the merger should be reviewed for relevance.[22] Also, the point is made (especially as it relates to Bell Atlantic and TCI) that changes in technology and regulatory procedures have driven the recent spate of merger activity. As long as the literature keeps abreast of these changes and the strategic effects on the market are properly addressed, society can be well served by prudent decision making.

THE FUTURE

Some analysts consider the frothy atmosphere, in which companies are issuing billions of dollars of stock based on their visions of the future, as a sign of a dangerously overheated stock market.[23] In the new marketplace of ideas, debate will replace debt as active shareholders identify specific operating policies for their target corporations and then invent new mechanisms to get their message across to management.[24] New issues and new questions are raised with every merger. In the case of Bell Atlantic and TCI, the question of competitiveness and privacy in a restructured market was raised.

We can conclude that mergers, acquisitions, and takeovers are very important. They deserve constant vigil from lawmakers, regulatory agencies, and the media. Mergers present tremendous opportunities that society can benefit from.

Due to changes in the business environment such as increased global competition, changes in customer demand, increases in employee mobility, etc., companies have begun forming cooperative relationships with their competitors. Companies that are not large enough or do not have the resources to succeed on their own in this kind of environment are forced to unite with their competition. This can be good in that it gives insight into the productivity and efficiencies of the rival company. This arrangement can also add to company's resources and lessen its risks. The time and effort to create a workable environment is one of the disadvantages.[25]

The Carlson Companies, a worldwide network of hotels, restaurants and cruise ships, plans to merge with Thomas Cook, one of the oldest and best known names in travel, at an estimated $1 billion value. This merger would make the two companies' annual sales about $42.5 billion. The intent of the merger was to establish a huge leisure travel group in the UK and also to own a part of their financial services, said Douglas Cody, the Carlson's communication director.[26]

P&G'S HOTTEST NEW PRODUCT:
P&G *BUSINESS WEEK* ON-LINE

Procter & Gamble had set a goal to double its net sales by 2006 to $70 billion, but has missed its growth targets ever since. Because of this, P&G was forced to seek external advice. It has begun a structural shift, moving away from internal themes such as cost cutting and engaging in a global marketing blitz. This has come to be called Organization 2005, a shuffling of the hierarchy and a new product development process. The traditional bureaucracy will be shaped into seven global business units organized by category. They will develop and sell products all over the world.

Procter & Gamble is counting on about $8 billion from emerging international markets in order to reach their goal, which does not look very promising due to economic slumps overseas. But new CEO Durk Jager has stepped into the role of a champion of the global focus and is preaching the new structure to P&G managers.

GM has announced that it is merging its North American and international operations under a single president in a $14.5 billion investment over the next five years. This reorganization is like Ford's consolidation of its North American and European operations four years ago. These two organizations would be replaced by four regional divisions who would all report to the same person, G. Richard Wagoner, who will then be the head of a $135 billion per year business. The goal of the merger is to get rid of many redundant or overlapping committees. Mr. Wagoner will preside over a single strategy board for all global vehicle operations. In Asia the focus will be on increasing the market share in order to remains the world's largest auto manufacturer. GM only holds 4 percent of the Asian car market. GM increased equity in Suzuki Motors to 10 percent. In Latin America the market is very volatile, so production needs to be cut. In Europe the division is in a turnaround process and is the largest foreign operation.[27]

HOW TO PREPARE FOR SUCH ACTIVITIES

There are many ways to lessen the barriers and risks a company might face from investing in a potential market, such as the following:

1. Understand the market, its needs, and expectations.
2. Collect information that is reliable and relevant. This information should help in making decisions.
3. Understand the culture and how to conduct oneself during negotiations.
4. Find out who are the real decision makers in the deals.
5. Assess political risk.
6. In many countries, foreign ownership of land is prohibited; therefore, try to lease for a long enough period.
7. Show in the negotiation stage that you are a trustworthy partner. Make it explicit that you will obey the law of the land and that you will contribute positively to the host country economy.
8. In case conflicts arise, suggest an arbitration process to settle and clarify any disputes.
9. Make sure that you have the right to transfer a good portion of the earnings at the end of the year.
10. Understand that the market is full of opportunities.

ISSUES FACING MANAGEMENT
IN THE TWENTY-FIRST CENTURY

Today cross-border transactions, mergers, and acquisitions have become ever increasing. This fact, however, has not stopped the risks that are involved. Nor have all the barriers been lifted that could potentially help these proceedings. Not only do cultural diversity and language play a part in these intrinsic deals, but also financial, legal, and political differences. A crucial strategic issue confronting American business executives is how do we compete in the future. Complications arise due to the perception of competition based on the idea of a relationship. Aggravation by the tremendous economic changes taking place in today's global market and the expanding interdependence of national economies adds to the complication. A result is that many U.S. firms are trying to compete in tomorrow's global marketplace with yesterday's understanding of competition. New arrangements, such as a strategic alliance, have emerged between companies to have a more comprehensive form of cooperation.

It is essential to understand that mergers and acquisitions have changed tremendously in the last two decades. From the 1960s through the 1980s, mergers and acquisitions were done mainly for expansion or diversification purposes. In that period of time, management had the resources and adopted the mergers as a corporate strategy to increase sizes and market share of the company. The merger was vertical, horizontal, or conglomerate.

The mergers and acquisitions of 1993 through the year 2000 are completely different. The merger is merely done for sharing the research and development activity, sharing technology, expansion, and for building competitive advantage. Most of the mergers were completed to create sustainable competitive advantage in a global market. The examples that were mentioned in this chapter are reflections of these types of mergers and acquisitions, including the merger of Mercedes-Benz with Chrysler, McDonnel-Douglas with Boeing, Pepsi with Lipton Tea, and Alltel with 360 Communication.

Consider the time period between 1980 and 1993. This period witnessed a divestment in so many companies who had diversified just a few years ago as a type of expansion. These companies discovered that their expansion positions were not necessarily appropriate, and therefore they divested their strategic business units that did not match their expected performance. This period, therefore, witnessed many attempted takeovers and hostile takeovers. Because hostile takeovers and putting the company into play were very costly strategies to corporations who were going through restructuring, this affected the target companies, but also society and the government. Many states established laws and regulations to make it difficult for companies or corporate raiders to take advantage of target companies. The author was directly involved in preparing and testifying in support of Senate Bill 1310 in Pennsylvania. This bill was presented to restrict hostile takeovers in the state of Pennsylvania. It is considered the toughest bill in the country. After long debate in the Capitol Hill of Pennsylvania, the Senate decided that this bill was in the best interest of the state, and therefore they approved it to be Pennsylvania Act of 36, 1990. The appendix attached to Chapter 8 contains the full written testimony of the author.

NOTES

1. "Mad Dogs and Mergers," *Economists* (15 November 1997), 18.
2. Thomas L. Wheelen and J. David Hunger, *Strategic Management and Business Policy*, 7th ed. (Upper Saddle River, N.J.: Prentice Hall, 2000).
3. John Pound, "Beyond Takeovers: Politics Comes to Corporate Control," *Harvard Business Review* 70 (March–April 1992): 83–93.

4. Randall Smith, "Higher Stock Prices Are Feeding a Revival of Merger Activity," *The Wall Street Journal*, 14 October 1993, A1.

5. Ken Hanley, "Hostile Takeovers and Methods of Defense: A Stockholder Analysis," *Journal of Business Ethics* 11 (1992): 901.

6. George Anders, "The 'Barbarians' in the Boardroom," *Harvard Business Review* 70 (July–August 1992): 79–87.

7. Pound, "Beyond Takeovers," 87.

8. William Beaver, "Is the Stakeholder Model Dead?" *Business Horizons* 42, issue 2 (March–April 1999): 8.

9. Peter Kostant, "Exit, Voice and Loyalty in the Course of Corporate Governance," *Journal of Socio-Economics* 28, 3 (1999): 204.

10. Andrea Foote, "Tea by Two (Pepsi Lipton Tea Partnership)," *Beverage World* 115 (May 1996): 36; according to Eric Reinhard, Pepsi's business unit general manager, "General Re Shareholders Approve Hathaway Merger," *Renters Limited* (September 1998).

11. Harvey Meyer, "My Enemy, My Friend," *Journal of Business Strategy* 9 (September–October 1998): 42–45.

12. Ibid.

13. Stephanie N. Mehta, "Alltel Confirms Plan to Buy 360 in Stock Deal," *Wall Street Journal*, March 17, 1998, B6.

14. Wheelen and Hunger, *Strategic Management and Business Policy*.

15. Cited by Cynthia Wood and Richard Porter, "International Mergers and Acquisitions: New Rules for Emerging Markets," in *International Business Strategies: Economic Development Issues*, ed. Abbass F. Alkhafaji and Zakaria El-Sadek (Apollo, Pa.: Closson Press, 1997).

16. Ibid., 6.

17. P. L. Zweig, "The Case against Mergers," *Business Week*, 30 October 1995, 122–130.

18. J. L. Roberts, D. Kneale, and L. Landro, "Bell Atlantic and TCI Are Poised to Share New Interactive World," *The Wall Street Journal*, 14 October 1993, A1; and Albert R. Hunt, "Bell Atlantic–TCI: A Merger Democrats Should Like," *The Wall Street Journal*, 21 October 1993, A23.

19. Jolie Soloman, "Big Brother's Holding Company," *Newsweek*, 25 October 1993, 38–43.

20. Randall Smith, "Higher Stock Prices Are Feeding a Revival of Merger Activity," *The Wall Street Journal*, 14 October 1993, A1.

21. Joseph B. White and Gregory L. White, "GM to Announce Major Reorganization; Wagoner to Lead Merged Operations," *The Wall Street Journal*, 6 October 1998, A8; Robert L. Simison, "GM to Carry Out $14.5 Billion Plan to Expand Globally over Five Years," *The Wall Street Journal*, 5 October 1998, A27.

22. Harvey Meyer, "My Enemy, My Friend," *Journal of Business Strategy* 9, 5 (September–October 1998) 42–45.

23. Ibid.

24. Pound, "Beyond Takeovers."

25. Adapted from Meyer, "My Enemy, My Friend."

26. Adapted from "Carlson and Thomas Cook to Merge Leisure Travel in Britain," *The New York Times*, 6 October 1998.

27. White and White, "GM to Announce Major Reorganization."

Chapter 11

The Stakeholder Concept and Its Contemporary Influence

Stakeholder participation in corporate governance provides a basis for better internal control and less government regulation. This chapter will examine the stakeholder concept and how management perceives its importance in corporate governance. Two hypotheses are proposed: The first states that the stakeholder, or corporate constituency concept, is a reemerging concept that is articulated today as a result of an evolutionary process. It is true that the actual birth of the word only recently occurred (in 1963). But the corporation's relationship to society and societal liens held by stakeholders upon corporations has been evolving for decades. The second is that as the level of management pertaining to power and responsibility increases, the level of acceptance of stakeholder participation decreases. For example, Sternberg in 1996 argued against the stakeholder concept, saying that it is the corporation's responsibility to maximize long-term owner value.[1]

It is asserted that although stakeholder influence has been legally recognized for over a century, upper level management has only recently begun to recognize its virtues as a tool that can be used for proper corporate governance. Companies do not exist in a vacuum. Many groups interconnect with the corporation and have a vested interest in its activities. They are the constituencies that affect, or are affected by, the achievement of corporate purpose and objectives.

Modern times impose a need for balance in all arenas of human endeavor. Businesses are not exempt from this conjecture of working towards balance between economic objectives and the broader needs of society. They do not exist in a vacuum, nor are they static. Many groups are interconnecting circles within this sphere. There are many groups with an interest in a corporation's activities. These constituencies either affect or are affected by the achievements of the corporate purpose and objectives. To elaborate, a "stakeholder refer[s] to those groups who have a direct interest in the survival of the organization and without whose support the organization may cease to exist."[2] The constituency circles presented to the corporation in the scales of balance include stockholders, employees, governments, unions, management, major suppliers, major creditors, major customers, competitors, communities, and community leaders.[3] In order for the company to do the right thing, it should balance the interest of all stakeholders and not just the concerns of the stockholders. The concept of corporate responsibility to societal requirements has coursed throughout the historical development of modern capitalist economics.

The assertion that the stakeholder concept is a revolutionary, new theory is inaccurate. It is true that the concept was defined three decades ago, but the corporation's relationship to society (as groups of affected constituencies), and societal liens held by stakeholders upon the corporation, have been evolving for many decades.

THE RECENT HISTORY OF THE STAKEHOLDER CONCEPT

Stakeholder theory emerged in the 1970s through people like William R. King, David I. Cleland, S. Turnbull, W. Rothschild, and Igor Ansoff. Rogene A. Buchholz feels that if the stakeholder concept is to be taken seriously, the corporation must become a multipurpose institution producing economic and social betterment.[4] The author in 1984 and 1989 expanded the stakeholder concept further to include a stakeholder board of directors, which would establish a business code of ethics and a corporate social audit.[5] Freeman and Gilbert expounded upon three levels of analysis useful in the development of the stakeholder model: the rational level, the process level, and the transaction level.[6]

The *rational* level is a view of the business in its larger environment. This deals with the relationships between the firm and the general stakeholders, or those groups who, generally speaking, can affect the firm. The specific stakeholders within each general grouping should be identified, as should their specific stake(s). It is important to note that the stakeholders and their respective stakes are not absolute and likely will change over time. An important point is that stakeholders often have multiple roles that can result in conflict. Networks and coalitions are also typical of the relationships between stakeholders and stakeholder groups. Freeman and Gilbert point out that stakeholders are multidimensional in that their stake may be an equity interest, that of a "kibitzer," or a market stake, and that those categories are to be analyzed in terms of the influence the particular stakeholder may actually have. They discuss the crucial difference between what the firm perceives a stakeholder's interest to be and what the interest or stake actually is. If the two do not have some common ground in this area, it will be difficult, if not impossible, for the firm to act in a manner that is responsive to the stakeholders' interest.[7]

The *process* level focuses on how the organization deals with the stakeholders. It is necessary to evaluate the procedures and processes used to fit with the external environment. Three analysis proposals are provided for the evaluation at this level: portfolio analysis, long-range strategic planning process with pertinent stakeholder related questions included, and the stakeholder audit.

The *transaction* level is referred to as the "bottom line" for stakeholder management. It encompasses particular questions relating to how managers and stakeholders interact and what resources are available for use in the interactions. It is this level where the actual face-to-face stakeholder management takes place. This is also where cooperation or confrontation will occur.

Interwoven within the three levels of analysis is the issue of business ethics. At the rational level, the business should address two areas of ethical concern. The business will at least in part determine what networks it will be a part of and the institutional identity it desires to develop. The second area is the precise determination of the stakeholders' actual stakes and generally the chosen responses to them. The process level contains two additional ethical concerns. These are the establishment of rules and procedures for dealing with each stakeholder and how the firm copes with routine matters. Freeman and Gilbert recommend that the development of an ethical code would be beneficial at this level. The authors also expand the concept of stakeholders to include internal elements as well as external.

The concept of external affairs (EA) managers is an expansion of the rather outdated model of the public affairs manager. It is proposed that the role of the external affairs manager should be as an advocate of both the stakeholder and the firm itself. As such, it is a boundary-spanning function where information is the most essential element and communication is the key to success. Freeman and Gilbert close with an agenda for theory and practice.[8] They list four areas for research and practice. They are (1) a need for experiments by managers in attempting to improve stakeholder relationships; (2) a need for systematic examination of the connection between ethics and strategy; (3) the concept of management as having a fiduciary responsibility to stakeholders; and (4) the development of management theory in terms of its cohesiveness with the human purpose.

In the theory development forum "Shifting Paradigms: Societal Expectations and Corporate Performance," from the *Academy of Management Review* in 1994, Thomas Donaldson and Lee E. Preston observed that there is a lack of cohesiveness regarding the use and description of the concepts of "stakeholder," "stakeholder model," "stakeholder management," and "stakeholder theory."[9] They have concluded that the three aspects of stakeholder theory—descriptive accuracy, instrumental power, and normative validity—are interrelated and mutually supportive and that the normative base of the theory is the most fundamental. The authors stated that stakeholder theory is unarguably descriptive. It presents a model describing the corporation as a constellation of cooperative and competitive interest possessing intrinsic value. The model may be tested for descriptive accuracy and can serve as a framework for testing any empirical claims. The theory is also instrumental. There is an important connection between the practice of stakeholder management and the achievement of corporate goals. They further state that the fundamental basis of stakeholder theory is normative and involves acceptance of the fact that stakeholders have legitimate interests in corporate activity. This is identified by their interest in the corporation and that interests of stakeholders are of intrinsic value and their merits are not founded solely on their ability to further others' interests.

The authors also propose that stakeholder theory is managerial. Stakeholder management requires simultaneous attention to the legitimate interests of all appropriate stakeholders. Stakeholder theory does not

1. Presume that managers possess the sole right to corporate control and governance.
2. Resolve who stakeholders are or evaluate their claims to corporate stakes.
3. Imply that all stakeholders have equal say in processes or decisions.

Donaldson and Preston stated that an analysis of the stakeholder model shows that there is no one interest that takes priority over the others and that all participants expect to benefit from their association with the organization.[10]

Interestingly, they suggest that many firms are actually practicing stakeholder theory now, whether they know it or not. They found that a significant number of managers believe that they must satisfy a wide variety of stakeholders other than the shareholders. This assertion is buoyed by the fact that at least twenty-nine states have adopted statutes that in essence permit boards of directors to focus concern on a host of nonshareholder constituents, including employees, creditors, suppliers, customers, and local communities. These statutes have in turn been supported by the courts and are in effect establishing "stakeholder law" by recognizing the impact of business on constituents other than those historically recognized.

In 1992, the American Law Institute report, *Principles of Corporate Governance*, affirms the central corporate objective of "enhancing corporate profit and shareholder gain."[11] However, it extends qualifications of that stance by making it clear that the corporation must abide by law, and may "take into account ethical considerations" and engage in philanthropy, "even if corporate profit and shareholder gain are not thereby enhanced." The commentary continues: "Such behavior is not only appropriate, but desirable. Corporate officials are not less morally obliged than any other citizens to take ethical considerations into account." Making the case that stakeholder theory is normatively based, Donaldson and Preston targeted two points for consideration regarding implications for managers: (1) recognition of stakeholders by managers (and other stakeholders); and (2) the role of managers and management function.[12]

Assuming that managers select activities and direct resources in order to benefit stakeholders, the problem then becomes one of how stakeholders are identified. They contend that stakeholders are identified by the actual or potential harms and benefits that they receive or expect to receive as a result of the organization's actions or inaction. Their belief is that the ultimate managerial implication is that managers should attempt to respond to stakeholders because it is a moral requirement of management function. Their conclusion is that "the most thoughtful analysis of why stakeholder management might be causally related to corporate performance resort to normative arguments."[13]

EVOLUTION OF CORPORATE LAW

Corporate law has its roots in the nineteenth century with the integral purpose of serving public issues such as education and utility regulation.[14] But, state issued corporate charters have produced a conflict of claims throughout their history. Corporate directors have been charged with maximization of shareholder wealth, but they are also charged with meeting changing and conflicting social responsibilities. The corporation is not a social institution, but it does have social responsibilities.[15]

The legislative power of the state is to enact laws that regulate corporate charters, and to promote the order, safety, health, and overall welfare of society.[16] The states are protected by the Constitution and thus are an outgrowth of the federal government system.[17] The judicial branch, vis-à-vis the Supreme Court, has opined the nonshareholder (stakeholder) influence for over one hundred years.

In 1876 in *Munn v. Illinois*, the Supreme Court found public use of a corporation considerable when a corporation provided free social goods and services for nonshareholders (i.e., employees), and the court disallowed a shareholder complaint. In 1914, insurance companies were deemed affected with a public interest.[18] The court "recognized the central public interest underlying the earliest corporate charters."[19]

After 1900 the court began to clearly define the right and responsibilities of the corporation (and thus management). In *Dodge et al. v. Ford Motor Co. et al.*,[20] the court stated, "A business corporation is organized primarily for the profit of the stockholders."[21] Henry Ford's intent was to increase employment and spread the benefits of his industrial company to the "greatest possible number, to help them build up their lives and homes."[22] The precedent permitted Ford's duty and in fact the duty of the stockholders owed to the general public. Still later, the court stated, in the case of a lawyer, that "duty to society as well as to his client involves many relevant social, economic, political and philosophical considerations."[23]

Social pressures of the 1920s and 1930s influenced the court and the government and resulted in increased regulation. The ever-changing definition of corporate governance continued to evolve. The responsibilities and liabilities of corporate boards of directors were continually examined in light of the dynamics of world events and societal needs. The impact of the increasing number of occurrences of mergers and hostile takeovers in the 1980s was profound, particularly upon this evolving definition.

The Business Judgment Rule protects the right of the board of directors to consider stakeholders as having an interest in corporate performance, as long as their decision to do so is absent of bad faith, fraud, or self-action.[24] In fact, directors have been deemed "reasonable" in taking stakeholders' interests into account. The rule allows the development of strategies that would protect the shareholders, employees, and management. This precedent is repeated throughout the law. In *Revlon, Inc. v. MacAndrews and Forbes Holdings*,[25] the court held that concern for various stakeholder constituencies is allowed when directors are faced with takeover (which is assumed to be hostile), as long as the related stock benefit of the shareholders is considered.

A claiming suit that involved T. Boone Pickens in a hostile takeover attempt further enhanced these stakeholder characterizations. The board of director's duty owed to the shareholders as well as the allowance of stakeholder consideration was stated in the court's opinion in

Unocal Corp. v. Mesa Petroleum Co.[26] Though the fundamental duty of the board is to protect the stockholders from harm, through interpretation of the Business Judgment Rule, the Court empowered the board to take into consideration the impact of a hostile takeover upon constituencies other than shareholders. Specified constituents included creditors, customers, employees, and the community in general.

The evolution from Ford (limiting the corporation's power to introduce stakeholder claims in their balance) to sanctioning such consideration is illustrated in recent law. In *Paramount Communications, Inc. v. Time Inc.* (1989), the court opined that the board's prime (but not only) duty was to maximize shareholder wealth. The board of directors was not obliged to change their strategies (including stakeholder consideration), to exclude the stakeholder in the balance.[27] After years of proxy battles within America's corporations, at least large shareholders are finding that managers are beginning to take them seriously. Investors outraged by lousy financial results slammed the door behind chief executives at General Motors, IBM, American Express, and Westinghouse. There have been two rule changes by the Securities and Exchange Commission (SEC), America's securities regulator, which have given shareholders newfound strength. One change is that fuller disclosure of executive compensation packages has put managers on the defensive. The other has made it easier for shareholders to communicate with each other and with managers and has removed barriers to effective shareholder action.[28] Active participation of the stakeholder in corporate governance will enhance the voice of the board in the organizational affairs. This will increase the effectiveness of the board and will satisfy shareholders and investors.

The Supreme Court has not provided the only discourse on the evolution of the stakeholder approach to corporate governance. The academic community has provided prolific amounts of literature. This literature builds the foundation for the hypothesis that top level management (i.e., corporate powers) do not currently embrace the rightful claim made by stakeholders. In 1994, academia proposed that the defined term "stakeholder" is not within the corporate power's working vocabulary.

Berle and Means studied the balance of duty owed to stockholders and to society. Among their now famous conclusions was one that is pertinent to this study. Berle suggested that the powers of all affected groups be enhanced, including stakeholders (specifically employees and consumers).[29] Restated, a balance is needed between the social responsibility owed by the corporate enterprise and the board's understanding of what they owe.[30] Milton wrote, "Sound consumer and labor relations increasingly have been made complimentary goals to the objective of profit maximization."[31] When the balance is uneven, the corporate loss may not only include fewer profits, but also a weakening ability to attract bright young minds. Mahoney concludes that social responsibility and financial growth are inseparable. One without the other is impossible today. Yet a clear, positive relationship between an increase in profitability and an increase in corporate social responsibility has not been proven.[32] Proof of a positive relationship would perhaps be the greatest influence on top management to accept stakeholder theory.

Another step in the evolutionary process has been the dramatic increase in the corporate social responsibility of a board committee. This type of committee was nonexistent in 1971, but within five years, they existed in approximately 5 percent of corporations. By 1982, over one-third of the Fortune 1350 corporations had a public–corporate responsibility committee.[33] In fact, Johnson & Johnson cited their central responsibilities in their credo, including, in order, the customer, the employees, communities, and stockholders.[34]

A Harris survey conducted in 1987 illustrates that society is clear on prioritizing social responsibility and profit maximization. The survey results indicated that nearly nine of ten adults surveyed agreed that corporations should be required to notify employees and communities in advance of closing an operations facility.[35]

Posner and Schmidt illustrated that management has a different view from that of the public. They polled top level management regarding the importance of various stakeholders. A high degree of importance was placed (equally) on customers and employees. A moderate degree (4.5 on a scale of 7) was given to the general public, and, curiously, the same weight, (4.5) was given to stockholders.[36]

THE STAKEHOLDER CONCEPT

The Stanford Research Institute (SRI) is credited with creating the word "stakeholder" in 1963. The term was used to counter the notion that stockholders were the only group to which management of a corporation needed to respond. The original definition of stakeholder was "those groups without whose support the organization would cease to exist."[37] Since 1963 the stakeholder concept has continued to develop, and the academic community has extolled its virtues. R. Edward Freeman in his book, *Strategic Management: A Stakeholder Approach*, defines stakeholders as "those groups who can affect, or are affected by, the achievement of an organization's purpose."[38] Sturdivant and Vernon-Wortzel define a stakeholder as "any individual or group who feels that they have a stake in the consequences of management's decisions and who have the power to influence current or future decisions."[39] The definition used here is that "stakeholders are those groups who have direct interest in the survival of the organization and without their support the organization would cease to exist."[40]

Stakeholders primarily consist of a mixture of those who have external or internal and direct or indirect influence on a corporation. For instance, a director on a board would have both internal and direct influence since he or she would be in charge of corporate governance of the company. Alternatively, a social activist who is a member of a group like the Sierra Club would only be able to influence a company externally and indirectly. The issue is that all stakeholders have a stake, to some degree, in a corporation and should therefore be allowed some commensurate degree of influence on that corporation.

The business community, especially managers, has not embraced the stakeholder concept and is just beginning to comprehend its implications. After accepting the total quality management philosophy, companies established quality teams. They paid close attention to customer needs. Those two groups are the major part of the stakeholder approach. If you take good care of your employees by empowering them, and satisfy customers, the financial issues will be taken care of.

WHY SHOULD CORPORATIONS CONSIDER STAKEHOLDERS?

Stakeholders are many in number and can wield a considerable amount of power. Companies that do not give stakeholders the attention they desire may find themselves out of business or with a substantial lower market share. During the 1970s U.S. automakers were producing automobiles of questionable quality, which caused many consumers to turn to higher quality Japanese automobiles. U.S. automakers have been working for the past fifteen years to overcome this problem, which has cost them over 25 percent of their market share. The government has stiffened pollution controls in recent years. If companies do not comply with the local communities, regulators such as the EPA, International Environmental Concern (ISO 14000), and the media will scrutinize them.

Sturdivant and Vernon-Wortzel focus on the recent problems with nuclear power plants. They give examples of how stakeholders became opponents of nuclear power after the Three Mile Island radioactive leak. Demonstrators locked themselves to chain-link fences that surrounded the nuclear plant under the watchful eye of the media. The public-interest groups have prevented nuclear plants from coming "on line," and the Nuclear Regulatory Commission (NCR) closed the Peach Bottom plant because workers were sleeping on the job.[41]

These examples give some indication of the effect stakeholders can have over corporations. Corporations should consider stakeholders because stakeholders expect corporations to be socially responsible. Social responsibility encompasses the economic responsibilities of a business to produce goods and services, which are of value to society, so it can repay its creditors and stockholders. It has legal responsibilities to obey laws and ethical responsibilities to follow the generally held beliefs about how one should act in society. It also has discretionary responsibilities, which are voluntary obligations that a corporation assumes. Each stakeholder falls under one or more of these umbrellas; therefore, it is very difficult for a company to avoid consideration of stakeholders at any planning or decision stage.

CORPORATE GOVERNANCE

Corporate governance is a concept that refers to the mode of structure and power that determines the rights and responsibilities of various groups involved with operating an organization. Since the mid-nineteenth century, American corporations have been chartered by the individual states with the understanding that the purpose of any corporation is to serve the public interest. Companies that supplied transportation, water, insurance, and banking were among the first to be incorporated by the issuance of state charters. Up until the twentieth century, state legislatures passed laws of incorporation that were very general. Some corporate promoters were even allowed to design and write their own charters. The overall result of their creativity was that noncontrolling shareholders were exploited and oppressed. The net result was that the federal government began passing legislation in an attempt to protect the nonmajority shareholders. This in turn led to more standardized rules regarding the issuance of charters by individual state governments.

The dawn of the twentieth century ushered in a different conception of the fiduciary duties of boards of directors. No longer could boards do what was in the best interest of the company without considering the effect of its actions and decisions on all the stakeholders of the company. The fiduciary role could be summed up by three main criteria:

1. Courts recognized the underlying central public interest of corporate charters.
2. The director's duty was to act in the best interest of the corporation; this was considered synonymous with the maximization of the current stock price.
3. The shareholder was not to be left without protection; the directors had to consider the interest of others who had a stake in the company when taking action or making decisions.

Traditional (agency) theory of corporate governance evolved to include the shareholders as owners of the corporation. As owners their role is to provide capital by buying shares of stock and to elect a board of directors whose loyalties lie with the shareholders. The board of directors' main role is to oversee and evaluate the performance of management and to take corrective action when performance fails or falters. Part of the board's responsibility is to evaluate management's performance and to adjust the level of compensation to a level commensurate with performance. There has been mounting criticism that this system of control has failed to achieve the goal of protecting shareholder interests.

One of the difficulties with the operation of traditional governance theory has been that in the United States there are many shareholders with small and/or extremely diverse holdings, and historically these investors are not capable of exerting sufficient influence to sway boards of directors to comply with their obligations. According to Berle and Means, there was a shift in corporate ownership away from the owners and into the hands of professional, self-perpetuating managers who picked their own successors and have been answerable mainly to themselves.[42]

The trend in American corporate ownership since World War II has been toward short-term profit taking by small investors whose interest in a corporation was to see how fast their investment could produce a return. It soon became obvious to managers that if they were to be able to protect their own futures, control of the corporations would have to fall to them. And take control they did: Frederick E. Rowe, Jr. explained in a 15 February 1993 article in *Forbes* magazine that most managers (and boards) have taken the attitude that "if you don't like the way we run the company, sell your stock."[43] Thus chastised, the shareholder is left with two options; sue for fraud, waste, or mismanagement, or propose an alternative slate of directors and mount a proxy fight. Both are expensive and very difficult to pursue with no promise that the desired outcome will be achieved. What is needed is a method of balancing power and control of the corporation to provide equity for the shareholders, while also protecting the interests of other stakeholders such as employees, suppliers, customers, as well as government, union management, competitors, and communities, among others (see Figure 11.1).

Stockholders are faced with the challenge of controlling the actions of and removing ineffective and incompetent managers. One mechanism that is designed to give shareholders a chance to voice their approval or disapproval of management is the stockholder meeting. In the past, these meetings were little more than an opportunity for stockholders to get heated up and vent a little steam. But, with the SEC's new proxy and executive compensation disclosure rules, there is a new

Figure 11.1
The Stakeholder Model

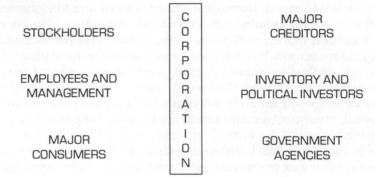

era of corporate governance. According to Louis M. Thompson, Jr., president and CEO of the National Investor Relations Institute, "Shareholders now have greater access to proxy statements. They can nominate dissident board candidates along with the selected management nominees. They can vote on individual proxy proposals. And they can communicate among themselves without first filing with the SEC. This is truer in today's technology than ever before. Shareholders now have greater access to proxy statements and other important issues in the organization through the Internet, and e-mail." In short, shareholders now have a greatly enhanced opportunity to involve themselves in company operations."[44] When these changes are coupled with the newfound direction of institutional investors to target boards of directors with their concern about corporate performance and other corporate governance issues, boards realize they must address investor relations. This is a role that top management handled in the past. Does this new strength and activism ruin managers' abilities to manage effectively? According to Frederick E. Rowe, Jr., "It is reasonable to expect a management to clearly communicate its business and financial strategies to its owners. It is reasonable to expect management to invest its discretionary cash flows profitably. It is reasonable to expect management to eliminate fat and extravagant perks. It is reasonable to relate compensation to performance."[45] Basically, Rowe believes that if a company (management) is not doing what is reasonable, shareholders will now legally be able to gather their collective strength to force managers to comply with their desires.

Part of the responsibility for dethroning some of corporate America's management kingpins falls to the formidable, but heretofore mostly silent, institutional shareholders. After years of inertia, they are now beginning to see their role more clearly and are beginning to flex their collective muscles. Some of these investors have tens of billions of dollars to invest and have little choice but to hold the equities of many of America's largest companies. More and more the performance of the funds is dependent upon the performance of these big companies whose shares they must own more or less permanently. This fact puts fund managers in the position of having to take a direct interest in the underachieving firm.[46] America's financial institutions hold 45 percent of all American corporate equity and have mostly remained silent, enjoying their dividends and seldom, if ever, even wagging a finger at corporate managers. However, this is slowly changing. Though the numbers are still relatively minute, "The number of resolutions on corporate governance from institutions or organized groups of shareholder activists has doubled since 1989."[47]

The next governance mechanism is the board of directors. Because board members are elected through stockholder votes, they are legally accountable for a company's actions. Insider and outsider directors provide valuable information and resources to the board at large. Critics claim, however, that insiders often abuse their position and sometimes can present information that puts management at an unfair advantage. Critics also claim that many CEOs dominate the company and board of directors and in effect handcuff the board and prevent it from taking appropriate actions. But corporate boards are beginning to react to the pressures put forth by the institutional investors. The previously mentioned ousting of the former heads of GM, IBM, and Sears are examples of the reactions those boards had to financial and institutional constituents. There is also the issue of the threat of legal action against boards. As Rowe pointed out, "As a matter of law, the duty to manage a corporation resides in its board of directors.[48]

BOARD STRUCTURE

Another area of research concerning an effective board is the structure of the board. Within the composition there are three different variables: size of the board; inside versus outside directors; and the type of board leadership. The interest in board structure is in response to the belief that boards are dominated by CEOs and that directors do not receive periodic information and do not interact with the corporate staff. The result is that the board responds to management analysis rather than being active in the planning process. A study by Chaganti, Mahajan, and Sharma in 1985 showed a higher rate of corporate bankruptcy among companies with small boards. Another study conducted by Provan in 1980 revealed that there is a positive relationship between board size and its performance.[49]

Several studies have been conducted on the issue of inside versus outside director participation. A 1955 study by Vance showed a positive relationship between the number of insiders and financial performance. By contrast, a study conducted in 1982–1983 by Baysinger and Butler suggested that increasing outsiders' means increased board independence from management and increased objectivity by directors. This is believed to be a result of multiple perspectives that outside directors bring with them to a company. Another study by Baysinger and Butler in 1985 showed that companies with more outsiders on their boards outperformed their competitors from 1970 to 1980. Yet another study conducted by Schmidt in 1975 and 1977 showed no relationship between the companies' financial performance and the number of outsiders.[50]

A second attribute that is related to company performance is that of the board's characteristics. Several studies show that certain characteristics encourage or limit potential interlocks, ensure a firm's access to vital resources, and determine the board's ability to monitor company performance. Provan conducted a study in 1980 that showed that directors were expected to deal with internal and external circumstances that would enhance a company's performance. Therefore, directors are expected to possess an appropriate level of education, training, and experience. They also need to establish links with political, competitive, and financial collaborators.

Previous research on board processes can be summarized as follows:

1. An ineffective decision-making process weakens a board and its ability to contribute to the company.
2. Boards are under public scrutiny for rubber stamping managerial decisions.
3. Process is important for explaining how boards contribute to strategy, exercise control, and make executive compensation decisions.

Research on board process has been limited for a number of reasons including, but not limited to the following:

1. The impact of contextual forces on board variables has been widely ignored.
2. There is a tendency among researchers to suggest reforms without sufficient description of board attributes.
3. Emphasis on universal analytical approaches has handicapped efforts to develop models.
4. Inadequate research samples have not addressed the range of questions asked.
5. There has been a failure to utilize boards in an efficient manner.
6. Measures of organizational performance have been restricted.

The increase in marketplace competition requires a high level of excellence for corporate governance. Boards of directors must take an active part in governance in order to create this level of excellence.[51] While what is needed are strong, competent, motivated directors, the corporate governance system makes being a director unattractive and possibly a dangerous proposition. What is needed is to remove the incentive for shareholders to file lawsuits. Also, by increasing the amount of compensation and long-term rewards for directors, perhaps they will spend more time with their respective companies.

Corporate boards of directors are the primary mechanism for ensuring that management works in the best interests of shareholders. It should be apparent that insider directors lack independence in their ability to fulfill their responsibilities. Because they are subordinate to management once outside the boardroom, it is believed they will vote in favor of management more often than not. But, while increasing outsider representation on the board is necessary, it may not be enough to overcome the power that many CEOs have. Two additional suggestions consist of requiring officers and directors to own substantial blocks of corporate stock and increase the extent to which officer and director compensation is contingent on performance.

ETHICAL IMPLICATIONS

Management acts as the agent for various stakeholder contracts and stakeholders have throughputs of value equivalent to the power they have over management. In an article entitled, "A Stakeholder Apologetic for Management", by Arthur Sharplin and Lonnie D. Phelps, it is stated that "assuming that management strives to optimize other than its own [interest] appears heroic, to say the least."[52] The authors found managers of large corporations to be ethical in regards to their stakeholders. They see this power as being roughly proportional to the value contributed through the organization in reference to other stakeholders. Perhaps the authors have overlooked the fact that some managers put profit before the interests of others. Perhaps poorly designed cars and trucks with gas tanks that explode in low-speed, rear-end collisions would never have reached consumers if stakeholders had been able to have more of an impact on corporate policy and business practices. This is just one example of how the stakeholder approach could have made a positive ethical contribution.

Because the term "ethics" is hard to define, government has often had to step in on society's behalf in order to resolve conflicts, and the result is usually more government regulation of business. The stakeholder approach could go a long way to slow, or even stop the further encroachment of unwanted government regulation, even without a written code of ethics to follow, as the combined values and beliefs of stakeholders would be similar to those of society:

1. To devise prescriptive and proactive policies on issues concerning the corporation and its interactions and relationships with those individuals and groups having an interest in or being affected by the company.
2. To benefit the company by allowing for smooth, effective, unbiased decision making that promotes efficiency, effectiveness, and productivity by all concerned corporate employees.
3. To benefit the external environment and its constituents by prevent damages to or impositions upon their property or persons.

CONCLUSION

It is proposed that utilization of a stakeholder board will serve to stabilize the environment within which a corporation operates and in so doing allow long-term prosperity that will positively affect and influence all constituents. Being so governed and providing only positive (nonnegative) effects, the corporation can be less constrained and provide greater benefits to its internal and external environments and constituents.

NOTES

1. E. Sternberg, "Stakeholder Theory Exposed," *Corporate Governance Quarterly* (Hong Kong) 20 (March 1996): 4–18.
2. Abbass F. Alkhafaji, *A Stakeholder Approach to Corporate Governance* (New York: Quorum Books, 1989), 31.
3. Ibid.
4. Rogene Buchholz, *A Business Environment and Public Policy: Implications for Management and Strategy Formulation* (Englewood Cliffs, N.J.: Prentice Hall, 1996), 459–503.
5. Alkhafaji, *A Stakeholder Approach*.
6. R. Edward Freeman and D. R. Gilbert, Jr., "Managing Stakeholder Relationships," in *Business and Society*, ed. S. P. Sethi and C. M. Falbe (Lexington, Mass.: Lexington Books, 1987), 397–423.
7. Ibid., 399.
8. Ibid., 407.
9. Thomas Donaldson and Lee Preston, L. "The Stakeholder Theory of the Corporation: Concepts, Evidence," *Academy of Management Review* 20 (1995): 65.
10. Ibid.
11. Buchholz, *A Business Environment and Public Policy*, 459.
12. Donaldson and Preston, "The Stakeholder Theory," 80–82.
13. Ibid.
14. Buchholz, *A Business Environment and Public Policy*.
15. Steven Wallman, "The Reemergence of the Corporate Constituency Concept," unpublished, Washington, D.C., 1990, 6.
16. Murray L. Weidenbaum, *The Future of Business Regulation* (New York: Anacom, 1979), 98.
17. Buchholz, *A Business Environment and Public Policy*, 104.

18. Yerachmiel Kugel and Gladys W. Gruenberg, *Ethical Perspectives on Business and Society* (Lexington, Mass.: Lexington Books, 1977), 97.

19. Ibid.

20. Wallman, "The Reemergence of the Corporate Constituency Concept," 13.

21. Ibid., 16.

22. Ibid., 20.

23. Ibid.

24. Ibid., 23.

25. Ibid., 27.

26. Ibid., 28.

27. "American Corporate Governance: Shareholders Call the Plays," *The Economist* 32 (24 April 1993): 83.

28. W. L. Hill and T. M. Jones, "Stakeholder Agency Theory," *Journal of Management Studies* 29 (1992): 131–154.

29. A. Berle and G. Means, *The Modern Corporation and Private Property* (New York: Macmillan, 1932), 8–9.

30. Robert B. Reich, *The Work of Nations* (New York: Knopf, 1991), 41.

31. Abbass F. Alkhafaji, *A Stakeholder Approach*.

32. David Mahoney, *Growth and Social Responsibility* (Princeton, N.J.: Princeton University Press, 1973), 20.

33. Ibid., 22.

34. Kenneth E. Aupperle, "An Empirical Examination of the Relationship between Corporate Social Responsibility and Profitability," *Academy of Management Journal* 28 (June 1985): 446.

35. Heidrick and Struggles, *Profile of the Board of Directors* (Atlanta, Ga.: Heidrick and Struggles, Inc., 1983), 5.

36. The Business Roundtable, *Corporate Ethics: A Prime Business Asset* (New York: The Business Roundtable, 1988), 82.

37. Wheelan and Hunger, *Strategic Management and Business Policy*, 235.

38. R. Edward Freeman, *Strategic Management: A Stakeholder Approach* (Boston: Pitman, 1984), 31.

39. Frederick K. Sturdivant and Heidi Vernon-Wortzel, *Business and Society: A Managerial Approach* (Boston: Irwin, 1990), 70.

40. Alkhafaji, *A Stakeholder Approach*, 36.

41. Ibid., 113.

42. Berle and Means," *The Modern Corporation*, 39.

43. Frederick E. Rowe, Jr., "Hurrah for October 15," *Forbes* 15 February 1993, 39.

44. Louis M. Thompson, Jr., "Shareholder Relations: A New Role for the Board," *Harvard Business Review* 71 (January–February 1993).

45. Rowe, "Hurrah for October 15."

46. Anonymous, "Getting Rid of the Boss," *The Economist* 326 (6 February 1993): 13.

47. Anonymous, "Getting Uppity," *The Economist* 318 (16 March 1991): 76.

48. Rowe, "Hurrah for October 15."

49. T. Carter Hagaman, "Outside Director: Small Companies," *Management Accounting* 3 (February 1992): 18.

50. Buchholz, *A Business Environment and Public Policy*.

51. William A. Sahlman, "Why Sane People Shouldn't Serve on Public Boards," *Harvard Business Review* 68, 3 (May–June 1990): 28.

52. Arthur Sharplin and Lonnie D. Phelps, "A Stakeholder Apologetic for Management," *Business and Professional Journal* 8 (Summer 1989): 41–53.

Chapter 12

The Liability of the
Board of Directors

Many changes in corporate governance have taken place since the 1980s. Today the board of directors has become more independent and attentive. The institutional investors have become more involved in corporate activities. The wave of hostile takeovers of the past decade indicated that the board was not carrying its job as expected by the stockholders. Management, on the other hand, proved that they are not effective in managing the organization on a day-to-day basis. Their loyalty to serve the shareholders is questionable. The combination of a weak board and less than effective management has contributed to the restructuring that took place in the past decade. There is a need to have an effective board to oversee management performance. This chapter will discuss the development of the board of directors and its changing role in the corporation.

In the past decade public organizations were structured under the traditional model in which management is considered the agent of stockholders. This structure provides management with the needed power to manage the organization their own way. On the other hand, the stockholders and their representative, the board of directors, are left with no real power.[1] This chapter will discuss some of the issues facing the board of directors in respect to the obligations owed to the shareholders. In recent years, the shareholders have been holding the directors liable for a variety of actions taken by them. This has caused many prospective members to think twice about taking a seat on the board. In the past, membership on the board was considered to be a prestigious position, as well as an easy way to earn some extra money. There are some members who belong to more than one board and may even be the CEO of another corporation. Needless to say, in these instances, their effectiveness is diminished when belonging to multiple boards. It will be difficult to become familiar with the operations of all the companies and be a productive member making effective decisions. The board of directors and top level management serve as agents for the owner of the corporation: the shareholders. As agents, management has a duty to maximize the wealth of the stockholders. In order to conduct their job, management had broad discretion protected by the expansive Business Judgment Rule, while at the same time stockholders are protected against excessive costs by management. The owners of the organization are also protected, at least in theory, from stealing or empire building of management by management's fiduciary duties of care and loyalty and by the legal structure of corporate governance.

Lately, increasing legal actions taken against board members as well as the expectation on the part of directors to give the company more of their valuable time has caused a decline in director membership. This increased liability has also been the cause for current directors to step down or retire in order to prevent the possible risk of a lawsuit against them. It seems ironic for individuals to turn down board offers when it has been shown that "most board members are paid a base salary of no less than $21,000 dollars per year for an average of 112 hours of work."[2] Accepting a board membership in the past did not always require the individual to be a part of the major decision-making process. In fact, members were chosen for who they were and not what they knew. For example, "Gerald Ford received a salary of $92,000 per year at the mining company Amax Inc., an industry in which he had no previous experience."[3]

The liability issue has also introduced different types of insurance policies to cover the possibility of future lawsuits. This has also forced a lot of companies to purchase this insurance to protect the directors and parts of the company. In fact, prospective board members may not accept positions unless the insurance is provided. With more lawsuits popping up, companies are looking at making directors purchase their own liability insurance.

HISTORICAL PERSPECTIVE

"The first boards in the United States were formed in the eighteenth century and were largely gentlemanly forums made up almost completely of the company's owners."[4] "The dominant figures of the boards that followed were men like Rockefeller, Carnegie, and Mellon, entrepreneurs who also owned large amounts of stock in the company."[5] At that time in the United States, these people made significant contributions to business and were willing and able to take the risks necessary to make their businesses prosper and established a nationwide industrial system.

Insiders and owners of the company remained in the majority on most board of directors until the 1960s when more outsiders began to become the focus in selecting future members. The opposite occurred by the time 1970 arrived, when the majority of board members were outsiders. Two of the historical precursors to the legal environment boards face today were the increase of outsiders on the board and the "second guessing" of the courts in regard to the Business Judgment Rule. The Business Judgment Rule "is one of the oldest and most fundamental building blocks of corporate America. This rule, which protects the directors' informed business decisions from judicial review," was shaken when, in 1985, the Delaware Supreme Court ruled that the Trans Union Corporation's directors had breached their fiduciary duty and were personally liable to the stockholders.[6] The Trans Union Corporation's case opened the flood gates for lawsuits regarding the liability of the board of directors.[7]

With increased legal liability, board members were running scared and stepping down, which forced corporations to hire professional recruiters to fill the empty seats. This caused companies to reflect on the fact that they should perhaps decrease the number of directors and return to having more insiders on the board. This was happening, though, at a time when management buyouts, stock repurchases, and takeover proposals were occurring at many companies. During these times, it was preferable to have more outside members on the board. Insiders have a tendency to go along with the CEO and are afraid to express their opinion, especially if it differs from what the CEO wants, since they feel they will lose their seat on the board. David J. Dunn, chairman of Prime Computer and three other companies, stated, "One reason directors do such a poor job is that boards are almost always structured in ways that inhibit the kind of give and take that should exist between independent overseers and the chief executive. Nearly all boards have subordinates of the CEO among their members. A company's situation has to become desperate indeed before the typical outside director will ask demanding questions that might imply criticism of the CEO in front of those subordinates."[8]

DIRECTOR'S RESPONSIBILITIES

Historically, the role of the board of directors has been viewed as one of accountability to the stockholders only. In recent years, this notion has changed due to revisions in current laws as well as the adoption of new laws, which are focused on environmental and social concerns. Little attention has been paid to whether the directors have a responsibility to their employees, customers and suppliers, creditors, and the community in which the firm is located.

In *Teck Corp. Ltd. v. Millar*, the Supreme Court of British Columbia evaluated the actions taken by the board of directors who were involved in a takeover situation. The judge in this case felt the directors had the responsibility to investigate all aspects of the other company and should have looked at the pros and cons of the effects that the takeover would have on the employees, the community, and the shareholders. In his decision, he did not specifically state that the directors had this obligation to other constituents but recognized the legitimacy of the concern for others. This caused a more contemporary stance to be taken, which recognizes that the primary duty of the directors is to the shareholders; but in fulfilling this obligation, the directors must also take into consideration other constituents who may have an interest in the company and its effect on society.[9]

As members of the board, directors are required to be loyal to the firm and stockholders and to properly disclose all matters concerning the operation of the corporation to all affected parties, and also to exercise a moderate standard of cares in the management of the company and execute the requirements of the Employee Retirement Income Security Act of 1974. As well as the fiduciary duties previously mentioned, directors have the responsibility for electing the officers of the firm and establishing the policies and objectives of the organization. They are expected to safeguard corporate assets, mail annual statements of financial results to stockholders, approve financial matters, delegate authority to members of management to conduct the daily operation of the company, and ensure that the rules and regulations of the corporation are updated and enforced.[10]

A director is required to exhibit and exercise a duty of care to the corporation. He or she must act in a way that protects and considers the best interests of the firm. One way to view this is the director should give the corporation the same concern that would be taken in the performance of his or her own affairs. Directors who are members of more than one board must especially take note of this "duty of care" responsibility. Knowledge of corporate opportunities is another area in which director diligence is necessary.

Delegation of responsibilities to others by directors is limited to some extent by each state. Directors must be aware of these state statutes in which the firm has been incorporated. A good example of this would be the selection of the pension plan administrator covered under ERISA. If it is found that the board did not perform a thorough investigation in the selection process, but instead chose an individual as a favor or because of friendship, the board could be held liable for any losses suffered by the participants of the plan. The liability would be based on competency, not friendship.[11]

THE CHANGING ROLES OF DIRECTORS

Nowadays, members of the board are required to contribute a substantial amount of their time to the proper execution of their duties as a director. Many individuals are not willing to submit to the increased time demand and amount of work required of them. Directors are also fearful of being censured by the public for the actions they take as board members. But the most important issue giving individuals second thoughts is liability, or the possibility of being sued. In recent years, the risk has become greater, lawsuits have been increasing, and potential board members do not want to get involved.

Directors in today's world are essentially under a microscope and all their actions are carefully scrutinized. They are required to understand the nature of business of the firm as well as be able to comprehend the financial aspects and statements of the company. "Robert Mueller, chairman of Arthur D. Little, the Cambridge, Massachusetts research and management consultant firm, has served on 30 corporate boards during his career and says that now it takes more attention, and more diligence. The whole agenda has changed."[12]

Julia Walsh, the founder of a brokerage firm who has served as an outside director on several companies has had firsthand experience with the great toll serving a board can take on the board member, his or her own job, and family life. She spent half her time over a two-month period in 1984 working on board business for Esmark, who at the time was faced with a court battle against Beatrice. "This is quite a change since ten years ago, we would get a report from management, look at it, maybe ask a question, and that would have been it," Walsh admits."[13]

Boards of directors in the past:
1. Size fluctuated between thirteen and sixteen members.
2. Audit committees had an important role.
3. Directors usually came from the same segment of the population.
4. Boards in general were not effective.

LOSS ELIMINATION–WARNING SIGNS

The following is a discussion of several topics that could possibly eliminate or reduce the probability of loss exposure. They are avoidance, document signing, conflict of interest, the audit committee, due diligence, and authority.

One possible technique to lower liability loss for the director is avoidance. Although this may sound impractical, it is not. It simply means if you are a member of one board, it would be to your advantage to not become a member of another board of directors. This would especially be true if you were an officer or major stockholder in a competitive corporation. Being a member of only one board enables the director to properly serve that company.

As a member of the board, there are times when the director must sign his name to certain documents. Registration statements require verification and the signatures of the directors. "If the statements are found to contain material misrepresentation or omissions, the directors may be held personally liable to investors under the Securities Act of 1933."[14] A second document that requires a signature is the completed application for a board of director liability policy. All this is saying to the director is that he should carefully read everything and thoroughly investigate all matters to ensure the document's accuracy before attaching his signature to it. If there is a question, ask, and do not hesitate to express your disapproval.

Another way loss can be eliminated is for the director to be wary of any conflicts of interest. This comes into play when trading in company securities, especially if the director may have received some inside information about the stock and/or company. The best prevention here is not to sell or buy the stock of the company. "In addition, the director's spouse, children, parents, foundations, trust funds, or any entity in which the director has personal interest should not trade in the stock when the director is in possession of private information that might affect its price."[15]

Establishment of an audit committee should be an item on the board of director's agenda. This committee needs the full support of all the directors as well as members of top management in order to be effective. It should review the director's duties and minutes of their meetings and make sure the records of the corporation are accurate. Another area of responsibility is to ensure and require compliance with antitrust laws.

The area of due diligence was previously mentioned. This basically means that a director is required to exercise reasonable care in similar circumstances. "The difficulty of applying the standard of due diligence is that it is frequently difficult to tell what a prudent person would have done in a similar set of circumstances."[16] Regular attendance at board meetings, especially if a significant issue is to be discussed, should be the aim of all board members. To be effective in their jobs, they need to receive all pertinent information.

Last but not least is authority. State and federal laws define specific areas in which the directors have certain obligations. "Corporation laws impose liability on directors for such acts as improper dividends, loans to officers, loans to directors, and distribution of capital to shareholders where no provision is made to repay the debts."[17]

Recently, the trend has been to seek more outside directors to serve on the board. Having more individuals on the board who are not affiliated with the company should facilitate more objective decision making. These individuals are also less likely to just go along with management; rather, they will question their actions. "The Canada Business Corporations Act requires federally incorporated companies to have two outside directors sit on their board."[18] Some people believe there are drawbacks to having outside people serve on the board. One is the fact that the individuals may not have enough knowledge about the company to serve it properly. Another problem has become the limited supply of outside directors.

As stated earlier, prevention is always the best cure. The following are some warning signs that should alert board members to possible liability suits. Any one of these should prompt the board to investigate the matter further in order to prevent legal action against the firm. Touché Ross and Company compiled this list:

1. Insufficient working capital or credit.
2. An urgent desire on the part of management to support the price of the company's stock.
3. A dependence on a very few customers or transactions.
4. A declining industry with many business failures.
5. Many lawsuits, especially from customers.
6. Rapid expansion or numerous acquisitions, especially in diversification.
7. Collection difficulties from key customers.
8. Highly diversified operations, each division with its own separate accounting system.
9. Management domination by one individual.
10. Separate auditors for separate divisions.
11. Rapid turnover in key financial positions or in outside legal counsel.
12. Frequent changes of independent auditors or of personnel of the same auditing firm.
13. Any activity that smacks of illegal political contributions, slush funds, kickbacks, or bribes.[19]

THE CHANGING BOARD

Today, corporate boards are becoming more effective. The duty of the board is more clearly defined. Some of their duties include overseeing the performance of managers, the hiring and compensation of the CEO, and monitoring the internal control system in the organization. One of their important roles is to verify the financial reporting and legal compliance. Because of liability issues boards are more aware of their legal responsibilities. In fact, many boards hire their own legal advisor to council them on the technicalities of corporate performance. In many organizations the legal department is more loyal to the chief executive officer than to the stakeholders of the organization. They understand that the CEO of the company is the one that hires them and is in the position to fire them. Their job is to look for any possible illegal activities that could endanger the position of the organization. The boards of directors meet more frequently than in the past through the various committees. Some of these committees are the audit, nominating, and compensation committees. These committees are now consisting of entirely outside members. Those outside directors usually meet independently from the inside members of the board.

Today, outside directors are in touch with the major stockholders such as the institutional investors. Despite a strong resistance, the corporate bar has generally revised its position and has accepted these developments within the corporate governance. Eisenberg has called the acceptance of this new role by corporate directors a "fundamental change in its belief system about norms."[20] General Motors in 1994 presented a guideline that enabled the board to add a lead director. This has influenced other companies to present similar guidelines. The lead director will chair regular meetings of outside directors and monitor the annual review of the board's performance. These practices were unheard of ten years ago but have become an acceptable practice. The outside directors are becoming more involved in hiring the CEO of the corporation. That is exactly what happened to Campbell Soup.[21] These changes were so quickly accepted that the 1997 Business Roundtable Statement of Corporate Governance was established as a set of "mainstream" ideas that were recently rejected and thought to be radical. Directors now have to risk their reputations by being listed in articles like *Business Week*'s "25 Worst Boards" or the Council of Institutional Investor's list of "turkeys."[22]

Changes in the board recently:
1. The board size is decreasing to about thirteen members.
2. The number of committees and meetings has increased.
3. There are more outsiders or independent directors.
4. There are more women and minorities on the board.
5. Many companies are providing stock options for board members.

CAUSES FOR BOARD OF DIRECTORS' LIABILITY

A survey conducted in 1992 by the Wyatt Company of 1,501 firms showed that 24 percent of them have had at least one, if not more, claims filed against their directors in the past nine years. The survey also indicated that claims leveled off in 1991 but showed an increase in the dollar amounts of the claims that were filed. In 1991, the main causes of liability claims were found to be suits filed by employees for wrongful termination.[23]

Some of the causes for lawsuits filed against directors were due to changes in tax codes, federal legislation, and retirement acts. The passage of the Civil Rights Act of 1991 has given employees the right to sue their employers for discrimination, wrongful discharge, and sexual harassment. For the first time, employees were given the right to sue for compensatory as well as punitive damages under the act. The new legislation also gave the workers the right to request a jury trial. Having a jury present can increase the dollar amount of the settlement if charges of discrimination can be proven against the corporation, as jurors are likely to be sympathetic to defendants in this area. Effective July 1992, the Americans with Disabilities Act affected firms with more than twenty-five employees and in 1994 required compliance by all employers. This act was enacted to cover handicapped and disabled employees and requires employers to make reasonable accommodations for them. Employers who disregard the implications of this act and are not in compliance with it will endanger the firm and subject it to a possible lawsuit.

Another area where board liability might surface is if the firm is having financial problems and files for bankruptcy. In fact, "bankruptcies can even place the unqualified portion of a senior executives' retirement benefits in jeopardy," reports the National Union Fire Insurance Company in Pittsburgh.[24] There is increased likelihood shareholders will sue if the firm has not properly disclosed all the pertinent facts regarding the operation and financial condition of the firm. Lately, pollution has also become a "major area of exposure for directors and officers, noted Dan Bailey, a partner with Artner & Hadden in Cleveland. In some states, statutes go so far as to say that if a particularly senior officer could have prevented the pollution even if the officer knew nothing about it that officer is personally liable."[25]

Why do corporate directors have such a difficult time with liability to the shareholders? This question could be answered simply with three words: mergers, takeovers, and buyouts. These three situations make stockholders very uneasy since they all deal with changes in ownership. The board has the responsibility to make sound judgments in these cases and is relied upon to keep the best interests of the corporation and the shareholders in mind when taking action. In June 1991, "A U.S. Supreme Court ruling involving Virginia Bankshares, a company sued by its shareholders who alleged that its stock was significantly undervalued in a majority buyout. The shareholders held that corporate board members should have realized that their valuation of the shares had been too low; the court held them liable for the losses."[26]

Another example of this was the case of Allegheny International. The firm was having financial difficulties, yet decided to ignore them. The board opened the door for a lawsuit by ignoring the request of the stockholders to address the situation. The shareholders brought the suit against the chairman and CEO of Allegheny International, Robert J. Buckley, for recovery of corporate funds. Buckley had significant influence in the selection of board members and chose people because of their popularity and not experience; otherwise, this situation may have been avoidable. Alexander Haig, former Secretary of State, was one of the individuals chosen by Buckley. Because of Haig's inexperience, he was easily manipulated. If board members do not have the proper background, there is no possible way for them to make intelligent decisions. One of the main functions of the board is to provide a true analysis of the company and the CEO's performance. If they are able to accomplish this, problems such as this one can be prevented.[27]

LIMITING LIABILITY

Although there are few legal choices available, directors are not totally vulnerable. There are two approaches by which directors can limit their liability: (1) conducting themselves in a manner which prevents liability from arising, and (2) ensuring adequate protection exists should liability ensue.[28]

Directors should carefully consider all actions to be taken and make sure there are not personal conflicts that may interfere in the proper exercise of their duty as a board member. Providing a duty of care to the corporation can be difficult, but the director just needs to use some common sense in this area. Prior to final action and approval by the board, a few simple steps should be taken:

1. Investigate each situation thoroughly.
2. Check all records carefully.
3. Determine any alternatives.
4. Study the possible choices.
5. Make choices in the best interests of the corporation.

"Corporations are permitted to insure directors against losses incurred in fulfilling their corporate functions."[29] In fact, this is becoming a necessity for corporations if they want to find and keep directors. With increasing lawsuits in this area, the cost of the board of director insurance is on the rise.

Large- and middle-market banks were the first and second in line to report increased premiums. Utilities proved to be the business with the lowest incidence of premium increases as well as the class most likely to carry the insurance. The survey found that real estate and construction were the least likely businesses to carry board insurance.[30] The increase in lawsuits has also brought about the speculation that directors may have to carry their own liability insurance just as individuals purchase car insurance.

Legislation has been passed in the states of Delaware and Pennsylvania, as well as a few others, which limits the legal liability of corporate directors. For example, "Pennsylvania amended the statutes to shield directors of corporations, including banking and nonprofit organizations, from personal liability for any action or failure to act on behalf of the corporation unless such a failure was willful misconduct or recklessness. This legislation insulates directors from purely negligent conduct."[31]

Delaware, on the other hand, allows for broader exemptions and passed legislation in 1986 which would permit companies to add the agreement to their charter. However, there are two disadvantages of the Delaware legislation. They are that

1. "The legislation does not apply to prior acts, corporate officers, acts of intentional fraud, breach of the duty of loyalty to stockholders, or transactions whereby the director derives an improper personal benefit.
2. All or part of the legislation may be pre-empted by various federal regulations."[32]

All the legislation was intended to encourage qualified individuals to accept positions as directors. In most instances, it does not extend to officers of the corporation. Another benefit they were hoping to achieve from the Delaware legislation was a decrease in the premiums for board of directors liability insurance but that has yet to be seen.

BOARD OF DIRECTORS' LIABILITY INSURANCE

One way in which the corporation can protect the directors from the results of wrongful acts which may occur during the performance of their duties is to purchase board of directors liability insurance. The definition in one policy for wrongful act was stated as follows:

The term, wrongful act, shall mean any breach of duty, neglect, error, misstatement, misleading statement, omission or other act done or wrongfully

attempted by the Directors or Officers of any company, or any of the forego-
ing so alleged by any claimant, or any matter claimed against the Directors or
Officers solely by reason of their being Directors or Officers of such company.[33]

Under a board of directors' liability policy, the insured are the directors and officers of the company and not the company. Boards of
directors' liability policies were implemented to provide personal protection for the directors and not to protect the corporation against any
mistakes it might make. Depending on the insurer and the type of
policy selected, it may cover positions only or it may list the names of
the specific directors. When filing suit, a claimant must identify the
specific director, or the coverage does not apply.

The board of directors' liability policy has two parts:

Part A directly indemnifies directors and officers for defense costs and loss
arising from various wrongful acts—usually including errors and omissions—
defined in the policy. This coverage part applies to acts for which the corporation is not required to provide indemnity. Part B reimburses a corporation for
defense costs and loss it incurs on behalf of its directors and officers, as per the
indemnification provision in its bylaws.[34]

There are four essential items in the board of directors' liability policy
to which the organization must pay close attention:

1. Discovery period—This is a clause added to the contract which extends
   coverage for a limited period of time for claims that may arise prior to
   cancellation or expiration but not discovered until later.
2. Notification of new directors and officers—Any time new directors are
   added, the underwriter must be notified; otherwise, coverage could be
   denied.
3. Claims notification—The firm must notify the insurance company of any
   potential claims or face the possibility of denial of claims. Firms are sometimes hesitant to do this, as they fear an increase in their premiums will
   occur or coverage may not be available.
4. Severability provision—This clause is very valuable as it provides protection for the other directors if one director has knowledge of a wrongful
   act and the others do not. Some insurers want to eliminate this clause
   from their policies.[35]

Michael Rekruciak, vice president and manager of the professional
services department of Alexander & Alexander in Chicago, listed a
few other features that a corporation might want to include in their
board of directors' liability policies:

1. Removal of exclusions for failing to maintain insurance—This situation
   occurs if the business either forgets or purposefully neglects to insure cer-

tain property or liability exposures. In this instance, if the client can show that they are carrying all the basic coverage, the underwriter of the policy will usually remove the exclusion.

2. Wrongful termination coverage—This feature will protect against suits filed by disgruntled employees. The business should resist if the underwriter wants to exclude this item.

3. Advancement of defense costs—Usually the corporation would have to pay these costs themselves and then be reimbursed. Adding this provision to the policy permits the advancement of the costs to the directors, if involved in litigation, that may not be covered by the company's indemnification agreement.

4. Deletion of participation requirements—Previously, some policies had a provision that the insured would have to cover 5 percent of the losses above the deductible. In this way, they thought the director would give their full cooperation. Nowadays, this clause can easily be removed, as directors are personally liable, have their reputation to maintain, and will want to have the suit finalized as quickly as possible.[36]

In nonprofit organizations, the board of directors' liability policies usually have broader terms and less exclusion. Customarily, they cover the employees, trustees, and volunteers as well as the directors and officers. Deductibles are lower for nonprofit organizations than they are for corporate policies. In some instances, a policy has been written which covers the entire entity, which would never be seen in a corporate board of directors' liability policy.

All board of directors' liability policies will have certain exclusions. One of these may occur because the issue–action could be covered under some other type of policy. An example of this would be a suit for libel against the company, which would probably be covered under a personal injury policy. At the time that the Environmental Protection Act was passed, the board of directors' liability policies also excluded coverage for pollution loss. "Other exclusions eliminate coverage for loss involving personal profit or advantages to which a director or officer is not legally entitled, and for illegal salaries or bonuses paid to directors or officers without stockholder approval. Also excluded is coverage for violations of certain securities laws and for losses caused by failure to obtain and maintain insurance protecting corporate assets."[37]

The Wyatt Company surveyed 1,700 firms in 1988, as noted in an article written by James S. Trieschmann and E. J. Leverett, Jr. in *Business Horizons*. In this survey, they found that 26 percent of these firms did not purchase any form of board of directors' liability insurance. It indicated that large firms were more apt to purchase insurance than smaller firms. Of the firms earning assets of over $5 billion, 90 percent purchased insurance whereas only 46 percent of the companies who had assets under $50 million were purchasers of the insurance. Companies who did not purchase board of directors' liability insurance gave three reasons: (1) They felt they did not need the coverage, (2) the cost was too high, and (3) the coverage was not thorough enough.[38]

FOREIGN BOARD OF DIRECTORS' LIABILITY

What effect will the increase in the number of lawsuits being filed against directors and officers in the United States have on individuals who serve the same role in a multinational company? An examination of U.S. board of directors' liability contracts revealed three possible problem areas in a foreign subsidiary:

1. Definition of a director and officer.
2. Territorial scope of coverage.
3. Definition of a subsidiary.[39]

We will discuss each of these individually. First of all, the boards of directors' liability policies in the United States do not define a director and/or officer. State laws or a statement in the corporation's bylaws are what are relied upon to stipulate who and what the directors are. When dealing with a foreign subsidiary, the firm must examine the laws of the specific country to see if any definitions exist concerning the directors. For example, "according to a text on directors and officers insurance published by the Insurance Institute of London, the Companies Act of 1985, in force in the United Kingdom, defines an officer as a director, manager or secretary. And, while it does not contain a definition of director, it describes the role of director."[40] Therefore, the subsidiary needs to investigate the laws of each country in which it does business to ensure the proper individuals are covered.

Territorial limitations in most policies are usually few, if any. This only enforces the notion that all parts of the policy need to be examined carefully. As to the third area, "Since many foreign countries require domestic majority ownership of locally based corporations, ownership by a U.S. corporation is frequently restricted. Board of director's liability policies, however, generally define a subsidiary to be a company in which the policyholder holds at least 50% of the stock." *Fletcher v. National Mutual Life Nominees Ltd.* was a case tried in the High Court of New Zealand. In this particular instance, the outcome was based on principles of liability in negligence rather than liability for breach of statutory duty.[41] The liability of the board of directors and the auditors for the company was questioned due to information they were supposed to supply to a third party (which was in addition to the audited financial statements). The third party in this case was the trustee. The client in this case was a group of interrelated companies who provided money services on behalf of the group. Shares were offered to the public who invested, capital was raised by deposits, and the fund was consigned to a trustee under a trust deed. The company and its directors were required to file biannual reports with the trustee, as well as deliver the information to the auditors. A separate report was to be filed with the trustee by the auditors. The company suffered financial problems due to unsecured and undocumented intercompany loans, which forced them to file for insolvency. The depositors sued the trustee for their losses which amounted to NZ$25 million. After the trustee settled with the depositors, they filed suit against the auditors and directors to recover the amount paid to the depositors.

The court found the auditors liable, since they owed a duty of care to the trustee. Their decision was based on the fact that the auditors were to provide an independent report to the trustee on which the trustee was relying to be accurate. Since the auditors had to know about the impending financial problems of the company, the court found the auditors negligent in informing the trustee.

As for the directors, "The court maintained there was a close, proximate relationship between the directors and the trustee, and the directors knew full well who the report was for and why. Accordingly, they could not escape personal liability for any misrepresentations."[42] Even though there were only two directors' signatures on the report, the New Zealand court held the entire board liable. The court held that "they were all aware of the deed's requirements, the report was tabled for discussion at board meetings, all the directors gave their implicit, if not expressed, approval when the report was adopted, and none of the directors had any valid excuse for being unaware of the report's facts or contents."[43] Two of the directors tried unsuccessfully to exclude themselves from the suit. One claimed he had been out of the country for an extended period and had not participated in the board meetings. The other director had resigned one month prior to the company being declared insolvent. The judge decided, in both instances, the two had some knowledge of the circumstances of the company and were just as liable as the other directors. In this case, the judge found the trustee more liable and responsible for 65 percent of the claim; the remaining liability rested with the directors and auditors, who were accountable for 35 percent of the claim.

Besides reviewing the foreign laws regarding the liability of the directors, a foreign-based subsidiary must examine their policy on business ethics and their standard of conduct. If they do not have a code of ethics or rules of conduct to follow, these should be established. It would also be a good idea to investigate how litigation, if it should occur, is handled in specific countries. Strong repercussions would be felt by the parent company if a major incident should evolve in its foreign subsidiary; therefore, the parent company wants to be prepared and protected.

POSSIBLE SOLUTIONS

Now that we have seen some of the problems facing individuals who accept positions as directors, let's look at some resolutions. The following solutions to board room liability appeared in *Fortune* in 1987:

- Stock options for board members should be installed in every corporation. With stock options, board members can relate to the same concerns that shareholders have.
- Board members should be paid the prevailing wages for their duties.
- Boards should be kept small.
- The board should include as many outside directors as possible. To be an inside director, one must own a substantial amount of company stock.
- It would be beneficial to a corporation and its stakeholders to have an accounting firm randomly present with the board.
- A chairman without a full-time position should be involved in the board.
- Institutional investors must be concerned about the quality of directors.
- Too many directors are often overly concerned with making a quick buck. This is often done at the long-term expense of the corporation.
- The board's concern for high short-term earnings is probably the main issue of boardroom liability. Board members should have more concern for the long-term health of the corporation.[44]

The board of directors must accept the responsibilities and perform the functions for which it was established. Reviewing the actions of management to ensure that the company's objectives are being met as well as overseeing the performance of the officers and the CEO are duties the board should not take lightly. The board is responsible to insure that the best interest of the firm and its stakeholders is obtained. John Smales, retired chairman of Procter & Gamble, has proposed eight rules on how to build a better board of directors. These rules state that

1. There clearly should be a majority of outside directors.
2. The independent members of the board should select a lead director.
3. The independent directors should meet alone in executive session on a regularly scheduled basis.
4. The independent directors should take responsibility for all board procedures.
5. The board should have the basic responsibility for selection of its own members.

6. The board should conduct regularly scheduled performance reviews of the CEO and key executives.

7. The board must understand and fully endorse the company's long-term strategies.

8. The board must give an adequate amount of attention to its most important responsibility, which is the selection of the CEO.[45]

MINORITIES–FEMALES ON THE BOARD OF DIRECTORS

Regarding the issues related to the progress of African Americans reaching significant levels in corporations, it is important to keep in mind how African Americans executives view the corporate world.

Many African Americans have expressed frustration with what has been called the "glass ceiling." This term refers to a perceived invisible barrier to success that many African Americans, as well as other minorities, believe they have experienced in the workplace.[46] There are many complaints that the jobs they have obtained have only a limited career potential with little or no authority to make decisions. According to Pogue, among the most frequently cited criticisms are as follows:

1. Emphasis on affirmative action programs is declining as the federal government assumes a far less active role and voluntary compliance is sometimes less than adequate.

2. The often conservative business environment does not attempt to integrate or appreciate cultural differences.

3. African Americans lack internal support systems—the role models and networks that are vital to success.[47]

A growing number of corporations have come to the conclusion that these issues need to be addressed. Development of training programs that not only cover the skills required but enlighten individuals to the cultural differences surrounding them may encourage more minority participation at all levels of the organization.

The United States is experiencing a shift in its occupational structure. According to the Workforce 2000 report, the manufacturing sector is expected to shrink by 15 percent. A 1986 Rand study, "Closing the Gap: 40 Years of Economic Progress," predicts middle-class African Americans will continue to progress, but the less educated and poor of the nation will become even more isolated.[48]

Changes that must be made in American corporations are being dictated by the varying demographics. CEOs of major companies have begun to recognize the need to look at the educational, social, and environmental factors that have previously limited the opportunities of a wide segment of the labor force. The organizations that are willing to face up to those problems and respond in a positive manner will be better able to compete in a global, multicultural environment.

A study performed in 1989 by Korn/Ferry International, a leading executive search firm, as to the composition of boards of directors had the following results:

1. Board of directors averaged thirteen in number.
2. Board of directors averaged ten outside directors and three inside directors.
3. Ethnic minorities represented 33 percent of board of directors, a slight rise from 1987 when it was 31 percent, compared to 1984 when it was only 26 percent.[49]

Also facing that same "glass ceiling" in reaching the top of the corporate world are the many females in the workforce. Of the nation's managers–professionals, 46 percent are female but only 6.2 percent sit on a board of directors. Some of the top companies such as Walt Disney, Apple Computer, and Black & Decker do not have even one female on their boards. "The gap has several causes. Many boards remain cozy clubs, where chief executives interact collegially with peers. Some CEOs fear that women won't know, or observe, the unspoken rules—such as saving sticky questions for private conversations. Female directors also sense that CEOs worry that women will want to devote more time to women's issues, such as family leave."[50] A few other reasons for few women on boards are CEOs want people with previous experience as directors, which most women do not have, and they seem to look for women directors in the wrong roles, such as community activists, academics, or celebrities. Choosing the wrong individual gives rise to generalizations that no woman is qualified to do the job.

A solution for both groups is that the selection criteria for board of director candidates need to be modified. Nominating committees have to look deeper for qualified candidates and broaden the range of the eligibility list. Currently, they only look at current and retired CEOs and chief operating officers. Professional accomplishment, sound judgment, and experience are key elements to become qualified for the position of director. These qualifications can be found and developed in both minorities and females if an open mind is kept as to the valuable input these people can provide.

THE SUBSIDIARY BOARD
OF DIRECTORS' RESPONSIBILITIES

The board of directors of a company that operates abroad is called a subsidiary board. The board of directors of the parent company chooses the subsidiary board members. A subsidiary board can be a dummy board or an active board. A dummy board operates only by the letter of the law, not by the spirit. An active board operates as the subsidiary's highest authority by governing, discussing local policies, and in general being proactive. Host country legislation addresses the structure and board composition. "Ipso facto" is applied to local subsidiaries' board composition.

Most host countries legally require subsidiary boards. Their duties are that of a board of directors. Active subsidiary boards provide governance, advise management in key situations, meet a specified number of times per year, and assume legal responsibility. If an active board does not exist, the host government perceives that there is a low concern for their interests.

By becoming intermediaries between host country pressures and multinational corporations (MNCs), subsidiary boards can be a helpful link between the foreign subsidiary and the MNC. Subsidiary boards are an "added structural" intended to help MNCs deal with highly turbulent and heterogeneous task environments.

Subsidiary boards also offer operational and strategic advice to subsidiary management and relay local information to the parent company. An active subsidiary board can obtain proactive knowledge of local economic, political, and social conditions. In fact many joint ventures fail because of the deficiency in understanding cultural and behavioral factors. This usually results in insufficient training for future managers. It appears to be to a company's advantage to have an active subsidiary board.

Strategic uses of an active board are

1. Strategic windows—a subsidiary board learns of environmental changes in the host country and informs the parent.
2. Windows of understanding—when the subsidiary board uses prominent locals to create understanding between the MNC and the host.
3. Windows of influence—prominent local members of the board influence stakeholder groups to think in ways that benefit the MNC.

Japan's MNCs have the highest use of active subsidiary boards. They view subsidiary boards as having high importance in future dealings, and their subsidiary boards are an important means for understanding local country conditions. Japanese subsidiary boards are primarily utilized to

1. Approve subsidiary budgets.
2. Monitor the subsidiary's performance.
3. Participate in strategic planning.
4. Ensure local legal compliance.

5. Relay knowledge of local environment.
6. Minimize local political risks.

Japan's MNCs are the best structured to take advantage of active subsidiary boards because of their *ringisei* consensual decision making. Japanese are concerned with all stakeholders and receive input from them. This attitude flows over into their subsidiary boards.[51]

The Japanese subsidiary boards are a combination of environmental sensing, decision making, and advising roles. Sweden is the second highest user of active subsidiary boards. They view subsidiary boards as having a high future importance in host countries. Their use of subsidiary boards is consistent with their worker participation theory. They view subsidiary boards as a combination of environmental sensing, decision making, and advising. Sweden has mandated the use of active subsidiary boards in coping with local situations.

A number of factors can lead to a country's variations in the use of active subsidiary boards:

1. The parent company's home country.
2. The type of industry in which the company is involved.
3. The local legal and economic conditions of the host country.
4. The formal and informal structure of the parent company.
5. The management styles of the parent and subsidiary.
6. The degree of internationalization of the parent company.

MNCs who are involved in active subsidiary boards view their efforts as a valuable and worthwhile investment. The U.S. MNCs' subsidiary boards have a less active role. They view the future role of subsidiary boards to be of moderate importance. They lag behind in the use of subsidiary boards of strategic and operational entities to cope with uncertainties. Their subsidiary boards are primarily utilized to advise local management and provide knowledge of local economic, political, and social conditions. Two factors which lead companies to increase their demand of active subsidiary boards are (1) a greater national responsiveness, which implies that those country-level operations should be more independent and that decision making be more decentralized; and (2) the pressure for more integrated operations and centrally controlled decisions resulting from the strategic imperative of increased global efficiency.

However, many MNCs retain dummy boards, apparently not realizing the strategic uses of an active board. Some MNCs are not structured to take advantage of active subsidiary boards. Some MNCs do not want active boards because of the decentralization, apparent loss of power, and to control overall cost. This is the case with much U.S.

management today. They are not interested in active boards that might result in loss of power and control for management. An active local board is useful for policy and political advice, but not necessarily managing the company. A subsidiary board is chosen by the parent company board to help an MNC succeed in a foreign country. The evolution of the role of foreign subsidiary boards in selected situations is closely tied to the increasing scope of the MNC's activities around the world and the increase of host country involvement in controlling the direction of the MNC's activities. Most countries continue to request, as they have in the past, that subsidiaries of MNCs take national development policy objectives into account when mapping out corporate strategies.[52] If there are no actively participating directors, it is assumed by the host country that local needs and requirements are of low concern.

The board is responsible for ethical issues when faced with making decisions. If directors misguide the management, they are often left with an abundance of ethics to worry about. It is important that subsidiary executives and directors in the field support ethical conduct. The director's liability is rated in Japanese MNCs to be a reason behind changes in the role of subsidiary boards.

THE FUTURE

There has to be a balance on the board for it to be effective. The directors chosen to serve must have the necessary qualifications and not be selected because of friendship or notoriety. Performing their duties with the best interests of the company and the stakeholders in mind should be their main concern. Board members will lower their liability risks if they perform their jobs conscientiously and have the knowledge and incentive to investigate all actions thoroughly. All directors must be able to think for themselves, ask pertinent questions, and insist all information received is accurate.

An active subsidiary board can be a helpful link between the foreign subsidiary and the parent company. In fact an active subsidiary board can obtain proactive knowledge of local economic, political, and social conditions. These subsidiary board can contribute to the success of joint ventures and strategic alliances.

NOTES

1. Mark J. Roe, *Strong Managers, Weak Owners: The Political Roots of American Corporate Finance* (Princeton, N.J.: Princeton University Press, 1994), 222–223.

2. Laurie Baum, "The Job Nobody Wants," *Business Week*, 8 September 1986, 56; and Peter Kostant, "Exit, Voice and Loyalty in the Course of Corporate Governance and Counsel's Changing Role," *Journal of Socio-Economics* 28 (1999): 368.

3. "Professional Directors: So Many Boards, so Little Time," *Business Week,* 8 September 1986, 59.

4. Baum, "The Job Nobody Wants," 56.

5. D. J. Dunn, "Directors Aren't Doing Their Job," *Fortune,* 16 March 1987, 117.

6. Richard M. Leisner, "Leave the Tuxedo at Home," *Barron's,* 28 July 1986, 30.

7. Abbass F. Alkhafaji, "Liability of the Board of Directors," *Management Magazine* 4 (1994): 3.

8. Dunn, "Directors Aren't Doing Their Job," 117.

9. D.R.R. DuPlessis and B. A. Trenholm, "The Board of Directors: How Liable?" *CMA Magazine* (March 1991): 27.

10. James S. Trieschmann and E. J. Leverett, Jr., "Protecting Directors and Officers: A Growing Concern," *Business Horizons* 33 (November–December 1990): 52.

11. Gerard P. Panaro, "Discriminating Directors' Domain Features Fiduciary Responsibilities," *Business Credit* 95 (May 1993): 49.

12. Tony Mauro, "Liability in the Board Room," *Nation's Business* 74 (May 1986): 45.

13. Baum, "The Job Nobody Wants," 58.

14. Trieschmann and Leverett, "Protecting Directors and Officers," 55.

15. Ibid., 55.

16. Ibid., 56.

17. Ibid.

18. DuPlessis and Trenholm, "The Board of Directors: How Liable?" 29.

19. Trieschmann and Leverett, "Protecting Directors and Officers," 56–57.

20. Quoted in Peter Kostant, "Exit, Voice and Loyalty," 368.

21. John A. Byrne and Jennifer Reingold, "Wanted: A Few Good CEO's," *Business Week,* 11 August 1997, 64.

22. John A. Byrne, "Governance: CEOs Catch Up with Shareholder Activist," *Business Week,* 22 September 1997, 36.

23. Brian Christine, "Executives Now Come under Fire," *Risk Management* 39 (June 1992): 14.

24. Ibid.

25. Joyce L. Kehl, RIMS North Central Regional Coverage, "Directors' & Officers' Liability," *Risk Management* 40 (November 1993): 76.

26. Abbass F. Alkhafaji, *A Stakeholder Approach to Corporate Governance* (New York: Quorum Books, 1989), 65.

27. Christine, "Executives Now Come under Fire," 16.

28. Alkhafaji, *A Stakeholder Approach,* 66.

29. DuPlessis and Trenholm, "The Board of Directors: How Liable?" 30.

30. Mark A. Hofman, "D&O Claims Severity Still Rising," *Business Insurance,* 24 February 1992, 15.

31. Ibid.

32. Trieschmann and Leverett, "Protecting Directors and Officers," 59.

33. Ibid.

34. Ibid., 57.

35. Donna Pedersen Fitzpatrick, "D&O Makes It Easier for Managers to Manage," *American Agent & Broker* 65 (May 1993): 23.

36. Michael E. Rekruciak, "D&O Insurance: A Shield for Decision-Makers," *American Agent & Broker* 62 (August 1990): 75.

37. Ibid.

38. Trieschmann and Leverett, "Protecting Directors and Officers."

39. Ibid., 57.

40. Thomas J. Drag and Brian Smith, "Assessing Foreign D&O Risks," *Business Insurance* 24 (8 October 1990): 57.

41. Ibid.

42. Ibid.

43. Mindy Paskell-Mede, "Sharing the Blame," *CA Magazine* 123 (October 1990): 58.

44. Ibid., 60.

45. Alkhafaji, *A Stakeholder Approach*, 68–69.

46. Justin Martin, "Directors' Feet to the Fire," *Fortune*, 29 November 1993, 8.

47. "Black Executives Still Hitting a Glass Ceiling," *Business Week*, 21 December 1998, 106.

48. Rogene A. Buchholz, *Business Environment and Public Policy: Implications for Management* (Englewood Cliffs, N.J.: Prentice Hall, 1996).

49. Martin, "Directors' Feet to the Fire," 9; and Alkhafaji, *A Stakeholder Approach*.

50. Judith H. Dobrzynski, "The Glass Ceiling: A Barrier to the Boardroom, Too," *Business Week*, 22 November 1993, 50.

51. Buchholz, *Business Environment and Public Policy*.

52. Michael J. Rubach and Terrence C. Sebora, "Comparative Corporate Governance: Competitive Implication of an Emerging Convergence," *Journal of World Business* 33 (Summer 1998): 167.

PART III

GLOBALIZATION

This part will discuss the globalization effect on today's organizations. Globalization is a very important topic for studying transformation management. Although globalization was integrated into every chapter of this book, the next two chapters will deal exclusively with the increased globalization of business. This increase has produced a need for effective managers with innovative spirit, excellent communications skills, and the ability to design strategies in a competitive global market. Conducting business within a global environment presents great challenges to corporate managers. The two chapters in this part have been selected to examine global strategies and its impact on transformation.

Chapter 13

Strategy Design in a Global Market

The globalization of markets and interdependence of economies has continued to increase over the years. This has resulted in increasing competition, revolutionizing technologies, rapid changes in organizational structure, diversity of the workforce, increasing demands, and changing market and economic conditions. This also increased the complexity of organizational process. Restructuring, downsizing, contracting out, cost consciousness, bottom lines, delayering, and process reengineering are some of the terms used for unprepared companies. Global businesses are undergoing reinvention, restructuring, and revitalization to be able to compete in today's economy. Global companies are preparing for a competitive market by maintaining or raising standards of quality and planning strategically. This leads to an increased competitiveness of the company and customer satisfaction. Keeping up with modern technology is another way companies can stay ahead of their competitors. For instance, the Internet has practically brought businesses right into the homes of their customers. These types of communications give a definite advantage to businesses that are on the Net. The merging of companies also leads to better global competition, by pooling resources and becoming more diverse, companies have become a stronger force. This chapter will focus on the strategic aspects of going global and strategy development.

Companies faced with a global competitive environment have followed various strategies such as quality product and services, efficiency (low cost), responsiveness to market differences, and adaptability to change. It does seem that to survive in the global marketplace, where the goal posts are continually shifting, the adoption of quality management becomes obligatory for the management of all organizations. These strategies require commitment, flexibility, personal responsibility, and teamwork as well as efficiency for their resolution. These demands are beyond the reach of organizations led by overpaid executives internally generating fear and resentment among the members of the organization. The task of survival in many organizations depends on the degree of understanding of the corporate environment and how to take advantage of the opportunities that exist in that environment. Global competition has forced businesses to change the way things have been done in the past. If businesses cannot compete globally, bigger corporations may force them out of business. Global competitors, who can produce for less because they produce on such a greater scale, are dominating the market. The larger companies also have the capital to invest in new and more efficient technology. Corporations need to think more of a global scale than they used to in the past to survive. The merger of Daimler Chrysler, which was just formed within the past two years, is a good example. These two companies are thinking globally and preparing for harsh competition. In order to be ready in the future, they agreed to a $40 billion merger between both companies. Daimler Chrysler has clearly become a global competitor. This merger plans to make two powerful corporations even stronger. When you take the advantages that each corporation had and put them together, you have created a more diverse product line. Being able to sell a higher class type of car like the Mercedes along with the lower cost cars of Chrysler creates a broader market to sell to. These two companies will no longer compete with each other. This merger helps to eliminate a competitor, which is another advantage in this deal.

STRATEGIC MANAGEMENT AND STRATEGIC PLANNING

Numerous senior management and executives are recognizing the competitive potentials of quality improvements for many products or services. Management realizes the importance of the relationship between quality, productivity, and profitability. The key starting point to enhance the attractiveness of a product or service to the consumers is to be prepared for the necessary organizational changes. The customer's perception of higher quality and lower prices usually increases when the company improves performance and conformance. It is still very common for consumers to translate quality as value. Techniques include linking strategy and quality by developing a quality strategy, establishing goals and objectives, and implementing the plans.

One important tool applied by today's management is strategic management and strategic planning. It is a vital mechanism in today's environment. Companies who ignored strategic planning have suffered tremendously. Strategic planning helps management appraise the future and assess tomorrow's opportunities or challenges in order to gain competitive advantages. Managers who think in terms of today are behind the times tomorrow.[1]

To stay in business, corporations must compete in the global marketplace. To survive the new business challenge, global thinking and practice must permeate all corporate activities. To succeed in today's environment, companies must consider the global marketplace as their domain. The determination of the basic long-term goals and objectives, a coherent vision, the adoption of courses of action, education and training, and a follow-up by managers of all employees are the ingredients of success in the beginning of this century.

Strategic management permits the organization to take a course of action for the future that coordinates and balances all the contributions made by the entire organization. As the competitive environment is pushing most organizations to their limit, a fundamental rethink and a new approach to the application of strategic management is urgently required. Strategies designed are the methods adopted by organizations to ensure a successful performance in the marketplace and the appropriate allocation of corporate resources. The process of evaluating the organizational environment (domestically and internationally) and the selection of the appropriate course of action will be crafted in a comprehensive document called the strategic plan. Strategic planning is therefore the end result of designing a strategy. Planning must be flexible enough to absorb and respond, driving the organization forward and adapting to the current business environment.[2] The strategies designed must be ethical and socially responsible. Business leadership in complex advanced societies must develop and act upon a genuine socially responsible view of its role, to avert unprecedented and unwanted new social control by a distrustful public.[3] Since the competitive position is dynamic and ever-changing, the means to sustain it should be comprehensive and vibrant. A comprehensive approach is required because the organization must deal with the global aspects of the business environment and must include an analysis of current and potential competitors.

It is important that the strategists in the organization, those individuals who are most familiar with corporate internal and external realities, are the ones to design strategy. Those individuals or groups are in a position to transform the organization through planning, creativity, and innovation. Those who have access to all the relevant and reliable information available in their organizations about the environment must design the strategy. Sharing information and working with others to generate ideas is the cornerstone of building a healthy strategy. Transformational leaders must consider the global marketplace as the proper domain of the organization. The strategy design aids management in better predicting future events and possibilities. Willingness to expand internationally and changing or adopting a new organizational culture that fits the region or the area of expansion will give the organization the edge or advantage over competitors. In addition it will help them in better allocating resources and activities.

COMPONENTS OF STRATEGIC MANAGEMENT

The evolutionary process integrates decisions and actions into a vision of where the organization wants to be in the future, rather than allowing daily demands to determine the organization's future direction and position in the marketplace. That vision must be clear, comprehensive, challenging, and accepted, and it must stimulate unity of purpose among all members of the organization. A leader must develop the vision. When the leader changes, most likely the vision will change as well. It represents what the organization can become in the future.

Strategic management is a process that helps the organization to pursue desired results by designing the desired outcome and also the actions needed to achieve true results.[4] The necessity of global thinking and planning is certainly the transformation needed in today's business world. To ensure stakeholder interests are protected, the organization must design social and ethical strategies. The board of directors must be actively involved.

Strategic management enhances the organization's ability to gain a sustainable competitive advantage in the marketplace. There are two major components in strategic management. First is strategic formulation or planning, and second is strategic implementation. Strategic formulation is a process where organizations develop their vision, mission, guiding principles, objectives, and tactics for accomplishing their organization goals and objectives. A strategic implementation involves the execution of strategies set forth in strategic planning, monitoring progress toward their achievement, and adjusting, as necessary, strategic execution, which is implementation that achieves maximum efficiency and effectiveness.

Another key component vital to any strategic plan is the organization's mission statement. The mission statement describes the concept of the business and must provide the following: Who are we? What is our position now? What are we trying to achieve? Why are we trying to achieve that? Where do we want to go? How do we want to get there? How should we indicate over time how well it is going? Once these questions are answered, the organization needs to determine which organizational level should take the lead. In most organizations the CEO, the general manager, or the top level management starts the process and then gradually involves everyone in the organization. Strategic units, departments, divisions, and various committees are included in the process. Regardless of the level chosen, the organization as a whole must include every single person, and each must play a part in order for the planning efforts to flourish and ensure the success of the implementation. Someone who comprehends the necessity of this process acts as a mentor or coach and should champion the strategic planning idea. People who are involved and participating from the beginning are more responsive and supportive of strategic planning and the change it brings.[5]

Strategic plans must be designed in a way that the company can utilizes its strength to overcome some of the weaknesses as well as minimize the effect of threats and challenges. Environmental analysis is one of the most important and complicated steps in the process of designing future strategy. While taking all precautions to have strategic planning smoothly set in place, there are still stumbling blocks. Strategic planning increases communication vertically and horizontally. Executives who derive their power from controlling access to information may feel their power eroding. Therefore, strategic planning may be counter to their personal objectives. There can also be a perceived lack of control over operational and administrative challenges that are part of the plan. Many well-intentioned ideas are counterproductive without the direction of a strategic management. Managers already face intense, complex, and numerous decisions daily. The new issues identified in the planning process may be overwhelming and may be straining already limited resources.[6]

A strategic plan is vital in today's business environment. In order to be effective, a strategic plan must be action oriented. Implementation of the plan in a particular business must be a priority, geared to the specific aspects of producing the finished goods.

THE PLANNING PROCESS

Strategic plans must be specific and articulate as instruments meant to help steer an organization to prosperity. Plans must be flexible enough to allow an organization to seize new opportunities and react to dynamic market conditions. Circumstances usually change, and therefore the process must have some flexibility. The planning process is one of evolution; adjustments made are to achieve the mission. Change is good, because it is through change an organization can identify its weak points and decide to strengthen them. Otherwise, lost opportunities will result. In changing, an organization can strive for perfection. The diversity of people involved locally and globally must be considered. Management needs to establish an integrated approach to strategic management encompassing issues of profitability, productivity, quality, advanced production processes, innovation, market growth, corporate downsizing, public image, social responsibility, and other business goals as part of the quest to create and sustain a competitive position in domestic and global markets.

In today's global markets any strategy that is not aimed at sustaining a company's competitive position is doomed to failure. An organization's strategy must be thought of as a tool to realize competitive goals. Downsizing, contracting out, cost consciousness, bottom lines, delayering, process reengineering, organizational development, and management by objectives approaches to sustain long-term growth all suffer a major shortcoming. All of them address internal organizational issues but fail to link them to national and international environments. Competitive analysis views a firm as a dynamic entity that is linked to the national environment and to conditions in the global marketplace.

STEPS IN DEVELOPING
INTERNATIONAL STRATEGY

The steps to develop international strategies for expansion include the following:

1. Creating a mission, goals, and objectives. The mission of an organization is the reason for being. In a global environment where so many competitors are competing for market share, it is important for a global company to distinguish itself from others: How is this company different from others? What is the function it performs in this global market? The goals are general statements about a desired end. Companies can establish goals in the various functions such as in production, marketing, finance, and research and development. These goals are usually transformed into more specific objectives. A good objective must be specific and measurable (e.g., to increase sales by 5 percent in three years; to improve productivity by 5 percent by the year 2004).

2. Assessing the strengths and weaknesses of the company. The company must know the resources available and capabilities. This helps the organization in setting reasonable objectives. In addition this will assist management in assessing the type of expansion overseas. If the

company has already decided on certain objectives, they have the opportunities to modify them as needed after knowing their strength in resources and capabilities.

3. Benchmarking is very useful at this stage. The company compares itself with others in similar conditions. This stage will also help the company to choose its market carefully and avoid those areas that have proven to be troublesome to other organizations.

4. Analyze the environment of a particular country or region. This involves assessing the environment at the home country (parent location), host country (where the new subsidiaries will be located), and the international environment (such as the requirements of the World Bank, the World Trade Organization, or the United Nations). In this stage the company analyzes environmental variables (internal and external) in the various locations. Environmental analysis is often called a SWOT analysis, which refers to strengths, weaknesses, opportunities, and threats. In this stage the company's capabilities relative to its competitor are assessed as pertinent to the opportunities and threats in the environment for those firms.

It is important to mention that the company has a choice to eliminate countries with an undesirable or unpredictable environment. It has a choice to avoid countries with high political and economical risk. This might effect large numbers of less developed countries. The people of those countries are punished because of their type of government and leadership. This is an unfortunate situation. Therefore, it is highly recommended that global companies take some risk if it helps to improve particular areas for people. This can be used to promote stability in such areas. In some countries the people have less to say about the type of political and economic system in power. The country's level of economic development generally determines its economic stability and therefore its relative risk to a foreign firm. The country's ability to meet its financial obligations determines its economic risk.

5. Analyzing the environment involves assessing the relevant industry structures as they influence the competitive condition in the particular country being considered. Can the company compete in that industry effectively? The company must assess the degree of competition in that industry and the relative supply and demand for their product and services. It must also examine the potential revenue expected after the new competitors enter the market; and the infrastructure available in that particular country or region to support new entry. To be able to answer all these questions, the company needs to gather relevant and reliable information.

6. The company is now in a position to determine the type of product or service that will be used as a leader in their expansion. This will better help them in allocating organizational resources.

7. Determine the strategy of entrance in this market. The company is now in a position to consider the advantages of various strategies available to them. The firm will take into account the availability of suppliers and human resources capabilities. It will take taxation, negotiation, and other relative arrangements into consideration.

The choices the company has to make when deciding on foreign investment depend on the type of strategy they will use when they first enter a new country or a new region. The company can use exporting, licensing agreements, franchising, international joint ventures, strategic alliances, and contract manufacturing. The company may also use more than one of these strategies when first conducting business in the new country. Exporting, licensing, and franchising are the least risky of all entry into new markets. Exporting requires little investment and usually the company can get out of the new market faster if restrictions dictated by the host country change conditions.

Other strategies include fully owned subsidiaries and other forms of foreign direct investment. This requires that a company establish subsidiaries to control its activities abroad (see Figure 13.1).

In summary, every organization needs a clear mission statement along with a vision for the future. In order for the company to adapt a successful global strategy, it is necessary for them assess their strengths and weakness before setting their overall objectives. Benchmarking with their competitors can be beneficial to their future strategies. It is advisable that if the early assessment of the international market is not significant, they should ignore that market. The company should consider only those markets or regions that the political and economic conditions consider reasonable. The organization needs to assess the environment of that particular region (home environment) to test the suitability of expanding there. This assessment requires relevant and reliable information. It is advisable to avoid countries with undesirable or unpredictable environments. Once the company selects a suitable market, they must design the strategy to enter that market. The company must respond to the following questions: Can we compete effectively in this market? What type of entry strategy should we apply? What types of modifications of current products or services are needed? The availability of suppliers, human resources, and the infrastructure are important elements of corporate composition to consider.

THE EFFECT OF GLOBALIZATION

Even total quality management was partially successful in sustaining competitive advantages. In the implementation of TQM, most organizations lack strategic vision. They drift into a program route rather

Figure 13.1
Global Strategic Planning Model

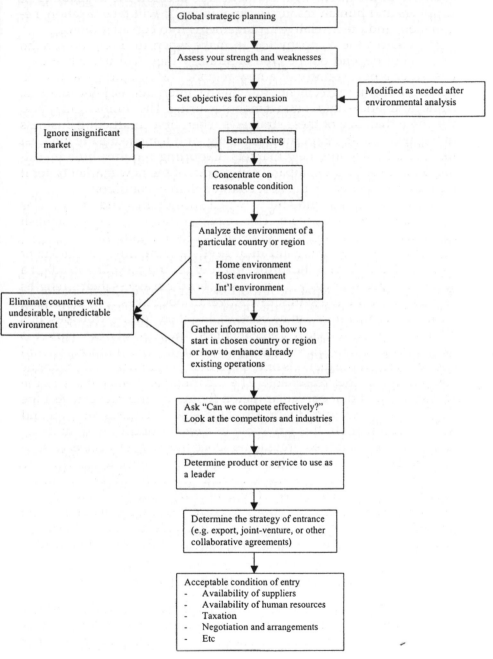

than adopt a strategic approach. The result has been a widespread failure in the implementation of TQM. It has been reported that about 67 percent of TQM attempts fail. Therefore, organizations need to adopt a strategic management approach to the quality process in order to ensure the effective and efficient implementation of TQM. Strategic application of TQM can only be effectively developed if organizations are aware of their key strengths, weaknesses, opportunities and threats.

Every company or industry is affected by globalization. The extent to which these companies or industries are successfully building entry barriers to import competition will determine their competitiveness. The strategic decision of each producing industry as to whether to compete in international markets by import or export depends on the type of product produced. If the industry produces homogeneous products, then it will be highly affected by import competition. A study in 1980 reported that imports have been shown to have their strongest negative impacts on profit in industries producing homogeneous products; the impact also has a strong positive interaction with concentration. The more concentrated the industry, the greater the negative impact of imports. In an industry producing a heterogeneous product, imports may have little or no impact on profitability or may even have a positive impact if the import facilitates price discrimination by the domestic producer. On the other hand, the impact of exports on industry profitability can be negative if the product is homogeneous and the industry unable to practice price discrimination.[7] The issue that must be dealt with by the strategist is how to protect the current market against growing imports. Companies can choose between specialization and diversification of their product line. By diversifying its product into related products, the company may increase its market share and satisfy its customers needs. The company will decide between market share or differentiation. With a variety of selections the company's hope to reduce or eliminate the imported goods chances to gain market share. If the imported goods succeed in penetrating the market, product diversity will gradually increase and other domestic products will be affected. This is what happened in the electronic and the automobile industries. The company can specialize in one or a set of related product lines in order to increase its economies of scale and gain a protected cost advantage that can work as a barrier to new entry. The higher the barrier to entry, the more protected domestic markets are against growing imports. The high barrier to entry will also make it difficult for a potential company to enter this market. A good example of that is the American semiconductor industry. This industry decided to manufacture more specialized integrated circuits in the face of low-cost imported semiconductors. Another example is AT&T trying to enter the cable business.

Both specialization or diversification strategies can also be used by companies competing in the international market. A diversified product line provides the needed diversity to match consumer taste in a variety of markets. The company can build a competitive advantage if consumers view these diversified products as quality products. A more specialized product line provides a wider basis for economies of scale. This will give the company a low-cost advantage in the international market. In both cases—diversification and specialization—to be successful, a company must have the ability to defend itself and its domestic market from imports while seeking competitive advantage in export markets.

TRENDS

A number of recent trends currently command attention, as they influence strategies. These trends are global competition, operations strategy, total quality management, information technology, time reduction, technology transfer, worker empowerment, environment issues, and training and development. Most of these trends relate to competition, particularly global competition, and the impact on corporate management styles. Successful implementation of a strategy requires the creation of a "fit" between the external and internal factors. The external environment of the organization can be measured in terms of the following factors: competitors, suppliers, customers, potential competitors, financial–capital, government–regulation, and labor unions. For example, in recent years, the competitive strategy of lowering costs has received much attention in the airline and health care industries. Cost control strategy is used in order to protect a company from competitive forces arising in these industries and to cope with regulatory changes. Organizations pursuing a low-cost strategy are expected to stress internal efficiency and protection of their domain. Low-cost strategy is appropriate in a stable and predictable environment.[8] British Airways, a very successful company, announced in 1996 a cost-cutting program that was designed to take $1 billion out of the business by the year 2000.[9] This measure was taken to protect the company's market share in the future. Management of British Airways (BA) expected that other major European airlines would catch up and pass BA in terms of cost efficiency.

Hospitals have also used many different bases, such as differentiating by types of technology, quality of medical support staff, patient support services, and quality of services offered. In general, hospitals pursuing this strategy have tried to offer patients a differentiated service that provides value to them by satisfying their unique needs. Differentiation strategy is associated with dynamic and uncertain environments. Differentiates also emphasize growth, value innovation, and learning, and will be interested in external expansion to achieve profitability.

The general framework suggested by Porter in 1980 for competitive analysis and strategy formulation has been applied in the airline and hospital industry for quite some time. A recent study by Kamalesh of one hundred hospitals indicated that about 36 percent of the hospitals put a primary emphasis on cost leadership. The hospitals in this group place average emphasis on the differentiation strategy, while about 28 percent of the hospitals in the sample showed below average emphasis on cost-leadership strategy. However, the primary emphasis was on the differentiation strategy. It appears that hospitals in this group were primarily using differentiation as their competitive strategy. The rest of the hospitals, about 36 percent, were characterized by an above-average emphasis on differentiation. The hospitals in this group are also high in terms of cost-leadership emphasis. Therefore, it appears that hospitals in this group are pursuing a combination of cost leadership and differentiation strategies. Using Porter's terminology, these hospitals are labeled as "stuck-in-the-middle."[10]

CONCLUSION

The globalization of markets and interdependence of economies has continued to increase over the years. Companies must assess the effect of this increasing competition on their strategic positions and learn how to protect their market. Managers who think in terms of today are behind the times tomorrow. They should consider the global marketplace as the proper domain of the organization. The strategy selected must aid management in better predicting future events and possibilities. In addition it should help in better allocating corporate resources and activities.

NOTES

1. Alan Scharf, "Secrets of Strategic Planning: Responding to the Opportunities of Tomorrow," *Industrial Management* 33 (January–February 1991): 9–10.

2. Gerald Edgley, "Strategic Planning," *Association Management* 44 (March 1992): 77–80.

3. Kenneth R. Andrews, *The Concept of Corporate Strategy* (Homewood Ill.: Irwin, 1987).

4. Nancy R. Daly, "Planning for Action," *Association Management* 43 (August 1991): 59–62, 107.

5. Edgley, "Strategic Planning," 79.

6. Ibid.

7. Thomas Pugel, "Foreign Trade and U.S. Market Performance," *Journal of Industrial Economics* 29 (1980); and Philip Turner, "Import Competition and the Profitability of United Kingdom Manufacturing Industry," *The Journal of Industry Economics* 29 (1980): 19, 32.

8. Kumar Kamalesh, "Porter's Strategic Types: Differences in Internal Processes and Behaviors," *Business Research Yearbook, IABD* 6 (1997): 890.

9. Alan Mitchell, "Corporate Dieting Can Make Your Company Fat," *Management Today* (May 1998): 42.

10. Kamalesh, "Porter's Strategic Types."

Chapter 14

The Strategic Alliance

Today international business has increased competition around the world. Companies are spending a great deal of resources and time on international expansion. These companies search for profitable new markets using variance strategies such as mergers, acquisitions, joint ventures, and alliances. While more than half of all mergers fail, about 90 percent of the strategic alliances in successful companies and about 37 percent in the low success companies usually succeed.[1] In the past decade strategic alliances and partnerships between companies have increased tremendously. A recent report by Booz, Allen, and Hamilton indicates that between 1994 and 1996 about 20,000 alliances have been formed worldwide. More than half of these alliances were between competitors. In fact, between 1990 and 1996, a total of 36,000 alliances of various kinds were formed in the rapidly blurring information technology–based industries alone.[2]

This chapter will focus on strategic alliances and their importance in today's competitive environment. It will highlight differences between strategic alliances and joint ventures, trends in corporate alliances, management–leadership positions within alliances, and problem solving.

Many firms are realizing that it is almost impossible to remain independent in a competitive and global market. Instead, firms are turning to partnerships, such as strategic alliances, to compete in the global market. Rapid environmental changes create a setting where it is important to locate alliance partners as opposed to tackling the problems alone. Companies discovering that strategic alliances can provide growth at relatively small cost to firms are involved in this process. Alliances usually improve the efficiency and productivity of both firms involved in addition to sharing risk and investments. Strategic alliances date back to the early 1900s. For example Royal Dutch and Shell formed alliances in the early part of the 1900s. However, they have become even more popular in the past two decades. The main reason why strategic alliances are booming is because of various synergies that both partners accrue. Some of these synergies are in the areas of information, intellectual property, and marketing effort.

An important requirement for a strategic alliance to work is competition through cooperation. This allows the firms involved to still compete while maintaining a competitive advantage. Along with cooperation, mutual learning will also encourage transfer of knowledge. Each partner will continually try to meet or exceed the expectations of the alliance in order to acquire a competitive advantage. Many companies have attempted a strategic alliance in the past decade. In fact, the number of alliances is growing daily. However, the failure rate of alliances is also high. For example, IBM and Cable & Wireless formed alliances to improve competition. However, it did not work, and their profits declined. Corel Corporation and Dragon Systems are partners in creating a Corel WordPerfect software that recognizes speech. The alliance will bring together high quality experience to create new technology.[3] Although some alliances fail, the majority do succeed. In fact, several firms have multiple strategic alliances. For example, Avid has alliances with such firms as Pluto Technologies International, Intel Corporation, Kolby, Panasonic, and Silicon Graphics.[4] This chapter will discuss the importance of this arrangement in global markets.

DEFINITIONS

A strategic alliance takes place when two or more companies agree to undertake a specific project or cooperate in a selected area of business. This kind of cooperation can be either short or long term. This association enables the partners to take advantage of the benefits of synergy regardless of their sizes and locations. The term strategic alliance covers a wide range of collaborative agreements that include joint ventures and other forms of collaboration. In the past decade there has been a boom in strategic partnership relationships in the United States as well as in many European and Asian countries. For example, in 1997 more than 15 percent of sales from the top one thousand U.S. companies came from alliances of one type or another as compared to only about 5 percent just ten years ago.[5] These alliances often take place between very diverse business firms such as retail, information technology, and manufacturing, just to mention a few.

Strategic alliances are defined as partnerships between two or more firms that decide that they can better pursue their mutual goals by combining their resources, including such things as finance, management, technology, or competitive advantage.[6] An alliance is formed also when two or more companies share a strategic information system (e.g., banks that share the same ATM network). This type of collaboration is usually difficult to break.

An agreement between corporations to transfer technology, research and development projects, marketing rights, or capital is a strategic partnership unless a separate business entity is created. Either type of affiliation may develop into temporary partnerships that are dissolved once the objectives have been reached, or they can become long-term, permanent associations. In a broad sense, a strategic alliance can involve nearly any contractual arrangement between two or more businesses.[7]

GLOBAL ALLIANCES

Globalization refers to the increasing trade between countries of the world and the gradual decrease of trade barriers. It is the integration of worldwide operations and the development of quality products or services that are accepted by international customers. Developing an alliance with a company in a foreign country enables easier entry into that country market. Knowledge of government regulations, distribution channels, local customs, and spending habits are strengths brought to the venture by the foreign partner.[8] For example, foreign oil producers view U.S. refineries as outlets for their oil and as a means to stabilize their earnings through diversification. Some ventures include: Texaco and Saudi Arabian Oil's forming of Star Enterprises, Unocal and Petroleos de Venezuela S.A.'s forming of Uno-Ven, and Shell Oil and Petroleos Mexicans's forming of Deer Park Refining LP. Some recent examples of these alliances are Lucent Technologies with Phillips of The Netherlands, Disney with Infoseek (an actual equity stake), Intel with Kodak, Intel with Hewlett-Packard, Toys R Us with Amazon.com, Business Week with America Online, Yahoo with Visa, and countless others.

Alliances are both a cause and effect of knowledge-intensive competition. According to Badaracco, collaboration fosters the movement of knowledge as firms learn from each other in order to perpetuate the "globalization of knowledge," which has become the hallmark of the modern business climate since the 1980s.[9] In general, strategic alliances allow organizations to combine their skills and resources to strengthen the organizations' competitive advantage. A strategic alliance also minimizes the gaps between organizational capabilities and it provides access to other organizations. It is believed that it might be faster and more efficient for an organization to access knowledge through a strategic alliance.

Strategic alliances are formed to help both partners. They are formed to increase growth, provide better revenue opportunities, and to improve productivity. Strategic alliances have consistently produced about 17 percent return on investment among the top two thousand companies in the world for nearly a decade. This percentage represents 50 percent more than the average return on investment that these companies produce overall.[10] When entering an alliance, both parties should feel they are being treated fairly. The future objectives for both parties should be the same. This will encourage both sides to do everything they can to meet the expected goals and serve their customers more effectively. In order for an alliance to work, both sides must communicate and share knowledge and information regularly.[11] The idea of sharing information is also known as a learning alliance. Firms must learn how to interact with each other and learn about their partner and how they operate in terms of technology, skills, and decision making. While managers learn about their partners, they must also remember to remain focused on the goals and not become dependent on one another. Strategic alliances can take many forms, ranging from being very simple (Lucent and Phillips) to being very complex, like the ones between Kodak and Intel and Intel and Hewlett-Packard, which involve sharing of resources, technical as well as financial.

WHY ESTABLISH COOPERATIVE RELATIONSHIPS?

Alliances can also take many forms, such as joint legal agreements, joint ventures, buying equity stake in a company, and development agreements for a specific product. Businesses form strategic alliances and joint ventures to gain strategic advantage. They may seek new technology to improve or create products and to gain entry into difficult markets. Another motive may be to acquire fresh sources of raw materials and resources. Other reasons include the desire to spread the risk and expense of developing new technology or launching large projects, to reduce competition within an industry, and to take advantage of economies of scale. Alliances have also increased due to the improved economic as well as political conditions in many developed countries.

In 1997, about 60 percent of U.S. CEOs had a positive view of alliances compared to only 20 percent five years ago. Even the electronics and computer industries, which initially encountered alliance-related difficulties, have started to reap the benefits of partnerships. Of the top one thousand public U.S. corporations, alliances make up 15 percent of revenues. Sales from the average U.S. alliance are approximately $80 million—a huge increase from $30 million in 1987. In Europe they are approximately $250 million.[12] According to Jeff Stiely of Kurt Salmon Associates, a strategic alliance can result in more efficient processes, buyer role changes, elimination of quality control duplication, and elimination of charge backs. These transactions can be performed with less cost-alliance partners.

The rationale behind development of this type of corporate governance ranges from reduction in transaction costs to strategic initiatives and organization and leadership preservation motives. Therefore, alliances are strategies used to improve competitiveness and reduce cost.

TYPES OF ALLIANCES

There are as many types of alliances as there are reasons for collaborating. Lynch discussed various types, four of which will be examined here. Operating affiliations are formed to establish a marketing or manufacturing presence in a foreign country. These international joint ventures enable the home country partner to ease into the market due to the country-specific knowledge of the host country partner.[13] IBM, for instance, has formed at least eight hundred alliances since 1990, AT&T has formed about four hundred, and Hewlett-Packard has developed more than three hundred.[14]

A small technology company can enter the market by allying itself with an established firm, thus creating a technology–manufacturing–marketing alliance. A producer of computer chips or software who competes in a fast-paced, volatile market needs to introduce and distribute these products rapidly since technology becomes obsolete in a short time. The focus is on development and sales and distribution are entrusted to a partner that has a reputation, credibility, and established channels (e.g., marketing ability). A case in point is a small manufacturer of microfilm technology, Energy Devices Corporation. They signed an agreement with 3M, which permitted the sale of their product through 3M's distribution network of business product centers.

The research and product development alliance consists of several companies who join together to reduce the risk of developing a new technology or product. They often begin as a strategic alliance, the precursor to a technology–marketing joint venture. Sematech (Semiconductor Manufacturing and Technology Institute) has formed a consortium of fourteen high-tech companies to produce high-speed computer chip technologies. These companies cooperate in the development of computer science research, sharing their technological expertise as well as the high costs and risks. In return, they are entitled to employ the advances generated at Sematech in the formation of new products.[15]

An interesting type of collaboration is the spider-web joint alliance. Distinctions between competitors are blurred because of the complex arrangement of interconnections. The telecommunications system in the United States is a good example of this intricate strategy. Martin-Marietta, an aerospace and communications conglomerate, led the bidding alliance against AT&T for a $4.5-billion contract federal telecommunications system. Joining Martin-Marietta, who provided the capital and management controls, were the regional bell operating companies, providers of local communications services and access to national networks. These included US Sprint, itself a joint venture whose contribution was long-distance carrier service; Northern Telecom, an American subsidiary of a Canadian firm, and Bell Northern, a Canadian research facility who designed the network and provided technical support.[16]

JOINT VENTURE AND STRATEGIC ALLIANCES

Joint Ventures

A joint venture is a cooperative business activity formed by two or more separate organizations for strategic purposes which creates an independent business entity. This arrangement usually spells out the role and responsibility of each partner. It discusses the important issues between partners such as allocation of ownership, operational responsibilities, financial risks, and rewards to each member.

Joint ventures occur because the corporations involved do not wish to or cannot legally merge permanently. Joint ventures provide a way to temporarily combine the different strengths of partners so that an outcome of value to both is achieved. For example, in 1990 the pharmaceutical firm Merck agreed with the chemical giant DuPont to form a new company called DuPont Merck Pharmaceutical Company. Under this agreement the two companies owned DuPont's entire pharmaceutical operations in a 50–50 partnership deal.

Merck provided the new company the foreign marketing rights to some prescription medicines plus some cash. In return, Merck got access to all of DuPont's experimental drugs and its small productive research operation.

STRATEGIC ALLIANCES

A merger is slightly different from a strategic alliance. A strategic alliance is when two firms carry out a specific project or cooperate in a selected area of business, which can be temporary. Through this merger the two companies can take advantage of the benefits of synergy. When these companies actually merge they will have to determine a new mission and goals for the organization because the previous mission and goals were for two separate companies.

Traditionally, the term strategic alliance covers a wide range of collaborative agreements that include joint ventures and other forms of collaboration. A strategic alliance can be defined as an agreement between two or more organizations, without regard to the sizes of the companies involved or their locations, in pursuit of global competitive advantages. Strategic alliances have become more popular in the past two decades.

In 1989, Actel Corporation, a small California startup chip maker which had limited production capabilities, negotiated and signed a deal with Matsushita to produce a special chip product called a programmable gate array.[17]

More recently, IBM and Japan's Toshiba had strategic alliances in technology development. They agreed to develop the hottest new product in the electronics industry—flash memory devices. This strategic alliance is pitted against an alliance between Intel and Sharp.

In these examples, none of the four firms could have achieved a leadership role alone, due to the relatively high costs of technology development. For example, the basis for Intel to consolidate with Sharp was the fact that Sharp had the technology and the resources to develop and manufacture the next generation of more powerful flash devices. Intel, on the other hand, had the experience in consumer market devices such as electronic diaries, portable computers, and audio–visual equipment. Thus, the interdependencies are mutual in strategic alliances, and the need is to jockey for market position in an increasingly competitive global marketplace. Several multinational firm alliances have already occurred. Two examples from the airline industry are mentioned here. Recently, USAir and British Airways formed one of the strongest global alliances in the airline industry. During this alliance, USAir believed that this was its opportunity for success, since British Airways is considered one of the world's largest airlines. This alliance provided USAir with access to the huge global market covered by British Airways. Further, British Airways also gained access to the lucrative American market, which is well served by USAir. However, this alliance came to an end two years ago. British Airways formed a collaboration agreement with American Airlines, and US Airways (formerly USAir), is now trying to merge with United.

In addition, a few years ago KLM Royal Dutch Airlines invested $400 million into Northwest Airlines, which has resulted in a tremendous profit drain and has yielded few synergies.

WHY ESTABLISH COOPERATIVE RELATIONSHIPS?

Strategic alliances have increased in various industries in recent years. Companies in retailing, manufacturing, computers, and information technology are going international by expanding vertically and horizontally. It has drawn intense attention not only of academics but also of legal entities such as Department of Justice (DOJ). One of the main reasons for such expansion is the global economy.

The global economy is encouraging trade between countries and regional economic blocks with a gradual reduction of trade barriers. Globalization promotes an open economy in which capital and other resources can be transferred easily from one country to another. This requires companies to expand globally to build competitive advantages and to find better suppliers, productive facilities, marketing, and distribution opportunities around the world. In order to expand, companies are in need of a great deal of information about the market overseas and new technology. How to gather and process information before expansion is an important element in the future success of any business. Of course not all firms can afford to have well-developed information technology departments that are able to effectively provide the needed information. In addition, technology and the knowledge of how to use it is very costly to many organizations. Therefore, companies learn to share technological resources with one another. One of the popular and inexpensive ways to develop a global strategy is through strategic alliances. Therefore, many multinational companies have expanded through strategic alliances. For example, Intel and Kodak have formed strategic alliances. Kodak obtained access to Intel's technology in processing pictures, while Intel got access to a potentially huge market in photo processing—albeit in a digital format. In this case technology was the main reason for such cooperation. The companies that develop their global operations through such integration will have access to new markets and wider opportunities for trade. In some cases, cooperation arrangements are established with local companies to reduce political and economic risk. While multinational companies establish a presence, local companies benefit from increasing sales and revenue. The local company can either repackage the existing product or remove some existing limitations on the part of the local consumer. Strategic alliances are easy to form and dissolve. It is not so when a company establishes a relationship through foreign direct investment. This requires a substantial amount of capital to be invested. However, a substantial amount of capital is not required for strategic alliances.

In many cases, companies may possess the product and/or technology, but may not be effective in marketing the product. The intention therefore is on how to expand the market. An example of this type is the cooperation between Disney and Infoseek. Infoseek is the Web portal service, while Disney is the media giant. They both formed a type of alliance whereby Disney will get to feature its products and services and Infoseek will get the marketing muscle and exposure as a result of this association. Alliances are formed to increase growth, provide better revenue opportunities, and improve productivity. When entering an alliance, both parties should feel they are benefiting from this arrangement. In order for an alliance to work, both sides must communicate and share knowledge and information regularly. The auto industry and the pharmaceutical industry have established arrangements where competitors join together to conduct shared research.[18]

THE STRATEGIC APPROACH

Before venturing into an alliance, a company should first evaluate its own strategic position in order to have a clear picture of the strengths it will bring to a venture and the weaknesses it cannot overcome alone. Strategy encompasses a wide spectrum of ideas and thoughts. Strategy involves the long-term objective of the organization and the course of action that allocates resources to achieve those objectives. Strategy invites management to take advantage of the opportunities that exist in the global market. A company's goals are shaped by the strategic position it chooses. These goals, based on a realistic plan, will facilitate the future success of a firm in a rapidly changing environment by maintaining its direction, while enabling it to respond to or anticipate the fluctuating business climate in which all firms operate. When deciding whether to form a strategic alliance, there is a lot to consider. The firm should decide what the main strengths of the organization are and what they would like to acquire from another firm. Important questions to ask when evaluating a strategic alliance are as follows: What is the reason for forming a strategic alliance? Is your potential partner right for you? And does this fit your business plan? Firms should also predict how the alliance would affect the firm and consider possible alternatives other than an alliance.[19]

When choosing a partner, it is important to have a set of criteria for a partner and to consider a number of candidates. As discussed earlier, prospective partners should have complementary technology, skills, and resources. It also helps if the prospective partner has a compatible corporate culture, such as values and behaviors. The prospective partner should be willing to contribute something specific which would benefit the alliance. There are several aspects to consider once the essential partner selection has been narrowed down. It is vital to consider such qualities as top management abilities and goals, financial and physical resource capabilities, past performance, and the firm's trustworthiness. Evaluating a firm's trustworthiness involves such things as questioning employees, determining their relationship with suppliers and customers, and checking their strategic alliance history. It is important to learn as much about prospective partners as possible. This is the only way to know how they operate. The main criteria when choosing a partner is to make sure that consistent goals are established and the firms are compatible with each other.[20]

After a partner has been chosen, it important to evaluate how the business will run. Values and expectations should be established to achieve the best outcome. Roles and responsibilities should be defined, along with a mission statement and a project plan. It is important to have regular meetings to allow feedback from both sides and eliminate problems. Both partners should build trust, dedication, and mutual interests. Monitoring and evaluating the firm also will help eliminate problems. Managers should remember to keep the goals of the combined entity first and foremost; the goals of the alliance entity are what is important, not the goals of the individual firms. Partners need to share information and skills in order to learn more about each other. Both partners should be prepared to dedicate resources to the alliance. For example, skillful and competent people should be allocated to work on this agreement. Global competition is increasing, and in order to compete successfully it is important to build a competitive advantage. A strategic alliance is one important strategy to do just that. The global environment changes rapidly, and this creates a setting where it is important to locate an alliance partner so that there can be a sharing of risk and investment. It is important to find a partner that compensates for a weakness in the firm and who will help in solving organizational problems.

RESTRUCTURING THE ORGANIZATION

After deciding on the strategic direction for the company, management must then consider two important factors: corporate structures and coordinating mechanisms. The restructuring of the organization depends on a number of elements. These elements include the size, technology, and the chosen strategy. Other elements include the environment in which the firm operates, as well as differences in time, language, cultural attitudes, and business practices. Management must align corporate structure and culture to ensure the smooth implementation of the chosen strategy. Changes in corporate structure are therefore important to accommodate the internationalization process of the company. In general, organizations are culturally reluctant to change.

This expected change must be planned. Management needs to be proactive in anticipating the kind of changes required and be prepared. For example, after assessing their strength and resources, Ford established a strategic alliance with Mazda. Ford learned much from this type of cooperation. Both companies are building and institutionalizing a skill base to enhance their position in the world market. Ford redesigned some of their departments following the Mazda example. It is advisable that companies learn about the process of change and how to increase business value through such changes. Companies should conduct partner assessment on a regular basis. Alliances require setting priorities and providing adequate training for management and employees. Top level management is expected to restructure the organization to be more receptive to such changes. This means assessing corporate culture of both companies and finding out how it influences behavior within the organization.

Therefore we must understand that
1. Organizational change is an evolutionary process.
2. Companies need to be disciplined in following an alliance process.
3. Companies should conduct partner assessment regularly.
4. Alliances should be built on trust, dedication, and mutual interests.
5. Selection of the right management is a crucial factor.
6. Culture and its impact on behavior is a critical factor.
7. Both partners should be prepared to dedicate adequate resources to the alliance.

POWER, CONTROL, TRUST, AND ETHICS

After analyzing the capabilities of each partner, reviewing the alternatives, and developing a strategy, the players must devote their attention to other fundamental issues. The first consideration is delegation of power and authority. Power can be defined as the ability to get things done, mold and control, or dominate and enforce. Friction can be reduced if these issues are addressed in detail as they apply to specific operations (e.g., who will contribute what resources, which personnel will be involved in the venture, who will make product–production decisions, and how will the profits be allocated?). This step is important because it will build the level of trust that will shape the future relationship. Any collaboration, like a marriage, has a better chance of achieving success if it is based on a foundation of trust and candid communication. Ethics, the platform for moral behavior, basically establishes right from wrong and how one acts in accordance with that knowledge. It is also important for partners to provide adequate resources to the alliance.

The point to be made here is that all partnership agreements must be based on trust, commitment, and ethical behavior—not just at the executive level, but all the way down the line—in order to ensure open communication and a successful business arrangement. A strategic alliance requires the active engagement of the top people of the organizations in the process. Top level management must build mutual trust and patience in developing alliances. They must provide commitment to seeing that both sides come out winners. Choosing your partners with these goals in mind will insure the success of your relationship.

MANAGEMENT AND LEADERSHIP

When all associates attempt to share equally in the day-to-day duties of management, the venture is prey to a high rate of failure. One partner should maintain operating responsibility and rely on flexibility and diplomacy in administration as the companies learn from and interact with each other. Leadership, trust, and commitment are important facets in managing an alliance.

As in any project or initiative, effective leadership is the key to success in these cooperation arrangements. A good leader is the one who exhibits enthusiasm for the project and persuades other management and employees to share in this venture. Successful alliances require the support of organizational teams. Teamwork is the essential element of collaborative agreements. This must be exerted at the top level of such agreements in order to serve as an example down the line to all employees. It is usually difficult to achieve when there are several companies involved in the strategic alliance. To ensure the fairness of such agreements to all parties involved, committees must be established to oversee the level of cooperation. It is obvious that there will be problems to overcome due to cultural and managerial differences. Management should prevent this from taking place as much as possible. Frequent management meetings to discuss potential trouble spots and finding alternatives might reduce tension. Effective meetings are conducted to identify problems, not to finger point and assign blame. Effective teamwork requires evaluating each situation as it occurs and finding an acceptable solution. Therefore, communication is a fundamental skill that is essential to the fruitful development and implementation of any business collaboration. In addition, strategic focus on long-term goals is a necessity. All partners in a venture are in pursuit of a mutual advantage that depends on the constant exchange and advancement of knowledge.[21]

The following list describes how to build a successful strategic alliance:

1. Identify your company's position. Identify your strength, weaknesses, resources, technology, and competitiveness.
2. Benchmark with competitors in the market. Identify what needs to be done to enhance your competencies.
3. Identify all potential partners that fit your needs.
4. Develop a strategic plan for future expansion.
5. Evaluate each partner on same criterion.
6. Make selection that complements your business.
7. Define a working relationship through an objective evaluation of both companies.
8. Redesign and eliminate duplication of processes and infrastructure between partners.
9. Define metrics of the partnership.
10. Understand and share risks, rewards, and benefits.
11. Set long-term goals.
12. Continue to evaluate this and other options.

TRAPS IN THE FORMATION OF STRATEGIC ALLIANCES

Cultural differences, a distinguishing factor in an international venture, necessitate an in-depth understanding of culture, language, customs, and norms. Misunderstandings over relationships, communication, and behavior can destroy the chances for a successful arrangement. This goes both ways: Not only must the American manager adjust his mannerisms, but the foreign manager must also adapt. The degree of "compromise" depends on which country the alliance will operate in. Here again, effective communication is an essential factor. Differences in personality, management styles, and culture can be used advantageously to spark creativity. The old adage, "Opposites attract," is a positive endowment if it encourages the parties to view a situation from new, expanded perspectives, leading to a wider range of alternative solutions in a given situation. The strongest partnerships are based on equal contributions. Nobody should have a position as a second-class partner, as this leads to discord and power issues. The motivation for forging an alliance—to complement each other's strengths and compensate for weaknesses—ideally leads to an equitable disbursement of responsibility, free of the perception that one of the ventures has contributed more and therefore is in a position to dictate to the others, which promotes an oppressive climate.

In summary, joint ventures are formed between companies to complement each company. Real synergy requires that a company join forces with another because each alone cannot achieve what the joint venture could achieve. Strategically dissimilar partners make good alliances when their combined resources complement each other. A thorough knowledge of a firm's strengths and weaknesses is necessary in order to determine what is lacking, how to correct for it, and whether a partner can supply it. Perform an identical scrutiny on potential allies. Ideally, the differences will complement each other. A compatible working relationship is vital to a successful venture. The key is to find common ground so that both companies can set acceptable objectives for their alliance. It is not easy to create chemistry between the companies involved unless all benefit from this project.

NOTES

1. J. R. Harbison and Peter Pekar, Jr., "Institutionalizing Alliance Skills: Secrets of Repeatable Success," available at <http://www.strategy-business.com/bestpractice/98208/page2.html> (1996).

2. Ash Vasudevan, "Successfully Managing Your Alliance Portfolio," available at <http://www.amiltd.com/allianceportfolio.html> (1999).

3. News release, "Corel Corporation and Dragon Systems Announce Strategic Alliance," available at <http://www.corel.com/news/1998/january/dragon-agreement.htm> (26 January 1998).

4. News release, "Avid Strategic Alliances," available at <http://www.avid.com/corporate/alliances/strategic/strategic.html> (1999).

5. Maneesh K. Sharma and Parsad Bingi, "The Alliance Trend in Corporate America: A Wealth Maximizing Strategy?" *Business Research Yearbook, IABD* 6 (1999): 226–230.

6. Helen Deresky, "Cross-Border Alliances and Strategy Implementation," in *International Management: Managing across Borders and Cultures* (Upper Saddle River, N.J.: Prentice Hall, 2000), 257.

7. John R. Harbison and Peter Pekar, Jr., "Strategic Togetherness," *Across the Board* 34 (1997): 56–62.

8. Robert Porter Lynch, *The Practical Guide to Joint Ventures and Corporate Alliances: How to Form, How to Organize, How to Operate* (New York: John Wiley & Sons, 1990), 19.

9. Joesph L. Badaracco, Jr., *The Knowledge Link: How Firms Compete through Strategic Alliances* (Boston: Harvard Business School Press, 1991).

10. LeNoir Thackston, "Increasing Your Profit through Alliances," available at <http://www.strategicmkt.com/new.html> (February 2000).

11. Paul Freeman, "When Competitors Form Alliances," *Puget Sound Business Journal* 17 (1997): 18.

12. Ibid., 21.

13. Lynch, *The Practical Guide to Joint Ventures*, 98.

14. Freeman, "When Competitors Form Alliances," 18.

15. "MCI & Microsoft Announce New Stragic Alliance," available at <http://www.microsoft.com/corpinfo/press/1996/jan96/mcimspr.htm> (29 January 1996).

16. Ibid.

17. Sharma and Bingi, "The Alliance Trend in Corporate America," 226–230.

18. Samuel Poss, "How to Create a Successful Strategic Alliance," *Los Angeles Business Journal* 25 (July 1999): 28.

19. J. Gimba, "Strategic Alliances: When You Don't Want to Go It Alone," available at <http://www.anet-cgroup.com/greg2.htm> (2000).

20. Lynch, *The Practical Guide to Joint Ventures*, 104.

21. Sharma and Bingi, "The Alliance Trend in Corporate America," 226–230.

Suggested Readings

Adams, W., and Brock, J. "The Structure of American Industry," 9th ed. Englewood Cliffs, N.J.: Prentice Hall, 1995.

Alkhafaji, A. *Competitive Global Management*. Delray Beach, Fla.: St. Lucie Press, 1995.

Benson, Tracy E. "TQM: A Child Takes a First Few Faltering Steps." *Industry Week*, 5 April 1993, 16–18.

Biberman, J., and Alkhafaji, A. *Business Research Yearbook*. Saline, Mich.: McNaughton & Gunn, 1995–2000.

Biekert, Russell. *CIM Technology: Fundamentals and Applications*. South Holland, Ill.: Goodheart-Willcox, 1993.

Blanchard, Ken. "Maximize Your Training Investment." *Quality Digest* (Association for Quality and Participation) (October 1992): 14.

Cole, R. "Reengineering the Corporation: A Review Essay." *Quality Management Journal* (July 1994): 77–85.

Costin, Harry. *Management Development and Training: A TQM Approach*. Orlando, Fla.: Dryden, 1996.

Costin, Harry. *Strategies for Quality Improvement*, 2d ed. Orlando, Fla.: Dryden, 1999.

Couger, J. Daniel. *Creative Problem Solving and Opportunity Finding*. Danvers, Mass.: Boyd & Fraser, 1995.

Crosby, Philip B. *Quality Is Free: The Art of Making Quality Certain*. New York: McGraw-Hill, 1979.

Crosby, Philip B. *Quality without Tears*. New York: McGraw-Hill, 1984.

DePinho, Joseph. *The TQM Transformation: A Model for Organizational Change.* New York: Quality Resources, 1992.

Ernst & Young and American Quality Foundation. *International Quality Study.* 1991.

Federal Quality Institute. *Presidential Award for Quality 1993 Application*. Washington, D.C.: Federal Quality Institute, May 1992.

Frost, Peter J., Mitchell, Vance F., and Nord, Walter R. *Managerial Reality: Balancing Technique, Practice and Values*, 2d ed. New York: HarperCollins, 1995.

Garrity, Susan. *Basic Quality Improvement*. Englewood Cliffs, N.J.: Prentice Hall, 1993.

Ginnodo, W. "Abstract of TQM History and Principles." *Tapping the Network Journal* (Quality and Productivity Management Association) (Spring–Summer 1991): 31–34.

Goetsch, David L., and Davis, Stanley B. *Total Quality Handbook*. Upper Saddle River, N.J.: Prentice Hall, 2001.

Hill, S., and Wilkinson, A. "In Search of TQM." *Employee Relations* 17, no. 3 (1995): 8–20.

Hunt, Daniel V. *Quality in America: How to Implement a Competitive Quality Program*. Homewood, Ill.: Business One Irwin, 1992.

Johnson, Michael D., and Gustafsson, A. *Improving Customer Satisfaction, Loyalty, and Profit*. San Francisco: Jossey-Bass, 2000.

Kanji, Gopal K. "Total Quality Management." *Carfax Publishing* 11, no. 1 (2000).

Kiemele, Mark J., and Schmidt, Stephen R. *Basic Statistics: Tools for Continuous Improvement*. Boulder, Colo.: Air Academy Press, 1992.

Kinlaw, Dennis C. *Continuous Improvement and Measurement for Total Quality: A Team-Based Approach*. San Diego: Pfeiffer, 1992.

Omachonu, Vincent K., and Ross, Joel E. *Principles of Total Quality*. Delray Beach, Fla.: St. Lucie Press, 1994.

Richardson, Terry L. *Total Quality Management*. Albany: Delmar, 1997.

Senge, Peter. "Building Learning Organizations." *Journal for Quality and Participation* 15, 2 (March 1992): 30.

Sinn, John W., Recker, L., and Duwve, Kristina. "Back to the Basics: Science, Math, and Technology." *Quality Progress* (April 1993): 31–33.

Stephanou, S. E., and Stephanou, F. S. *The Manufacturing Challenges: From Concept to Production*. New York: Van Nostrand Reinhold, 1992.

Stewart, Greg L., Manz, Charles C., and Sims, Henry P., Jr. *Team Work and Group Dynamics*. New York: John Wiley & Sons, 1999.

Tichy, Noel M., and Devanna, Mary Anne. *The Transformational Leader*. New York: John Wiley & Sons, 1990.

Townsend, Patrick L., with Joan E. Gebhardt. *Commit to Quality*. New York: John Wiley & Sons, 1990.

Watson, David. *Managing Strategy*. Philadelphia: Open University Press, 2000.

Index

ABOUT THE AUTHOR

Abbass F. Alkhafaji is Professor of Management at Slippery Rock State University of Pennsylvania, where he teaches a range of courses, with a special emphasis on strategic and international management. Author of several books and recipient of awards for research and teaching, he is founder of the International Academy of Business Disciplines. He is also a consultant and trainer. His two previous books published by Quorum are *A Stakeholder Approach to Corporate Governance* (1989) and *Restructuring American Corporations* (1990). He holds a Ph.D. in management from the University of Texas at Dallas, an M.B.A. from Bowling Green State University, Ohio, an M.S. in accounting and an M.S. in economics from North Texas State University, and a B.A. from the University of Baghdad.